The Weight of Freedom

D1117897

THE AZRIELI SERIES OF HOLOCAUST SURVIVOR MEMOIRS:
PUBLISHED TITLES

ENGLISH TITLES

Album of My Life by Ann Szedlecki
As the Lilacs Bloomed by Anna Molnár Hegedűs
Bits and Pieces by Henia Reinhartz
A Drastic Turn of Destiny by Fred Mann
E/96: Fate Undecided by Paul-Henri Rips
Fleeing from the Hunter by Marian Domanski
From Generation to Generation by Agnes Tomasov
Gatehouse to Hell by Felix Opatowski
Getting Out Alive by Tommy Dick
The Hidden Package by Claire Baum
If, By Miracle by Michael Kutz
If Home Is Not Here by Max Bornstein
If Only It Were Fiction by Elsa Thon
In Hiding by Marguerite Élias Quddus
Joy Runs Deeper by Bronia and Joseph Beker
Knocking on Every Door by Anka Voticky
Little Girl Lost by Betty Rich
Memories from the Abyss by William Tannenzapf / *But I Had a Happy Childhood* by Renate Krakauer
My Heart Is At Ease by Gerta Solan
The Shadows Behind Me by Willie Sterner
Spring's End by John Freund
Suddenly the Shadow Fell by Leslie Meisels with Eva Meisels
Survival Kit by Zuzana Sermer
Tenuous Threads by Judy Abrams / *One of the Lucky Ones* by Eva Felsenburg Marx
Traces of What Was by Steve Rotschild
Under the Yellow and Red Stars by Alex Levin
Vanished Boyhood by George Stern
The Violin by Rachel Shtibel / *A Child's Testimony* by Adam Shtibel
W Hour by Arthur Ney
We Sang in Hushed Voices by Helena Jockel

The Weight of Freedom

Nate Leipciger

To Mercy

Remember & Share

Nate

11/11/15

FIRST EDITION

THE AZRIELI FOUNDATION
www.azrielifoundation.org

Cover and book design by Mark Goldstein
Endpaper maps by Martin Gilbert
Map on page xxxiii by François Blanc
Family Tree on pages xxxiv–xxxv by Keaton Taylor

LIBRARY AND ARCHIVES CANADA CATALOGUING IN PUBLICATION

Leipciger, Nate, 1928–, author
    The weight of freedom / Nate Leipciger.

(The Azrieli series of Holocaust survivor memoirs; 7)
Includes index.
ISBN 978-1-897470-55-8 (paperback)

1. Leipciger, Nate, 1928–. 2. Holocaust, Jewish (1939–1945) – Poland – Chorzów (Województwo Śląskie) – Personal narratives. 3. Holocaust, Jewish (1939–1945) – Poland – Łódź – Personal narratives. 4. Holocaust, Jewish (1939 – 1945) – Poland – Sosnowiec (Województwo Śląskie) – Personal narratives. 5. Jewish children in the Holocaust – Poland – Biography. 6. Holocaust survivors – Canada – Biography. I. Azrieli Foundation, issuing body II. Title.

DS134.72.L43A3 2015   940.53'18092   C2015-906563-1

MIX
From responsible sources
FSC
www.fsc.org   FSC® C004191

PRINTED IN CANADA

The Azrieli Series of Holocaust Survivor Memoirs

Naomi Azrieli, Publisher

Jody Spiegel, Program Director
Arielle Berger, Managing Editor
Elizabeth Lasserre, Senior Editor, French-Language Editions
Farla Klaiman, Editor
Elin Beaumont, Senior Educational Outreach and Events Coordinator
Catherine Person, Educational Outreach and Events Coordinator,
    Quebec and French Canada
Marc-Olivier Cloutier, Educational Outreach and Events Assistant,
    Quebec and French Canada
Tim MacKay, Digital Platform Manager
Elizabeth Banks, Digital Asset and Archive Curator
Susan Roitman, Office Manager (Toronto)
Mary Mellas, Executive Assistant and Human Resources (Montreal)

Mark Goldstein, Art Director
François Blanc, Cartographer
Bruno Paradis, Layout, French-language editions

Contents

Series Preface:
In their own words...

In telling these stories, the writers have liberated themselves. For so many years we did not speak about it, even when we became free people living in a free society. Now, when at last we are writing about what happened to us in this dark period of history, knowing that our stories will be read and live on, it is possible for us to feel truly free. These unique historical documents put a face on what was lost, and allow readers to grasp the enormity of what happened to six million Jews – one story at a time.

David J. Azrieli, C.M., C.Q., M.Arch
Holocaust survivor and founder, The Azrieli Foundation

Since the end of World War II, over 30,000 Jewish Holocaust survivors have immigrated to Canada. Who they are, where they came from, what they experienced and how they built new lives for themselves and their families are important parts of our Canadian heritage. The Azrieli Foundation's Holocaust Survivor Memoirs Program was established to preserve and share the memoirs written by those who survived the twentieth-century Nazi genocide of the Jews of Europe and later made their way to Canada. The program is guided by the conviction that each survivor of the Holocaust has a remarkable story to tell, and that such stories play an important role in education about tolerance and diversity.

Millions of individual stories are lost to us forever. By preserving the stories written by survivors and making them widely available to a broad audience, the Azrieli Foundation's Holocaust Survivor Memoirs Program seeks to sustain the memory of all those who perished at the hands of hatred, abetted by indifference and apathy. The personal accounts of those who survived against all odds are as different as the people who wrote them, but all demonstrate the courage, strength, wit and luck that it took to prevail and survive in such terrible adversity. The memoirs are also moving tributes to people – strangers and friends – who risked their lives to help others, and who, through acts of kindness and decency in the darkest of moments, frequently helped the persecuted maintain faith in humanity and courage to endure. These accounts offer inspiration to all, as does the survivors' desire to share their experiences so that new generations can learn from them.

The Holocaust Survivor Memoirs Program collects, archives and publishes these distinctive records and the print editions are available free of charge to educational institutions and Holocaust-education programs across Canada. They are also available for sale to the general public at bookstores. All revenues to the Azrieli Foundation from the sales of the Azrieli Series of Holocaust Survivor Memoirs go toward the publishing and educational work of the memoirs program.

～

The Azrieli Foundation would like to express appreciation to the following people for their invaluable efforts in producing this book: Doris Bergen, Sherry Dodson (Maracle Press), Barbara Kamieński, Therese Parent, Allegra Robinson, Keaton Taylor, and Margie Wolfe and Emma Rodgers of Second Story Press.

About the Glossary

The following memoir contains a number of terms, concepts and historical references that may be unfamiliar to the reader. For information on major organizations; significant historical events and people; geographical locations; religious and cultural terms; and foreign-language words and expressions that will help give context and background to the events described in the text, please see the glossary beginning on page 267.

Introduction

Born in Chorzów, Poland in 1928, Nate Leipciger was among the 11 per cent of European Jewish children under sixteen years old living in what became the theater of World War II who survived to its conclusion. That alone makes him extraordinary. Then too, the percentage of child survivors was not uniform across Europe; at perhaps 1 per cent, the rate for young Jews in Poland was lower than elsewhere, as was the survival rate (10 per cent) for Polish Jews in general.[1] And Jacob Leipciger, Nate's father, with him throughout the Holocaust years, saw war's end as well. That, too, marks him as extraordinary.

Yet, in key aspects Nate's history was typical as he shared the fate of his coreligionists. For him, as for other Jews, family emerged as the bedrock of his life. And, like others, Nate was astonishingly resourceful. At no point did he (or they) sit and wait for the next German blow. Certainly the Germans had the power; they decided what they wanted to do and when that action would unroll. And Nate, like the rest of European Jewry, sought ceaselessly within those narrow parameters to find ways to confront the harsh conditions the Germans imposed; to slip through their lethal net; to lay his hands on food to stay alive.

---

1 Debórah Dwork, *Children With A Star: Jewish Youth in Nazi Europe* (New Haven: Yale University Press, 1991), xxxiii. See, too, note 27 on pp. 274–5.

Nate was five years old when the Nazis came to power in Germany in 1933. They pursued their antisemitic agenda relentlessly. Relying, at first, on individual emigration, they threw Jews out of their jobs and made it impossible for Jewish families to earn a living. Facing poverty and no prospects for a better future, many German Jews fled. The *Anschluss* of Austria in 1938 gained the Nazis territory they wanted and Jews they didn't. Berlin sent Adolf Eichmann to Vienna to organize the mass emigration of Austrian Jews. Again the Nazi strategy was successful. In total, of the 800,000 Jews who in 1933 lived within the area that in September 1939 comprised the Greater German Reich (Germany, Austria, Sudetenland, and Bohemia and Moravia), more than 450,000 emigrated. The Germans' invasion of Poland from the west and, in accordance with a secret agreement with USSR, the Soviets' invasion from the east, changed the situation, however. For while the Nazis once more got land they wanted, there now was nowhere to send the more than two million Jews under German control, 550,000 of whom (the Leipcigers among them) lived in areas annexed by Germany and 1.5 million in rump Poland, the so-called General Government.

The Germans' solution was to push the Jews into enclosed ghettos.[2] There were exceptions, however, even in areas annexed to the Reich. And the Leipcigers, forced to relocate (October, 1939) from Chorzów to the larger nearby town of Sosnowiec, lived in such a region. While the Nazis pursued a program of "ethnic cleansing" in most of the annexed territory, deporting Jews and Poles out of the Germanized areas and into the General Government, the Reich's need to maintain industrial production in eastern Upper Silesia and

---

2 Debórah Dwork and Robert Jan van Pelt, *Holocaust: A History* (New York: W.W. Norton, 2002), 212ff.

the adjacent Zaglembie district meant that Poles and Jews, including the Jews in Sosnowiec, remained there.[3]

Sosnowiec counted some 130,000 inhabitants in 1938, of whom about 29,000 were Jewish. German troops, followed by the Einsatzgruppen, special squads to murder Polish leaders and terrorize the population, occupied the town on September 4, 1939, and soon set up a Judenrat, or Council of Elders. In the first days of the occupation, an officer commanding some German soldiers abusing a group of Jewish men suddenly demanded who among them were leaders of the Jewish community. Silence reigned until one Moishe Merin stepped forward. In his post-war memoir, survivor Konrad Charmatz remembered Merin as "a short, thin man with mousy eyes who was known as an idler, as a professional gambler, and who was always looking for a loan, which he would never repay."[4] The Germans appointed him the Judenrat chairman. The power he thus gained over his coreligionists did not improve his character. As Charmatz had noted, Merin sought easy money, and his position, with its contacts with Germans and control over Jews, provided multiple opportunities to achieve this goal. Forced labour and bribery led the list. [5]

---

3   See Debórah Dwork and Robert Jan van Pelt, *Auschwitz* (New York: W.W. Norton, 2008), 163ff.; Sybille Steinbacher, *"Musterstadt" Auschwitz: Germanisierungspolitik und Judenmord in Ostoberschlesien* (Munich: K.G. Saur, 2000), 92ff, 105ff.

4   Konrad Charmatz, *Nightmares: Memoirs of the Years of Horror Under Nazi Rule in Europe, 1939–1945,* trans. Miriam Dashkin Beckerman (Syracuse: Syracuse University Press, 2003), 14.

5   On Merin see Philip Friedman, "Two 'Saviors' Who Failed: Moses Merin of Sosnowiec and Jacob Gens of Vilna," *Commentary*, vol. 21 (1958), 479–491; and Philip Friedman, "The Messianic Complex of a Nazi Collaborator in a Ghetto: Moshe Merin of Sosnowiec," in Ada Friedman, ed., *Roads to Extinction: Essays on the Holocaust* (New York and Philadelphia: The Jewish Publication Society, 1980), 353–364.

To protect the German "purity" of the old Reich, Heinrich Himmler, in charge of "ethnic cleansing" in the annexed territories, ordered an internal police boundary (roughly along the former German-Polish border) that effectively imprisoned 850,000 Poles and Jews in a 2,000-square-mile area. This region was now called the *Oststreifen*, or Eastern Strip.[6] The Germans used cities in the Oststreifen, especially Sosnowiec and its neighbour Będzin, as a dumping ground for Jews from areas west of the internal police boundary. But the Germans did not order the establishment of enclosed ghettos in the strip. Not yet. In this, the situation of Jews in the Oststreifen differed markedly from that of Jews in Lodz or Warsaw. Thus, Nate's freedom to roam the streets and his frequent interactions with gentiles were typical for Sosnowiec Jews.

To facilitate their dealings with the nearly 100,000 Jews in the Oststreifen, the Germans established a Central Committee of Councils of Elders who represented thirty-seven Jewish communities in the strip, and appointed Merin as head. One of the Central Committee's main tasks was to provide forced labourers – Jacob Leipciger among them – to the Germans.[7]

With the invasion of Poland and the enlistment of German men in the armed forces, Jews in the annexed territories, including the Oststreifen, provided a new pool of forced labour. Heinrich Himmler appointed (October 15, 1940) the forty-one-year-old SS-Oberführer

---

6 See Steinbacher, *"Musterstadt" Auschwitz*, 75ff, 109ff.

7 Ibid., 121ff.; "Sosnowiec" in *Pinkas Hakehillot Polin: entsiklopedyah shel ha-yishuvim ha-Yehudiyim le-min hivasdam ve-ʿad le-ahar Shoʾat Milhemet ha-ʿolam ha-sheniyah*, eds.: Danuta Dabrowska and Abraham Wein Encyclopedia of Jewish Communities, Poland, 7 vols. (Jerusalem: Yad Vashem, 1976–1999), vol. 7, 333f. The entry on Sosnowiec is translated into English by Lance Ackerfeld, and made available on the internet by JewishGen. Inc. and the Yizkor Book project at www.jewishgen.org/yizkor/pinkas poland/pol7_00327.html.

Albrecht Schmelt, who was also police commissioner of Breslau, as his Special Representative for the Deployment of Foreign Labor in East Upper Silesia. In charge of Jews in the Oststreifen, Schmelt created a department that became known as the Schmelt Organization. Its headquarters were in Sosnowiec, and Schmelt ordered Merin to conduct a census of all labour-worthy Jews. With the information provided by Merin and his Jewish police, Schmelt built a comprehensive system of exploitation.[8]

The Jewish Council became an arm of the Schmelt organization. Merin believed that German dependence on Jewish labour would save Jews' lives. And he had reason to hold that notion. Living conditions for Jews in Zaglembie were far better than in the enclosed ghettos of Lodz, Warsaw, or other Polish cities. And Schmelt clearly aimed to exploit Jews' labour, not to murder them. Thus, when Jews like Nate's father were called up for forced labour service, they reported for duty. Carrot and stick: they thought that this was a way to survive – and they knew that if they did not show, the Jewish Council would punish their entire family by withdrawing everyone's food ration coupons.[9]

Schmelt, for his part, appreciated the financial potential of his human goldmine. He began to send labourers to camps set up near large ammunition plants, or railway yards at crucial junctions where their job was to enlarge the grounds. An uncompleted stretch of the Breslau-Gleiwitz autobahn that – with the possibility of a future war

---

8 Alfred Konieczny, "Die Zwangsarbeit der Juden in Schlesien im Rahmen der 'Organisation Schmelt,'" in Götz Aly, ed., *Sozialpolitik und Judenvernichtung: gibt es eine Ökonomie der Endlösung?*, Beiträge zur nationalsozialistischen Gesundheits- und Sozialpolitik, vol. 5 (Berlin: Rotbuch, 1987), 95ff.; Steinbacher, *"Musterstadt" Auschwitz*, 138ff.

9 Konieczny, "Die Zwangsarbeit der Juden in Schlesien," 101f.

with the Soviet Union – was considered of vital military importance, emerged as a major source of income for Schmelt.[10]

Men such as Jacob Leipciger who worked in the autobahn camps toiled for twelve hours a day. Heavy labour and lack of medical care took a high toll: many died and were buried just outside the camp grounds. The workers were not free to leave, nor did they get sick pay or any other worker benefit. But as they were paid (however small the pittance), this was still forced labour and not the slave labour of Auschwitz and other SS camps. And workers were fed real food; they were hungry but they did not starve.[11]

Schmelt and Merin made a fortune. Schmelt leased Jews for a daily payment of 6 RM (Reichsmark) per skilled worker and 4.5 RM for unskilled. He triaged the money unequally into his own pocket, the organization (for "room and board"), and to Merin. Merin did the same, keeping some for himself, turning over some to the Jewish Council, and allotting male forced labourers 0.5 RM a day and less to women. Schmelt demanded that Merin supply him with workers. Merin, in turn, imposed a minimum head tax of 10 RM – a high bar for the many impoverished Jews – on all able-bodied, non-essential personnel; anyone who could not pay was subject to forced labour. He pocketed a portion; the remainder supported the Jewish Council's nine departments: welfare; health; food; finance and budget; labour; education; statistics and archives; administration; and legal matters. While Merin profited enormously from Schmelt's organization, he

---

10 Konieczny, "Die Zwangsarbeit der Juden in Schlesien," 102f.; Steinbacher, *"Musterstadt" Auschwitz,* 145ff.

11 Yet life in these camps was harsh enough, as one of the few memoirs written by a Schmelt camp inmate reveals. See: Hans-Werner Wollenberg, ... *und der Alptraum wurde zum Alltag: Autobiographischer Bericht eines jüdischen Arztes über NS-Zwangsarbeitslager in Schlesien (1942–1945),* Manfred Brusten, ed. (Pfaffenweiler: Centaurus-Verlagsgesellschaft, 1992), especially 56ff.

also established a system of social support that included soup kitchens, milk for young children, child care centres for the children of
working parents, vocational training for young people, three orphan-
ages, five homes for the elderly, and a hospital in Sosnowiec. Unlike
their coreligionists elsewhere in former Poland, Jews in Zaglembie
did not sink into the direst poverty; they had clothes, food, and medical support. If conditions were not good on an absolute scale, they
were better than elsewhere. And that mattered. It nourished Merin's
megalomania that he was a modern-day Moses, a saviour of the Jewish people, and it fuelled the Zaglembie Jews' hope that they could
endure until the Germans lost the war.[12]

Germany invaded the Soviet Union in June 1941. As the war
against Russia claimed ever greater resources, the Germans re-
deployed the guards along the boundary that separated the Oststreifen from the rest of Upper Silesia.[13] Systematic deportations of Jews
from the area to Auschwitz ensued.[14] Some 1,500 Sosnowiec Jews
were sent to Auschwitz in May 1942 and another 200 Jews in June.
Smaller transports followed. The Leipciger family was not among the
targeted. They remained until the great selection and deportation of
Zaglembie Jews in August 1942. Some 50,000 Jews from Sosnowiec,
Będzin, and Dabrova were ordered to report to the Sosnowiec sports
stadium. Jewish youth movement leaders urged Jews not to go, to resist deportation. Desperately, they sought to organize underground
resistance cells and to make contact with Polish underground movements. All to no avail. Some advocated armed defense; others pressed
fellow Jews to flee. Both came to nought.[15]

Gestapo and Schmelt men conducted the selection. About 18,000

---

12 Konieczny, "Die Zwangsarbeit der Juden in Schlesien," 95ff.; Steinbacher, "Musterstadt" Auschwitz, 153ff. "Sosnowiec" in Pinkas Hakehillot Polin, vol 7, 333ff.

13 Steinbacher, "Musterstadt" Auschwitz, 285f.

14 "Sosnowiec" in Pinkas Hakehillot Polin, vol 7, 335.

15 Ibid., 335ff.

xxii THE WEIGHT OF FREEDOM

people who had papers showing that they were forced labourers returned home that night. More than 30,000 remained in the square, without food or water, for three days. Some 9,000 were selected for the Schmelt organization. The rest – the elderly, young, pregnant, and ill – were shipped to Auschwitz. Still Merin believed that his policy of cooperation with Schmelt had saved Jews. "I feel like a captain whose ship was about to sink and who succeeded in bringing it safe to port by casting overboard a great part of his precious cargo," he announced to the Jewish Council.[16]

By that time, Nate's father was a member of the Jewish police, and it is probable that his employment spared his family. The Leipcigers were among those released the first day; they remained in Sosnowiec until October 1942, when all of the remaining Jews in the city were forced to move to the adjacent suburb of Środula. Their reprieve lasted less than a year. The Leipcigers were deported to Auschwitz nine months later, on August 1, 1943.

Throughout those first four years of brutal oppression, the Leipcigers relied on each other for practical help and emotional support. Indeed, Nate's extended family emerges as the core structure of their existence. Nate and his sister, Linka, belonged to Zionist youth groups, and his parents had many friends and acquaintances. These networks were significant. But the family turned to each other to confront the many problems they faced. Nate's parents had marital difficulties before and during the occupation years. His father shorted the family financially, using his earnings on card games. He had affairs with women, including in the Środula ghetto. And when Jacob was deployed for forced labour in October 1939, Leah, Nate's mother, not knowing when or even if her husband would return, embarked upon a serious relationship with a Polish Christian. Yet the parents remained together and

---

16 Friedman, "Two 'Saviors' Who Failed," 483.

the family drew closer together as they faced difficulties and danger. "In the last year before the war … [t]alk of war was prevalent and we were all scared," Nate recalled. "Our family became more supportive of each other." Family provided the energy and ideas to find apartments and employment in Chorzów, Sosnowiec, and Środula. And they remained together even in the thick of deportation. "[T]he Nazis were selecting young people to be sent to labour camps…. My father suggested to my sister to go…. My sister refused…. She wanted to stay together as a family." And they did. Separated upon arrival at Auschwitz, Linka and her mother remained together. And when the Germans sent Nate in one direction and his father in another, Jacob approached the SS to make the case for his son to join his group.

The agency exhibited by Linka and Jacob in those instances marks the whole history Nate recounts, from the start of the war to the present day (2015). Soon after Jacob was deported to Nisko on October 16, 1939, he managed to escape and fled east to Soviet-held Lwów, where he chanced upon his wife's sisters, Zosia and Ruzia. "My father and my aunts decided it would be safer to return to German-occupied territory. They reasoned that the Germans, being a more civilized country than the Soviet Union, would treat their population in a more humane way." They were wrong, of course. But they made the best decision they could with the information they had. Nor was that the only time Jacob found a way out of the Germans' hands.

Time and again, each member of the family, like millions of Jews in Nazi Europe, confronted the ever more circumscribed and restricted circumstances with agency and resourcefulness. As they needed money upon arrival in Sosnowiec, Linka taught paying students Polish literature, Latin, and French. And, as they had Zosia's and Ruzia's many books in tow, she turned the collection into a lending library, charging 10 pfennig per book for a two-week loan. Leah, for her part, opened a home knitting business. And Nate sought a way forward no matter the difficulty. He too found ways to earn money for the family. Forced into the Środula ghetto, he and his friends built a basement bunker and an attic hiding place. Caught and incarcerated in the Germans' concentration camp system, he continuously looked to gain a foothold, no matter how slight. When the Germans conducted their notorious selections to identify the ill and weak to be gassed, he and his father hid by mingling with prisoners in other barracks. And when the Nazis conducted their selections to identify strong workers, short and skinny Nate stood next to inmates of equally small stature so that he would appear as robust as they. In camp after camp – Fünfteichen, Gross-Rosen, Flossenbürg, Leonberg, Mühldorf am Inn, Waldlager – he sought to be assigned work or to find a function that offered him opportunities to obtain extra food and afforded him protection from the common heavy labour that killed prisoners in months, and from the relentless elements (sun, snow, wind, rain) that wore down inmates working outdoors.

Trained as an electrician in Sosnowiec, Nate was detailed to skilled crews that worked inside and, often, in circumstances that yielded something to eat. "I worked with German and Czechoslovak civilians, which meant there was a possibility of obtaining some extra food," Nate recalled.

Looking like a child resulted in some expressions of sympathy.... At noon, the civilian workers received soup from the factory kitchen. The soup was not very good and many of them did not eat it. They could not give it to anyone, but they just left it a distance from where they sat.... I had bartered a canteen from one of the sheet metal workers in the plant and was able to transfer the soup quickly from their bowl into the canteen. If someone saw me take the soup, the civilian would say that I took it without his permission. If caught, both of us would be in trouble. I shared the extra food with my father.

Food was key. It kept meat on his bones, which helped him to look healthy and thus pass the Germans' selections. And it helped his immune system fight the many infectious diseases that felled prisoners daily.

In the camp system, food and relationships frequently intertwined. Nate, for example, organized a way to pass the soup he got from his co-workers to his father. And, anticipating food from them, Nate sometimes gave Jacob his bread ration. These were life-sustaining measures shared in an intimate circle of care that counted two persons: father and son.

But if food was a gift, it was also the currency of power. Choosing Nate as his sex-boy, his *pipel,* Janek, the barrack kapo in Fünfteichen, gave him a special place to sleep and "he would call me first to receive an extra portion of soup." Janek and his compatriots "had friends in the kitchen and were in a position to organize extra food." Nate cooked and served, and was allowed some of the leftovers "which I would share with my father." This relationship, at once abusive and "one of the things one does to survive" continued for several months until another young boy arrived in early 1944 and caught the kapo's eye. "He almost immediately became Janek's favourite and took my position, and I was relegated to mundane jobs cleaning and running errands. It also meant that my privileges were curtailed and I had less access to extra food." But privilege, power, and abuse are multidimensional, as Nate went on to reveal. "I knew that my time was up and I regretted it somewhat but it meant that the kapo would not abuse me any longer. It meant, too, that he withheld his affection and I was actually jealous of the other boy."

Many memoirs mention pipels, but as someone else, not the author. Nate, by contrast, identifies himself as a pipel. This is an extraordinary admission. Opening a typically sealed window onto sex and power among Nazi camp inmates, Nate offers a rare perspective on victims' choices, which he elaborates as the narrative continues. No longer Janek's sex-boy, Nate became another prisoner functionary's favourite. He had learned that the privileges that would accrue to him would help him endure camp conditions. Nate's new protector/abuser, Staszek, was both the camp scribe and the kapo of the electrical unit. He was in a position to ensure Nate got "more responsible and less physically taxing work" and "an extra portion of soup," both of which were life-saving measures. And Nate masturbated the older man in return.

The line between sexual abuse and sexual barter blurred. Yet the issue of power remained key, and this carried into Nate's post-war life in Germany. Sex became a weapon; an expression of victory and of dominance. Nate "justified sex with Germans as a triumph over Hitler.... It became an obsession to have sex with as many young German girls as possible." For the women, however, this was a form of sexual barter: they expected, and got, material goods such as stockings and coffee.

Nate and his father had been sent to Fünfteichen in mid-October 1943. The following year, the SS gained thousands of slave labourers, especially during the summer and fall of 1944. In August, Himmler was master of more than half a million prisoners; the count on January 15, 1945 topped 700,000. By that time, there were more than 650 satellite camps attached to factories and other production sites. Germans, who had once figured so prominently in the concentration camp population, now accounted for only 8 per cent of all inmates. Jews, by contrast, were perhaps a quarter of the entire camp population.[17]

By that point, however, the Allies were closing in on the Reich, advancing from both the east and the west. Located in lower Silesia, Fünfteichen stood in the Red Army's path. "By December 1944, the air raids became much more frequent and we could hear the roar of cannons," Nate recalled. "The question on everyone's mind was what would happen to us. Would the Germans kill us before the Soviet

17 Dwork and van Pelt, *Holocaust*, 363ff.

army got to us?" The answer soon came in the form of an order to leave the camp on January 21, 1945. It was the first leg of a murderous march to the west, deep into Germany.

Why the Germans bothered to force their prisoners west with such violence is still a mystery today. What is clear is that they were determined to evacuate the inmates before the Allies arrived. They no longer believed the prisoners would function as slaves. Nor were they interested in keeping the prisoners alive. On the contrary. As the SS moved inmates from camp to camp, the institutions still within German-controlled territory became massively overcrowded. The SS infrastructure cracked. Food – little of it as there was – arrived irregularly. Hordes of terribly ill human beings overwhelmed the minimal hygiene systems. The whole camp kingdom became a death trap. In the weeks and months that followed, Nate and his father were force-marched from one camp to another: Gross-Rosen, Flossenbürg, Leonberg, Mühldorf am Inn, and Waldlager.

The order to leave Waldlager came in late April 1945. In Nate's view, at the time, "[s]urvival depended upon the will to live." He believed that any chance for salvation lay in obeying the Germans' command. "To give up was like committing suicide," he contends. But the history he recounts suggests a very different conclusion. "I knew I could not keep up," he admits. He heard rumours that the SS would murder all who remained in the camp. "I did not care." Nate gave up; he and his father remained in Waldlager. They were not murdered, while many of those who marched out were killed by the Allies' bombs. Survival, in short, depended upon luck and fortuitous circumstances, not a "will to live." Many people who wished to live were murdered. And many of those who gave up like Nate nevertheless survived.

Nate and Jacob were among the staggering number of people freed by the Allies who fell under the definition of "displaced persons," or DPs. According to a UNRRA (United Nations Relief and Rehabilitation

Administration; the international body created to help the DP population) report, "Most of them were found in deplorable physical and
mental condition, particularly those who had managed to survive the
horrors of the Nazi concentration camps." Nate and his father were
freed on May 2, and by the end of that month "the total number liberated had reached 3,500,000." Most went home; by August, millions
of displaced persons had been repatriated. "It was estimated that by
September 1 the only displaced persons remaining would be those
who were either stateless or for one reason or another could not be
immediately repatriated," the UNRRA report concluded.[18]

Jews fell into this group. Jews amounted to a tiny fraction of liberated persons. But they were the most vulnerable. No one knew what
to do with them. Unlike other nationals (like Poles or Belgians), their
identity as "Jews" held no official political status; no Jewish government existed to call for immediate action on their behalf. And, for
their part, the end of the war and the collapse of the Third Reich
raised a searing question: Now where? The Jews who filled DP camps
in Europe faced a world as closed to them as it had been to Jewish
refugees desperate to leave Europe before the war. Including Canada.
"For two years following the end of World War II, Canada's gates remained closely guarded against most immigrants and European refugees," historian Adara Goldberg noted.[19]

The post-war influx of refugees to Canada began with a new
immigration policy announced by Prime Minister William Lyon

---

18 UNRRA, *Journal*, vol. 3, no. 4 (10 August 1945), 38.

19 Adara Goldberg, PhD dissertation, *We Were Called Greenies: Holocaust Survivors in Postwar Canada*, Clark University, 2012. (Forthcoming: *Holocaust Survivors in Canada: Exclusion, Inclusion, Transformation, 1947–1955* [University of Manitoba Press, 2015].) Page 57. See, too, Valerie Knowles, *Strangers at Our Gates. Canadian Immigration and Immigration Policy, 1540–2006* (Toronto: Dundurn Press, 2007), and Irving Abella and Harold Troper, *None is Too Many: Canada and the Jews of Europe 1933–1948* (Toronto: Lester & Orpen Dennys Publishers, 1982)

Mackenzie King on May 1, 1947. It aimed "to foster the growth of the population of Canada by the encouragement of immigration. The government will seek by legislation, regulation, and vigorous administration to ensure the careful selection and permanent settlement of such numbers of immigrants as can advantageously be absorbed in our national economy."[20] According to Goldberg, 1,866 Jewish immigrants entered Canada in 1947. The following year, the number jumped to 9,386, of whom 6,054 came through close relatives sponsorships.[21] Nate and his father were two, brought to these shores by Jacob's sole remaining brother, David Leipciger, who had emigrated from Poland well before the war.

It would be a comfort to imagine that immigration to Canada brought Nate's difficulties to an end. It did not: not for him, nor for any survivor. Twenty years old upon arrival, Nate faced the challenge of securing an education, employment, future prospects. And he had to navigate adjustment and adaptation to a new culture and its customs. All of that loomed large, while the assaults he had endured and the losses he had sustained went unacknowledged and silenced. "Few people were interested in our past," Nate recalled. Like other survivors, he concluded that "since no one listened, it was best to keep silent."

It is our good fortune that the silence came to an end. And, with this memoir, generations of readers will listen.

Debórah Dwork
Rose Professor of Holocaust History and Director of the Strassler Center for Holocaust and Genocide Studies, Clark University
2015

---

20 Canada House of Commons, *Debates*, 1 May 1947, 2644.
21 Goldberg, *We Were Called Greenies*, p.61.

Map

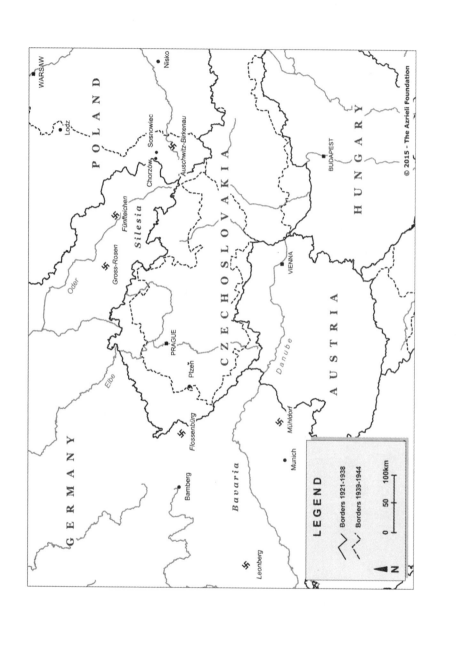

GERMANY

POLAND

WARSAW

Lodz

Nisko

Silesia

Oder

Gross-Rosen

Fünfteichen

Chorzów

Sosnowiec

Auschwitz-Birkenau

CZECHOSLOVAKIA

Elbe

PRAGUE

Plzeň

Flossenbürg

Bamberg

Bavaria

Leonberg

Munich

Mühldorf

Danube

VIENNA

AUSTRIA

HUNGARY

BUDAPEST

LEGEND

Borders 1921-1938

Borders 1939-1944

0   50   100km

N

© 2015 - The Azrieli Foundation

Nate Leipciger's Family Tree

PATERNAL GRANDPARENTS:
*Abraham Hersch Leipziger m. *Rudel Biernbaum

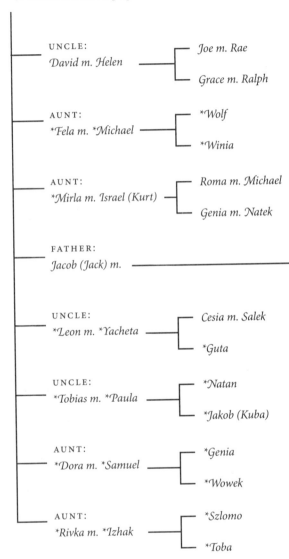

UNCLE:
David m. Helen
 — Joe m. Rae
 — Grace m. Ralph

AUNT:
*Fela m. *Michael
 — *Wolf
 — *Winia

AUNT:
*Mirla m. Israel (Kurt)
 — Roma m. Michael
 — Genia m. Natek

FATHER:
Jacob (Jack) m.

UNCLE:
*Leon m. *Yacheta
 — Cesia m. Salek
 — *Guta

UNCLE:
*Tobias m. *Paula
 — *Natan
 — *Jakob (Kuba)

AUNT:
*Dora m. *Samuel
 — *Genia
 — *Wowek

AUNT:
*Rivka m. *Izhak
 — *Szlomo
 — *Toba

MATERNAL GRANDPARENTS:
Shimon Percik m. Elka Hochman

AUNT:
Rosalia (Ruzia) m. Antek Uziemblo

AUNT:
Zofia (Zosia) m. Leszek Winiarz

MOTHER:
*Faigel Leja (Leah)

SISTER:
*Linka (Blima)

Nate Leipciger
born 1928
m. Bernice Collis

DAUGHTER:
Lisa m. Steven Pinkus

Jonathan

Mira

Jordana

DAUGHTER:
Ronda m. Cary Green

Daniel

Jennifer

Jason

DAUGHTER:
Arla m. Zvi Litwin

Joshua

Adam

Gary

*Murdered in the Shoah

In memory of my mother and my sister, and all those who were murdered in the Shoah and perished without a trace.

In memory of my dear and loving father, who saved my life, many times at the risk of his own.

To my children, grandchildren and their descendants.

To the March of the Living participants and leadership.

To all those who are dedicated to keeping the memory of the Shoah alive.

To my dear wife, Bernice, the love of my life, my confidante and most exacting critic, without whose encouragement, prodding and constant support this book would never have happened.

Acknowledgements

I owe a great thanks to the many wonderful and generous people who read my early manuscript and encouraged me to go on, when I often had doubts if it was a worthwhile endeavour: my wife, Bernice, my children and grandchildren, our good friends Alan and Louise Dabrow, Esme Gotz, Joyce Green, Alana Getzler Saxe and Sherri Rotstein Ettedgui. Our dear friend and family member James Purdon made a great contribution to the readability, clarity and flow of the narrative. My special thanks go to my granddaughter Mira Pinkus, who did the first edit of a very rough document and corrected many grammatical and spelling mistakes. Very important critical contributions and suggestions were made by the author Sarah Leipciger, and Margie Wolfe of Second Story Press, which resulted in the rewrite into a chronological timeframe. Dr. Franklin Bialystok was kind enough and generous with his time to do a historical review of the text, for which I am greatly indebted.

Foreword

I have written this narrative as a record, a legacy for the next generation, so that they may learn something from my experiences. I have written it as a survivor who has devoted over thirty years of his life to the events of the Shoah, searching for a meaning where there may be none. To this end, I studied the writings of survivors, historians, scholars, philosophers and theologians. As a survivor, I believe I have an obligation to the lost generations to teach the next generations what happened, who the victims were and what life they had, and what the world has lost by their demise.

Until 1972, my father was the storyteller – the keeper of records and anecdotes. He spoke in Yiddish, to his friends and closest of family. He never spoke publicly, though I think he would have done it well. I had asked him only one question: After all we had gone through, did he believe in God? He told me that his faith was unshaken and that he prayed every morning and evening. He attributed our survival to his belief in God and to his prayers. With his sudden and untimely death, the task of telling our history and suffering fell on me. Although I had occasionally spoken to the graduating confirmation classes in our synagogue and to friends, I was unprepared, insecure and too emotional to tell the story well.

Now I have spoken and taught in high schools, private clubs and universities. The audience listens intently and responds with sympathy and understanding. Many in the audience break down and I have to be strong for them; otherwise, I too would break down, and be unable to continue. People tell me that I relay my story with passion and that I am totally absorbed and appear to be reliving the events (I actually do), and that makes it real for them. Students have told me that my story was a life-altering experience for them and that I have greatly influenced their understanding of the Shoah. So many have encouraged me to write down what I have experienced, and this narrative is the result. I hope I have succeeded in this task. It would be a crowning event to my dedication to the memory of those who did not survive. It will hopefully help my family to grasp my life experiences in a meaningful manner. It will, I hope, make the point that hatred destroys not only the one who hates but also perpetuates hatred, discrimination and violence.

Prologue

It was May 2, 1945. A heavy, overcast sky fit the mood of the inmates in the infirmary. The air stunk with decay and death. The last evacuation transport had left the camp five days earlier. Only two guards and the commandant stayed guarding us. The end was surely near, but would liberation come in time? My father, one of the few still able to walk, shuffled among the bunks, helping others with a cup of water or shifting their bodies on the wooden bunks and thin straw mattresses. The daily soup, lukewarm and thin, had not yet arrived. Suddenly, the door burst open and a shout penetrated the putrid air. "The Americans are here! We are free! We are free!" No one moved; the long-awaited words were now incomprehensible to our minds. They promised life and freedom to people who knew only hunger, despair and death. Could it be true, or was it a trick? After a few seconds, the realization came upon us simultaneously. As a rupture in a dam, floods of emotion so long suppressed – joy, tears and laughter – were uncontrollably released. My father and I embraced, danced, laughed and cried with joy. We survived. We survived!

I was alive, free to go anywhere, but where would I go? To whom? Would anyone in my family be waiting for me? I should have been happy, but I was not. But I remembered a time when I was happy. It had been only a few years earlier, but to me it seemed like a lifetime.

Photographic Memories

I heard most of my early childhood stories from my mother, as told to her friends. One such story was how, in my preschool days, she would dress me up in a white sailor uniform, which I hated, and take me to her favourite café. She was fond of telling her friends how strangers would come up and say, "What a beautiful little girl." She knew I hated that story. She would also add how naughty I was: once, when a lady pinched my chubby cheeks, I kicked her in the shin and ran away. I remember seeing photographs of me with wavy blond hair, although I don't know where it came from, since my parents' hair was dark brown and straight. My older sister, Linka, had black, straight hair and envied mine. My mother would not cut my long, blond hair until I had to go to school.

My earliest recollection goes back to the first day of school, when I was five or six years old, in my hometown of Chorzów. I am fortunate to have a very good visual memory, almost a photographic one. When I see a scene, it remains with me for years and, if I revisit it, it becomes reinforced. I am sure that the first day of public school was a momentous occasion for some children, but the memory that comes to my mind is filled with anticipation, disappointment and joy. On that day, it was the custom for parents to send their children a colourfully decorated cone filled with things like candy, chocolate, crayons and plasticine. My parents, Jacob and Leah, warned me not to expect to receive one, as they could not afford it. At the end of the first day the teacher distributed the cones and I couldn't help but be disappointed. Yet, as I emerged from school, my parents greeted me with, "Where is your cone?" Apparently, my parents had tried only to diminish my expectations, because the cone they could afford was smaller than most. They sent me back into the classroom and there, on the teacher's desk, was my cone. I had left the classroom before the teacher called my name. The cone was small, but to me it was the biggest and greatest. I remember seeing a formal photograph of me with a beautiful big cone, which I am sure was not the one I received from my parents – it was likely a prop used by the photographer's studio.

I attended a public school where all the students and teachers were Jewish, and my mother had enrolled me one year earlier than I was eligible. She thought I was ready since I could count to twenty and back and I knew some addition. But I had difficulty sitting still in my seat, and I couldn't see the blackboard. The teacher complained to my mother that I did not pay attention and was disruptive in the classroom. The only time I paid attention was when we did arithmetic or drawing. I could draw well, and I coloured within lines at a young age. I also loved bible time each Friday, when a rabbi came to our class to tell us bible stories and hand out pictures that we were allowed to take home and colour.

My school trouble ended when I developed scarlet fever and had to be quarantined at home for months. As a consequence of my illness, I would end up having to repeat Grade 1. Not something that I was proud of. I remember the long days in bed and only being allowed to come out of bed carried by our maid. Through the window, I could see snow on the ground, and I wished I could go out and play with my friends in the yard. It was a very lonely time. My sister, Linka, had to move out because of the risk of infection, and she went to live with our grandparents. To my sister, this episode was a fantastic vacation because my grandmother doted on her. While Linka was living there, she became best friends with her gentile neighbour's daughter, Krysia. Later, during the war, Krysia and Linka managed to keep up their correspondence. Krysia never gave up on Linka, and she kept her photographs through the worst of times.

Linka considered me a nuisance because I always wanted to know what she was doing and tried to do the same. She was three years older than me and was very studious, even at age nine. I remember her wearing thick glasses that always slipped down her tiny nose. She loved to read books and was, in my eyes, my father's favourite. I admired her and was very jealous of her relationship with my parents, with my father in particular. When we did not fight over something or other, and when she did not ignore me because her friends were around, we were good friends and I loved to play with her.

My childhood experiences were governed by our family's economic circumstances, which varied widely in the early years of my childhood. External conditions, such as worldwide economic depression, affected not only my and my sister's education and vacations, but also the marital harmony of my parents. If our financial situation was good we received new clothing and new shoes, usually before holidays and especially the spring holiday of Passover.[1] In good times we had candy, toys, books and crayons. I knew we were not as well off as eight of my cousins, judging from the size of their homes and the vacations they took. I don't remember feeling bad or underprivileged – I was not demanding and was happy with what we had.

Our home consisted of two rooms, a kitchen and a bedroom. The kitchen floor was made out of pine boards that my mother scrubbed clean. My mother was very meticulous about the house, and kept it spotless. In the kitchen, for lack of floor space, a table stood folded against one wall; there was also a cabinet with a sink – although we had no running water – an iron stove and a rollaway bed. We called

---

1 For information on Passover, as well as on other religious, historical and cultural terms; significant historical events and people; geographical locations; major organizations; and foreign-language words and expressions contained in the text, please see the glossary.

the iron stove *kaczka*, the duck, because it consisted of a fire box and a chimney pipe that looked like a duck's neck standing on four thin legs. The stove was used for cooking and heating. Our water supply was in the unheated staircase and in the winter it was always fun to see my mother try to defrost it using rolled up, flaming paper, which I always wanted to hold. The washroom was also in the stairwell. Twice a year the stink was unbearable when the holding tank was emptied in the backyard.

The bedroom had a double bed, a crib, a sofa, a large clothing commode and a dining room table against the wall, which I remember being used only for Passover seders. In one corner of the bedroom was a large ceramic tiled heating oven and it was fired up only when someone was sick during the winter. It took a long time to heat up using coal briquettes, and I was told we could not afford them. I slept in the crib and my sister, Linka, slept on the pull-out couch.

We didn't have electric lights, but we had a gaslight in the kitchen. The gas was delivered through a coin meter and my mother had to drop a coin in every few hours to keep the lights burning. When we ran out of gas the pilot light went out and the lamp had to be re-ignited. Igniting the lamp was always a source of fascination to me. One had to turn on the gas and bring a lit match close to the element to light the gas without touching the element. If one touched it, the element would fall apart. My mother could do it without fail. During difficult times, there was many a day when we did not have a coin to put into the meter and we had to use a kerosene lamp or candles. At those times I was very worried about money and what we would do, and I remember that my sister or I often had to go to my grandmother's to bring home a meal. I never knew whether we had no money because my parents quarrelled or they quarrelled because there was no money. My maternal grandparents seemed to always come to our aid.

When both my parents worked, my sister and I were taken care of by a mother's helper, who was also our maid. She was a young girl from a large, poor German mining family and she spoke mostly German. Her family lived in company barracks that were small, single-storey shanty houses. Years later, I found out she worked for us in exchange for food and clothing. On special occasions, she received a few zlotys (Polish currency).

The helper was with us and our young cousins Roma and Genia one evening when my parents, my aunt Mirla – one of my father's four sisters – and her husband, Kurt Nadelberg, went out together. It was winter and the little iron stove was fired up. Genia and I were chasing each other when I ran around the stove and lost my balance, falling face down on the red-hot surface of the stove. My skin burned instantly. The maid acted quickly and applied butter to my face, but the butter was salted and it hurt terribly. I screamed uncontrollably, and fortunately our parents arrived a few minutes later. My mother had the presence of mind to crack some eggs and apply the egg white to my skin. My mother loved to tell the story and was proud of her quick action, to which the doctor attributed my scarless face and quick recovery.

When I started Grade 1 for the second time and went to cheder, after-school Hebrew classes, I could go anywhere I wanted without supervision. My parents knew I had a good sense of direction and I always found my way home. The only problem was that time meant little to me and I would get into trouble for being late for supper.

In cheder, the teacher picked on me. I complained to my parents but they sided with the teacher and warned me to behave and listen to him or my father would teach me a lesson with the *kańczug,* a whip. The teacher made me sit at the back of the room because the front rows were for the bright students, but I couldn't see the words he printed on the blackboard. He called me the "Blinder," blind one, and all the kids would laugh and pick up on it and call me by this nickname. I was bored sitting at the back and did not pay attention. The teacher would grab me by my ear (I blame him for my protruding ears) and drag me to the front and shout, "Read!" And I could not. He would make a great production of this as the class roared with laughter, which only encouraged him. The whole thing was such a painful experience that I stopped going. Instead, I would wander the streets until I saw the kids coming from the cheder, at which time I would go home. This worked fine until my mother asked the teacher for a report on my progress. All hell broke loose when he told my father that I was skipping classes. My father took it out on me with the *kańczug*. The next plan was to have the Hebrew teacher come to my home, but when I saw the teacher approaching the front door, I jumped out the window and disappeared. When I returned my father was there, ready with the *kańczug*. Finally, they gave up and my father attempted to teach me while he was shaving in the morning. This didn't last very long – my father had a short temper and would get angry whenever I made a mistake.

As a child, I feared my father. I thought he did not love me. No matter what I did, I could never gain his approval or support. My father never took note of how I made my toys – bi-planes and cars – out of wooden sticks and boards that I got from the grocer's or my grandfather's shipping crates. The harder I tried to please him, the more miserably I failed. I felt rejected and unhappy when I was with him. My sister was his darling. They would share stories and laugh together, which made me terribly jealous. Whenever I had a fight with my sister she would whack me but I was not allowed to hit her back. Apparently she had a problem with her eyes and there was a danger of retinal detachment.

I was convinced that my father thought she was brilliant and that I was just plain dense. I often overheard my parents talking about me; they thought I would not succeed in school and that I would end up in a trade that did not require much education. I was keenly aware of what my parents thought of me and I fell into the role. I had three strikes against me – I could not see well, I could not read well and I could not sit still. I must have been nine or ten years old when one day in our kitchen, I picked up my mother's glasses and, to my surprise, I could see the clock clearly from across the room and tell the time. Prior to this, my mother thought that I wanted to wear glasses because my sister did. This incident convinced her to take me to the optometrist and he prescribed rather thick glasses, which opened up a new world to me.

My feelings toward my mother were in sharp contrast to my feelings for my father. If my father was harsh to her, I felt her suffering and sided with her, despite not knowing what the dispute was. I only thought that whatever it was, she did not deserve the treatment she received from him. I loved her very much and as a child, I always felt I had her support. I loved to watch her work; no matter what she did, she did it skilfully, with flare and finesse. I loved the way she moved her hands and I could spend hours watching her cook. She thought that I should have been a girl and my sister a boy. This did not sit well with my father.

~

I was seven years old when Marszałek (Marshal) Józef Piłsudski died in 1935, and after that, my life started changing, fast. Some of my Christian friends, whom I had played with for years, suddenly became hostile. Gangs of youth would attack me and other Jewish kids on our way to and from school, calling us "dirty Jews" and yelling "Jews to Palestine." When I walked home from school, I took the main streets. If some boys tried to attack me I would stand against a wall and call "Mother!" as if I lived in that apartment, and they would leave me alone.

My curiosity often led me to different parts of the city, usually without incident, but once I took a shortcut from school through a small park. Halfway through the park I was accosted by a group of four or five Poles my age. At first I stood my ground as they started to push me around; even when one of them punched me in the chest I still stood my ground, swinging my wooden pencil case back at them. "This is one tough Żydek [small Jew]," remarked one, as he continued punching me in my chest. Another one threw a punch from the side that I did not see coming and I fell backwards. For a minute they paused, and then one of them unbuttoned his fly and said, "Let's piss on him." I rolled away, getting some kicks to my back, and made my escape. They followed me, calling me names. They chanted, "Away with the Jews, Jews to Palestine." I ran up to a woman, pretending to know her, and I walked beside her out of the park.

Most of the residents in our apartment block worked in the coal mine or the smelter and most of the boys, on reaching the age of sixteen, started to work in the mine. The coal mine was the lifeline of the city and extended under most of it, so it was not unusual when a street collapsed into the mine. One day while wandering through the streets, I came upon a large gathering of people surrounding a huge hole in the pavement. I could not believe my eyes – four horses and a huge wagon containing large barrels of beer had fallen through the roof of a mine.

Our backyard was ruled by an older boy and his gang of friends. To be accepted, I had to prove myself and do things that I knew were wrong, but I did them anyways and didn't tell anyone else about them. One of the things was to collect cigarette butts on the street for the older guys, who opened the butts and used the tobacco. When one of my father's acquaintances saw me and told my father what I was doing, I got a real beating. Other times, walking past a garden with overhanging lilac flowers, we cut some flowers and took them home. I presented the flowers to my mother and instead of getting a thank you, I got an interrogation as to where they had come from. She accused me of stealing them and promised punishment from my father. When I told my friends what happened they had a good laugh – their mothers had all thanked them for the thoughtfulness.

One of the storage lockers, at the far end of the yard, was our clubhouse, the entry door decorated with a skull and crossbones mounted on a wheel, which, when turned fast from the inside, made a bone-chillingly loud, squeaky sound. Above the roof of the clubhouse was a wall separating our yard from the others. For many years this wall represented the end of my world. Once I was tall enough and strong enough to chin myself up over the wall, my world expanded and I was allowed to join the older boys to raid the garden that lay behind. We would hop over the wall, grab the nearest thing we could and hop back over before the owner could come after us, yelling and screaming and turning the water hose on us. Our loot consisted of carrots and fennel that we ate raw.

The backyard was also where all domestic problems came out into the open. The wealthier people who were more educated and held better paying jobs than the miners lived on the second floor or third floor. The poorer families lived in the basement or on the fourth floor. There was no elevator in the building. We lived on the first or ground-level floor, which represented the middle of the economic ladder. Sitting on our windowsill provided a ringside seat to observe the goings-on in the yard. Whatever happened in the homes – fighting and swearing and shouting – carried over into the yard. It was not unusual to see a man beat his wife when she complained about his drinking and not bringing enough money home. One huge coal miner living in the basement apartment provided a show almost weekly when he beat not only his wife but also his children.

Until the last two years before the war, we were the only Jewish family in our apartment block and backyard; our neighbours were Polish or German. Before attending school, I spoke German or Silesian, a dialect that mixed Polish and German words, and that some considered slang. My aunts, who were very patriotic, had complained to my mother on several occasions that I must learn to speak proper Polish and not speak German or the gibberish Silesian language.

I was nine years old when another Jewish family, a tailor with a family of four kids – one, Iatzek, was my age – moved into the apartment complex. They were much more religiously observant than my family and did not go to our synagogue. Each Saturday the tailor spent the entire day in a *shtiebel*, a small prayer room next to my school building, praying with other men. Iatzek, my newfound friend, was not accepted by the backyard gang and was not allowed to be with them. I had to choose if I wanted to be part of the gang or spend time with Iatzek. Iatzek did not even go to my school; he went to a private school called a yeshiva, which was a Hebrew day school. His family must have been wealthier than all the other tenants, since they lived in a two-storey building at the back of our yard and had a private toilet and running water inside their apartment.

~

Our synagogue served Chorzów and the surrounding area. Rabbi Kohl was liberal Orthodox, clean-shaven except for a small Vandyke beard. He lived on the corner of our street and I passed his building, which had an elegant façade, daily. I was secretly in love with the rabbi's daughter, and she occasionally invited me and my friend to her home. The rabbi's apartment was beautiful, with high windows. It was an inviting, warm home with dark wood furniture and thick carpets. The rabbi's study was in one part of the home, so we had to play quietly so as not to disturb him. I wished to impress this girl in some way, but I always failed. I knew she liked my friend, and that made me extremely jealous. I used to dream about her being trapped in a jungle by lions and me, as Tarzan, rescuing her.

We were not very religious, in that we did not go to synagogue every week, but we did have a kosher kitchen and we were not allowed to cut paper or draw pictures on Saturdays, during Shabbat. On Passover morning, we had a ceremony to look for *chametz*, food, such as bread, that is not eaten on the holiday. After we finished sweeping the last breadcrumbs, which I suspect my mother intentionally placed on the floor under the table, we placed them on a wooden spoon and burnt both the spoon and the breadcrumbs in the yard. After that, our home was considered kosher for Passover and no *chametz* could be eaten until the end of the holiday. Our religious observance changed when our father obtained a stall in the city's main market hall in Chorzów and my parents had to go to the market on Saturday. Working in the marketplace was difficult, especially in the winter. I remember my parents wearing booties made from woven straw, which became a toy for me to try on and walk in for a while; as they were huge, I destroyed them in no time.

My mother's parents were what are considered today as liberal Orthodox, or Conservative Jews. They observed Shabbat and all the Jewish holidays, and kept a kosher home. My grandmother did not wear a *sheitel*, a wig; my grandfather was clean-shaven and did not wear a kippah. My grandmother, unlike us, had a baking oven and before each holiday we would assemble in her kitchen and bake goodies. For Chanukah, it was twisted pastry fried in oil, and at Purim, it was hamantaschen, a cookie traditionally eaten on the holiday. I loved to cut the dough and place the filling inside. I thought about this many times later, during the war.

My maternal grandfather, Shimon, was a glazier and his shop was a treasure trove for me. Every time I went there I came out with things to play with, such as coloured papers that were used to protect the corners of the glass during shipping, boards from the crates and other useful items. He even tried to teach me how to cut glass, which was not easy, as one had to apply even pressure and hold the glass cutter at an upright angle. After a few tries I was able to make a clean cut. One year my grandfather had a job installing a huge plate-glass windowpane in the new tallest building in the middle of town. He took me with him to watch the installation. A large crane lifted the glass from a truck and as it was moving it into place, almost in position, a corner of the glass hit the window frame and shattered into a million pieces. My grandfather stomped away angrily. I was upset and had a good cry. This image stayed with me for years. After the war, I met someone from my hometown and in reminiscing about our childhood in Chorzów, I told him how bad I had felt when my grandfather lost this huge pane of glass and all the money it represented. He assured me that it was insured and that my grandfather most likely made money on this mishap.

I loved my grandfather. He would take me to his favourite café on the weekend for a hot chocolate with whipped cream and a large slice of chocolate torte called Sacher Torte. My aunt Zosia had a cocker spaniel dog called Bijou that I always enjoyed playing with, and he would usually bring him along. I loved to spend time with my grandmother Elka as well. My sister and I would often go over to their home, which was across the street from my school. I did not see my father's parents often, since they lived about eighty kilometres away in Częstochowa, a long way from us.

Not far from my grandparents' apartment was a smelter yard. I could stand on a nearby bridge to have a bird's-eye view into the smelter to see the red-hot iron coming out of the furnace. In the yard, a huge ball suspended from an overhead crane was hoisted up and fell against large chunks of slag, breaking it into thousands of pieces and sending sparks in all directions. It was a beautiful show; I was mesmerized by the skill of the crane operator.

Every year since I can remember, my grandfather Shimon rented a farmhouse close to the town of Bystra in the summer. The farmer's family would occupy the attic or move to a dwelling above the barn. My grandparents, my mother, my sister Linka and I would spend two months in the village. There, I had the freedom to roam unsupervised. Decades later, when my wife made a flower garden, it reminded me of the magnificent flower gardens some of the farmhouses had. As the flowers ripened and went to seed, I helped to collect the seeds for drying, labelling and storing for the next year.

For me, summer was the best time of the year. For a few summers, we stayed in a farmhouse near a creek. The house had a large backyard with goats and chickens. We spent most days at the creek, building a dam to create a pool for swimming or wading. Most of us did not know how to swim but we spent hours on end playing in the water. On Fridays, a group of Hasidim, dressed in black, would come to the pool and we would have to leave, but we watched from behind bushes as the men removed their clothes and immersed themselves, in their underwear. We would burst out laughing and the rabbis would chase us away. At the time I did not know it was a cleansing ritual before Shabbat, called a mikvah.

On the weekends, my father, and sometimes my aunts, would come to the farm and bring all kinds of goodies. We would meet them at the railway station with a *droszka*, a horse-drawn wagon, and the driver let me sit next to him as we drove to the train station. Occasionally, he let me take the reins. I don't remember which excited me more – the buggy ride or the goodies we received.

When I was ten years old, we stayed at a working farm and could participate in the farm work. Although I was skinny and not tall, I was strong enough to participate in the chores, one of which was taking the cattle to pasture, which was a long walk from the farmhouse. I spent the day with one of the farmer's children, watching the cattle to make sure they would not stray into the neighbour's fields. It was a bit boring, so to amuse ourselves we would play hide-and-seek, chase each other or go off into the nearby woods to collect blueberries.

After harvesting and drying the wheat, we would also thresh the wheat kernels out of the husks on the barn floor with wooden threshers. This procedure – hitting the floor in a rhythm so as to avoid hitting the other threshers' sticks – was challenging. I was shy and spent a lot of time observing others before I would try. Another task was milking the cows. It looked really easy but when I tried it, it was very tricky to apply the right pressure to the teats and pull without hesitation. I was very proud to do it and had something on my sister, who wouldn't even try.

My sister spent some of her days at a Zionist summer camp. I didn't go, either because I was too young or my parents could not afford to send both of us. One Friday she took me with her to the camp and we all sat around a big fire, singing Hebrew songs. I knew most of the songs and could participate. This was one of the highlights of that summer. During the year, my sister and I belonged to a Zionist youth organization called Akiba, which, politically, was a centrist Zionist organization. We wore uniforms like the Scouts' – khaki shorts, white shirts and coloured scarves, the colour designating a different *kvutza*, group. We met each weekend and learned songs and played games, such as treasure hunts, and went on nature hikes. I belonged to Akiba because my sister did and she would take me to the meetings, but I would have rather belonged to the much more militant, right-wing organization known as Betar. I was envious of my friends who belonged there; they got to march with wooden rifles and play war games.

One particular summer, we were staying in a lodge in the mountains. I had a great time with a group of boys who were somewhat older than me. I was happy to be included in the group and tried hard to keep up with them. We ran through the grounds of the lodge and its long corridors, chasing each other and playing games while my father and his friends played cards for hours on end. All of his friends had boys in our group, but whenever one of the players wanted something my father would call my name and order me to fetch it. This meant that I had to leave the group to do the errand and would lose my friends in whatever they were doing. I was very angry and had a tantrum, shouting, "Why me? Why me?"

There were times when I disliked him even more, when for some reason he would have a fight with my mother and move out of the house. My father was supposed to give us money then, but he did not and my mother had to depend on her parents to provide for us. My mother would find out what club he was playing cards at and send me there to get the money. The man at the entrance never let me in but when he left for an errand I dashed in and approached my father. He just looked at me and dismissed me with a wave of his hand. I felt terrible, having to go home without anything. I think my mother understood how I felt when I arrived home in tears; she would embrace me and comfort me.

Although I never anticipated that my father's attitude toward me would change, and I was often afraid of him, I respected him. I thought he was a very smart man and could do anything and always knew what to do. I always felt safe with him. In retrospect, there were times when he showed his love for me. Once, after I had been having trouble skating, he took me to a skating rink. He tied my boots tightly, took me by my hand and, when I felt discouraged and thought I would never learn how to skate, he brought me a chair to hold on to. I learned to skate that day. I don't remember if he took me again, but to me it was a change in his attitude. And, in the summer before the war, my father, to my surprise, took me by taxi with him and his partner to go on their work tours, selling merchandise. Although their work had gone badly that day, my father treated me kindly and he even took me out to dinner. But it was not until years later that I found out how much my father loved me, and that he used his disapproval and discipline to teach me and make me a better person.

The Slow Roar

In the last year before the war, the situation between my parents was noticeably better. The situation for the Jews in Poland, however, became even more precarious. Talk of war was prevalent and we were all scared. Our family became more supportive of each other as the war came closer, but life still grew frightening. Jewish storefronts were smeared with paint that said "Żyd" (Jew), and "Don't buy from Jews." We heard stories of Jewish men and women being accosted by gangs of young men in the street, in broad daylight. My father was attacked once while carrying a suitcase full of merchandise. The gang was trying to rob him, but he fought them off, ending up with a bloody face and hands. He was near his sister's home and went there to clean up. After he washed himself, his sister would not give him a towel, and instead gave him newspapers to dry himself off. I don't think he ever forgave her.

In the summer of 1939, when we were on vacation, my grandmother Elka fell and broke her hip; she died shortly after. She was my first close relative to die, and I had difficulty dealing with the reality of her death. As I cried, my mother tried to console me by telling me that she was still with us, only in another form, that she had gone to heaven and was united with God. Her casket was taken to the train station to be transported back to our hometown, Chorzów, for burial. I sat next to the driver on the wagon that carried my mother, my grandfather and my sister. The driver even let me hold the reins so I would stop crying. As we drove through the town all the shopkeepers closed their stores and stood outside with their customers, watching us pass and paying the funeral procession their respects.

That year our vacation was cut short and we stayed in the city the rest of the summer. Everyone kept talking of war, and in our backyard, the kids' moods were subdued. Old veterans from the Great War, as it was called then, would sit on the steps in the evening and tell us what they had experienced in the war. They told us that this war would take much longer and there would no doubt be more deaths because the military would use poison gas and drop it from airplanes. They did not spare any details in telling us how painful that death would be. We sat quietly, getting frightened and more and more worried.

By the end of August, there were rumours that the Germans were amassing troops on the border only a few kilometres from Chorzów. Fearing an invasion, many people fled, including my father's whole family. His brother Tobias left his wool and knitted goods store in my father's hands. My father told my mother to take us north to Lodz, away from the German-Polish border. My grandfather Shimon organized the trip because my maternal grandmother was from Lodz and her family agreed to take us all in, including my grandfather. My father was of military age and in the Polish Cavalry Reserve, so he stayed behind and awaited a call-up. He was proud to have served in the Cavalry and felt it was his patriotic duty to serve. The Polish armed forces, however, were no match for the German armoured division and the war with Poland, when it came, ended quickly. He never got called up.

In the first week of September, a few days after we arrived in Lodz, the German army bombed Warsaw. In anticipation of a mustard gas attack, which we were told the Germans were sure to drop on us, we had to carry masks made of gauze impregnated with gas-absorbing chemicals whenever we left our home. As the German troops approached Lodz, people ran east to Warsaw and beyond.

My sister, mother, grandfather and I were eventually separated into various homes because no one could accommodate us all for any length of time. I stayed with a cousin who was my own age. His brother, who was about nine years older, was one of those who decided to drive east on his motorcycle. A few days later we heard that he was killed on the road by Nazi aircraft that were strafing fleeing civilians with machine guns. My cousin was inconsolable. In a moment of generosity, I gave him my cherished stamp album, which he had admired. It was my most prized possession, and I almost immediately regretted giving it to him. This album contained years of stamps that had been sent on postcards to my grandparents by their daughters Ruzia and Zosia, both of whom travelled widely to wonderful-sounding places like Paris, Rome and the island of Capri.

When the victorious Germans entered Lodz on September 8, 1939, I was eleven years old. It was an unforgettable and mesmerizing event. They marched in precision, column after column, with their shining boots and goose steps. What impressed me most were the tanks and motorized cannons. Every piece of equipment was clean and shining. It was an endless procession.

My enthusiasm was short-lived. Almost immediately, the Germans started to denigrate the Jews. SS men would grab Jews on the street and from homes and make them fill in the anti-aircraft trenches. There were almost no tools and people were forced to use their bare hands to do the work. The soldiers stood around laughing and photographers took pictures as some soldiers walked up behind men as they hunched over and kicked them in the behind so they would fall head first into the trench.

Early one morning, a group of SS soldiers invaded our courtyard. Through a loudspeaker they ordered all residents to come out of the apartments and assemble in the inner courtyard. If people did not respond quickly enough, they entered their homes, beat them and shoved them down the stairs. One apartment on the ground floor was a *shtiebel* where a group of men were at morning prayers. They forcefully pulled the men into the yard, still wearing prayer shawls and phylacteries on their head and arms. Then they cut off their beards and ordered them to dance while the photographers took pictures. Those who refused were beaten. Those who did not dance fast enough, to the Nazis' satisfaction, were beaten and left unconscious. No one was allowed to leave the courtyard and we stood there as if paralyzed, sobbing bitterly. We heard that this happened in many courtyards. In some cases the Nazis cut not only men's beards, but also parts of their faces, and men suffered serious injuries. This was an indication of what was to come.

About a month later, at the beginning of October 1939, my grandfather Shimon somehow obtained railway tickets for us to go back to Chorzów. There were travel restrictions in effect, and we were the only passengers in the boxcar; we sat in a corner on the floor. At checkpoints, soldiers looked for unauthorized passengers and Jews. My grandfather, who spoke fluent German, stood at the door with our papers, which stated we were not Jewish, and assured the soldiers that there were no Jews in our car. My grandfather did not look like a typical Jew – he was a stout and stately man with a clean-shaven face, and he dressed elegantly, with shirt and tie. He told them he was a *Volksdeutsche*, a German national living outside Germany. They believed him and moved on.

Our return to Chorzów and being reunited with my father made for a happy time, and we enjoyed the warm fall weather. But things were changing quickly. We were afraid to go out and meet our old friends; everyone mainly stayed in their homes. Although my sister and I were not supposed to listen to our parents talk about the war, and we pretended to be busy reading and playing, the close confines of our apartment made it impossible not to hear. My father told my mother what happened in the intervening month while we were in Lodz. My father had anticipated that as soon as the war started there would be a lot of vandalism and looting, so he had decided to take home as much of the merchandise from his brother's store as possible. The vandalism did not happen, but shortly after the Germans occupied the city he was told to report to the city hall, now under German control, and to bring the store keys. On arrival he was informed that the store had been confiscated by the German government and that he was not allowed to return there, and if he removed anything from the store it would be deemed theft against the Third Reich and punishable by death. He was given a receipt, which documented that the store was now the property of the Third Reich, and dismissed.

He was now confronted with the fact that he had all the merchandise at home and had to do something to hide it. He thought of Mrs. Ullmann, who was a friend of the family and was a German national and thus not likely to have her house searched. He transported all the material to her home and gave my mother an inventory list.

In the first week of October, the Nazis issued an order requiring all Jewish men between the ages of seventeen and forty-five to register and be prepared to go to work in the east of Poland. They were required to have winter clothing and a shovel or pickaxe, and on October 16 they were to report to the former Jewish public school. My father was one of them. That day, as I saw trucks loaded with men go past our street, I waved goodbye to my father. I could not contain my sorrow and I cried uncontrollably for a long time. On the way back to my apartment, I passed the bakery where we used to shop regularly. The owner was standing on the steps and saw me sobbing as the trucks passed. She called me over and told me not to worry. She told me that my father would soon come back. Somehow I believed her, hoping she was right.

My mother and Linka had accompanied my father to the deportation place; on their return home they were very sad but did not cry. They told me that they had no idea where he had been sent to and when he would return. Mother tried to keep us as calm as possible. All we could do was wait and hope for Father's quick return. I could not sleep, and continually worried what we would do. My sister was no help to me – I saw her speaking to my mother a lot but they

considered me too young and did not share their thoughts with me.
I wandered around aimlessly in the house, not wishing to leave and
face my now hostile neighbours, who once were my friends. I couldn't
understand the quick transition, and this I did talk to my sister about.
She had experienced the same change in attitude and told me she was
convinced that their parents wouldn't allow them to be with us or be
seen with us. There was just nothing we could do to change the situation. My sister immersed herself in books and I spent time with my
remaining duplicate stamps that were not in the album I had given
away. I spoke to my mother about my change of heart about giving
the album away, but she assured me it was the right thing to do. I accepted that and started to assemble a new album.

Our uncertain and idle time lasted until two or three weeks after the deportation of the men from our region. Then, we received
orders to leave Chorzów. Upper Silesia, in which Chorzów is located, was annexed to the Third Reich and our city was to be made
Judenrein – free of Jews. We were in a panic, unsure where we would
find a place to live and what we could take with us. We were then told
we could take as much as we could transport in one wagon. It was
hard for me to imagine what we could fit. Linka was busy making
inventory lists whereas I worried about taking my tools – although
there were not many, I cherished them. We had two households to
move. Grandfather and my mother made up a list of what they would
take from each household. My grandfather took the initiative and
went to Sosnowiec, where his family came from. Although located
in the annexed area, Sosnowiec had not been declared free of Jews.
There was an influx of people from surrounding areas into Sosnowiec
and my grandfather had a very difficult time getting a flat. Through
our family connections, my grandfather managed to get us an apartment. He also hired a horse and wagon to transport our belongings.

It was a foregone conclusion that any bulky furniture would have
to be left behind. We had to leave our dining room table, large wood-
en double bed and our huge wardrobe. Most of the furniture we took

came from my grandfather's apartment, including his bedroom furniture, two metal-frame beds and a huge amount of books. The books were my aunts' prized possessions and he did not think he should leave them. In the meantime, my mother went to Mrs. Ullmann to retrieve the wool my father had left with her. At first, she gave her only a small portion of the wool. When my mother confronted her with the list my father had left her, Mrs. Ullmann reluctantly gave my mother half of the wool. She told my mother that she was entitled to half because she had taken the risk of hiding it.

In Sosnowiec, our apartment at 12 Prosta Street was larger and much more luxurious than our apartment in Chorzów. Instead of an outhouse and a cold-water tap in the stairwell that froze up on cold nights, we had a full washroom with a bathtub, a toilet and a sink with hot and cold running water. There was a large bedroom and kitchen and we even had a locker in the cellar, where my grandfather brought sacks of potatoes, carrots and cabbage for the winter. We buried the potatoes and carrots in sand and chopped up the cabbage to be stored in a barrel to make sauerkraut. I was fully involved in this operation and I loved it. Nevertheless, I was afraid to go down to the basement by myself because there was no light in the stairwell and a candle threw large shadows on the walls. I overcame my fear by going into the corner of the stairway and kicking the wall to convince myself that no one was there.

Things were looking up in spite of being expelled from Chorzów. We were hopeful that my Father would soon return. With the wool and my grandfather's help, our finances seemed to be better. Mother even went to the market and brought home carp, which she let swim in our bathtub. This was a new experience for us and we played with the fish until Friday morning, when my mother took it and cooked it.

Life went on and we adjusted to the new circumstances. Without school, organized activities or community centres, I had a lot of time to run around the streets and get into mischief with other children. Parents had little control over their kids. Most men had been deported or sent to camps, and the absence of fathers contributed further to our unruly behaviour. There were several gangs, each with its own territory; fights would often break out not only among Jewish gangs, but also between Jewish and Polish gangs. The fights between the Jewish and the Polish gangs were much more serious because the Poles came equipped with rocks, sticks and iron bars. Most fights resulted in one or two kids getting hurt and then everyone scattered. In one of these fights I got hit in the face by a rock and one of the lenses in my glasses shattered; fortunately, no glass entered my eye. However, my mother made me pay a portion of the replacement cost because she blamed me for taking part in the fight.

A number of girls a bit older than me lived in our apartment building, and I was excited to meet them. My sister didn't join the girls' groups – she told me they were too young for her and she preferred to spend her time reading. She missed her friends from Chorzów and didn't make any new ones. She decided that since there was no public school, she would give private lessons in Polish literature, Latin and French to younger students. Linka had finished her first year of high school and she felt this would keep her busy and provide some income. My sister started to look for students to teach, and after a few disappointments, she managed to get some paying students. At first she let me sit in on some lessons, provided I behaved and listened to her. After a few days the novelty wore off and I didn't bother her and her students.

I had no trouble finding new friends, all of whom were Jewish since we now lived in a totally Jewish district. This was quite different from Chorzów, where we had lived in a predominantly gentile area of mostly *Volksdeutsche*. My life was much more fun with my new friends and freedom, without school and father's supervision. The presence of Jewish girls changed the atmosphere – the older boys flirted with the girls, teasing them, pulling their pigtails and running away. Some of the girls were in puberty and were less interested in skipping games; they congregated in groups, whispering and giggling. My older friends were more interested in girls and they too gathered in separate groups. At twelve, I was not interested in girls; besides, I was awkward-looking, small and skinny, and my shoulder blades stuck out. I wore thick glasses and had protruding ears – not exactly an attraction to girls. In addition, I was shy and could not easily make small talk. I was more interested in stamp collecting and playing hide-and-seek.

All of the boys in the neighbourhood tried to earn money and we had to compete for the available jobs. There was no such thing as allowance money, so anytime we wanted to buy something we had to ask for it or try to earn it. I managed to find two religious families who would not turn on the stove or make fires during Shabbat. They required someone to pick up their pots of *cholent*, stew, on Friday before Shabbat and take them to the local bakery to be placed in the hot oven overnight. Just before lunch on Shabbat, I would take the pots back to the family. I had to be in the bakery well in advance of the time the baker would take the pots out of the oven, because some boys would play tricks by interchanging labels on the pots so that some unsuspecting delivery boys would pick up the wrong pot. The boys thought it was a good sport to switch the pots so that some poor families would end up getting a good meal with meat and kishka, stuffed derma, instead of just potatoes and beans. One of my friends was the baker's son, and his job on Friday mornings was to brush the challah with egg white after it came out of the oven. I helped him, which usually meant that we were rewarded with a freshly baked pastry. I had a great time and thought little of the school I missed.

Life in the Jewish district of old Sosnowiec went on as best as it could. We thought that life was bearable, as long as it didn't get any worse. Our long hallway was piled up with my aunts' books, as was much of the bedroom, and I managed to get some bricks and boards from the backyard to make shelves. The shelves extended the full length of the long hallway, and with all the books lined up neatly, we could see what we had. My sister arranged the books – good Polish literature, novels and science on a variety of subjects – by subjects and authors. Soon, my sister became very popular because people wanted to borrow the books. She came up with the idea of turning it into a lending library to make some money to help our mother. My sister catalogued all the books and we numbered each one. We were ready for business. We charged 10 pfennig per book lent out for a two-week period. Business was brisk and we took in small amounts of much-needed cash. The news of the library spread, and even some non-Jewish people came to borrow our books. My sister was very diligent and recorded everyone's address.

After a month, we ran out of books. My task was to go out and collect the overdue ones. I had few problems with our Jewish readers, as most lived in our building or not far away. Collecting the books from the non-Jewish readers, however, was quite different. It was not easy to find them and some denied that they borrowed books from us. Quite often, they told me to get lost and called me a dirty, money-grabbing Jew. Some of the borrowers lived quite far and I had to venture into districts unknown to me. In some cases the address didn't exist and I quickly concluded it had been invented, that the borrower obviously had no intention of giving back the books. Other times, people chased me and tried to beat me up. Luckily, I was a fast runner. Only a few produced the books and returned them without a problem.

The next money-making scheme my sister came up with was to manufacture cigarettes. We bought empty filter tip tubes, tobacco and a tube-filling gadget. My sister made the cigarettes and I sold them on the street one at a time for 5 pfennig or whatever I could get. If a customer bought more than one, I lowered the price. That worked for a while but we had to sell a lot to make back our investment. Other boys got the same idea and there was soon too much competition, so it became unprofitable to continue.

My grandfather also tried to make some money and found a source for pocket watches, which the merchant convinced him were in demand by the Poles and that we could make a good return. However, what he did not tell my grandfather was that he sold literally thousands of these watches to so-called middlemen; when I went on the streets to try to sell the watches, I found that there was an over-supply of sellers and no buyers.

The wool that my mother had rescued was quickly diminishing and my mother and sister decided that instead of selling it they would open a home knitting business to make more money selling sweat-ers and dresses. This business flourished for weeks. My mother even hired girls to knit. My job was to sit for hours with my hands spread out with a skein of wool while someone made balls of wool, so I de-cided to make a device that would relieve me from this, using wood sticks and dowels. I never got to patent my invention, but I made a few and sold them to neighbours, and I was able to get out of the te-dious work.

In the fall of 1939, the city of Sosnowiec felt exciting and fright-ening at the same time. In our building lived many wealthy German Jews who had been evicted from Germany or other cities and regions of Upper Silesia. They seemed to have a lot of money and nothing to spend it on. Almost every evening, three or four of the men congre-gated in our kitchen for cards and drinking, bringing a large amount of food and sweets. They were my grandfather's friends and my moth-er couldn't object to their presence. She retreated to the bedroom or visited friends in the building.

My mother's uncle, Yehoshua Percik, the youngest of my grandfa-ther's siblings, lived with his wife, Helen, and four of their youngest children one floor below us. They had thirteen children in total, and the rest were older and lived on their own. Uncle Yehoshua spoke German perfectly and somehow obtained German newspapers. In the evening he would come up to our apartment with them and read aloud in German to the assembled men. He was a lively, spritely man, all of 1.5 metres tall, thin and very vivacious. Although he was small, he had a big, booming voice and he spoke and read well. He read with gusto and dramatic emphasis, describing in great detail the victorious advances of the German troops. The atmosphere was thick with fore-boding. The Germans seemed unstoppable, and the men discussed the situation in astonishment and fear. They expressed various troubling views of what it meant for us, but they agreed on one thing: the Germans would not leave Poland anytime soon. I was not supposed to listen, so I pretended to be busy doing something, but I heard everything. They assumed that I didn't understand the German language well enough to make sense of what they read, but even though I may not have understood every word, I understood enough to get the gist of the news. And I saw the pictures illustrating the devastation inflicted on the cities they conquered. I marvelled at the huge tanks and artillery. They called the war a *Blitzkrieg,* and at the speed the Germans advanced it was just that, a "lightning war."

I became the runner for the guests, even after the imposed curfew, to the local bar to purchase beer and cigarettes, which everyone smoked incessantly. I received good tips for each run and my only competition was Elsa, my uncle's youngest daughter. She was my age and was very pretty, with blond, curly hair and a big smile. I was told she looked like Shirley Temple, except her teeth were decayed because she ate too much chocolate. A Polish chocolate company had used her as a model and she had had an unlimited amount of chocolate. I tried to be her friend but she would not even look at me – although we were the same age, she considered me a child. The card players liked her and made sure that I shared my running duties with her, but she wasn't always around, so I got more of the jobs and tips. Some of my money went toward buying stamps to replace the album that I had given away.

The apartment was filled with the smell of smoke and beer. It seemed to me that these men had quite a lot of money and time to play cards. It was as if they knew they were on borrowed time and might as well enjoy whatever they could before it was too late. I had never encountered adults sitting around all day with nothing to do and drinking so much. My grandfather suffered from high blood pressure and my mother admonished him for drinking. I heard rumours that young people were partying all night and having sex parties. When I repeated what I overheard to my friends, they soon enlightened me as to what that meant.

My uncle Yehoshua, who was not a card player or drinker, turned his kitchen into a workshop and manufactured kaleidoscopes. I would sell them on the street together with the cigarettes, watches and whatever else I could find to sell. Elsa and I helped make the kaleidoscopes, but my uncle grew anxious to conceal his supply sources of glass and paper tubes, in fear that I would produce them and become his competition, which, much to his displeasure, I did. Actually, I created some innovations and we had a competition to see who could make a better kaleidoscope. In addition to inserting glass fragments, I inserted coloured beads that I took from my sister's jewellery box.

~

Slowly, progressively, life became more difficult. We were not enclosed into a ghetto per se; rather, police surrounded our whole area. We considered it an open ghetto. In November 1939, we were ordered to wear white armbands with a blue Star of David. The adults were upset by the requirement to wear armbands, which, to them, was a sign of denigration. I, on the other hand, felt a sense of pride. After all, the Nazis wore a swastika on their arms and we wore a Star of David. I naively took pride in the armband and starched it so it was straight, firm and clean. But it was easy to slip off the armband and infiltrate the Polish areas where Jews were not allowed to be, and buy goods and food on the Polish market.

Once, some of us were on the street near a theatre without our armbands. A young Nazi from the Hitlerjugend spotted us and became suspicious. It was in the early evening but there was a curfew for even the German youth; as soon as he approached we scattered but he caught one of my friends by the arm and ordered him to stand at attention. We all feared for him, thinking he would get into serious trouble, and possibly involve us as well. The Nazi berated him for being on the street after curfew with a group of other youth. My friend had fantastic presence of mind and courage. In perfect German, with a straight face, he lied flawlessly that he was a member of the Hitlerjugend from a different part of the city. He explained that he was waiting for his parents who were in the theatre to take him home and that the Polish guys who had run away were trying to attack him. We were all astounded that he kept his composure and stood his ground. That was the last time we stayed out past curfew.

Later, in 1941, we would be ordered to wear a yellow Star of David with the word "Jude," which had to be sewn onto each piece of our outer clothing. Wearing the yellow star, my mother explained, was an ancient method used to keep the Jews separate from the Christians. We were not allowed to leave the house without the yellow patch on our outer clothing. This made it much harder to mix with the Polish population.

Selling anything on the street was considered "black marketeering" and prohibited by the Nazis. To make a point, the Nazis convicted six men caught doing business on the black market and sentenced them to death by hanging. The hanging was to be public to let us know what the consequences of black marketeering were. A huge stage with a scaffold was erected – built high so that everyone could see – in one of the city's squares and everyone was compelled to attend. To me it appeared as though people wanted to attend this public display of barbarism. The square was ringed with four- or five-storey buildings, and all the windows were packed with onlookers. My family's friends had an apartment overlooking the square and we were invited to see the spectacle from a good vantage point, right across from the gallows. From the window, we could see the entire square and as far as I could see, the square and streets were packed with people. The mood appeared high, anticipatory, if not festive. No one had ever seen a public execution.

Soldiers and police surrounded the square as the six men were lined up on the scaffold. The executioners put ropes on their necks. A Gestapo official read a short verdict and the trap was sprung. It felt like the crowd uttered a shudder as the men fell through the trap. Their knees jerked, then dropped, and their bodies swayed. They were left hanging for twenty-four hours. The crowd's mood changed to sombre, and people left either crying or in silence. I heard that the families were allowed to retrieve the bodies for burial the next day. This exhibition understandably caused everyone to take notice, and my mother stopped me from going on the street to sell or trade.

Closing In

In February of 1940, we heard that my father was in Częstochowa, a mere seventy kilometres away from us. The news was electrifying. Up to this point, we'd had no information about his whereabouts or even if he was still alive. My mother had been thinking the worst – that he would not come back – and had tried to make a life for herself as much as possible. She had met a high-level Polish railway employee who helped us with food and other items. More importantly, he was a companion to her in a trying time. He was a widower and had two sons – one a bit older than me and the other my sister's age – and we were introduced to them. I visited their apartment on the main thoroughfare in an elegant building in the centre of the city and was very uncomfortable when I overheard the boys say, "We'd better be nice to him; he may end up as our stepbrother." I had an inkling that something was happening between their father and my mother, and once I walked in on them in the bedroom and saw them kissing. My mother told me that he was just a friend, but I realized it was more than that. I was shocked and wanted to talk to my sister about it, but I never did. By that time I understood that people had love affairs. My mother was young and beautiful and it was not surprising men found her attractive. Even as a young child, I remembered that my father had accused her of having an affair and hit her when he found her in a park with a man. My father had been away a number of months and the future was uncertain, so I guess having an affair with a Polish official of the railway would be helpful in providing for our family. Nevertheless, I felt pain and disappointment. The news of my father's homecoming changed all this, and I was overjoyed.

Due to travel restrictions, it took another three weeks before my father could find his way to us. Jews were forced to wear a white armband with a blue Star of David, and it had become illegal for them to travel. When my father boarded a train without the armband, a Polish man pointed him out to the Gestapo and he was arrested. He talked his way out of jail by telling them that he had come from the Soviet Union area and did not know the law; besides, he could not have found a vendor to buy an armband. After that, he mostly travelled by foot and cart because the railways were well patrolled and he could not risk being caught again. When he contacted us from Częstochowa, his troubles were not over – Częstochowa was in the *Generalgouvernement* area and Sosnowiec was annexed to the Third Reich, so he had to smuggle himself across the border. We were all terribly worried and hoped he would not be caught. When my father finally did arrive, he brought us news of our family in Częstochowa and we were overjoyed to hear they were all well.

Much of what my father had gone through since his deportation came to me in pieces as he related his experiences to my mother and his friends. When he was deported from Chorzów he was shipped to the eastern part of German-occupied Poland to a camp near the town of Nisko. Nisko was selected by the Nazis as a huge resettlement area for Jews expelled from Third Reich territory. On arrival in Nisko, my father managed to escape while the Germans were shooting at him and the only direction he could run was east. He travelled further east to the border between German-occupied Polish territory and Soviet-occupied Polish territory. We later found out that before the war, the Germans had signed a non-aggression pact with the Soviet Union, which came to be known as the Molotov-Ribbentrop pact. They agreed that when the Germans invaded Poland, the

Soviet Union would invade from the east and occupy the eastern part of Poland, including the territory known as Polish Ukraine and parts of Galicia. After crossing the border at night my father made his way to Lwów where, by chance, he met up with my mother's two sisters, Ruzia and Zosia.

Lwów was overrun with refugees and was certainly no place to bring a family. People lived in hallways and went from one place to another to avoid being caught without a job or a place to live, since this was cause for the Soviets to deport people to Siberia. Deportation to Siberia was thought of as certain death. My father and my aunts thought that the Germans, being from a more civilized country than the Soviet Union, would treat their population in a more humane way. Despite my father's experience of deportation from Chorzów, he reasoned that although the Nazis might not tolerate Jews in the annexed territory, they wouldn't bother people living in the *Generalgouvernement* territory. He assumed that since he no longer had a store and was willing to work, the Germans would not bother him. My father was a big, strong man and was not afraid of work. In 1919, at the age of seventeen, he had left his home in Częstochowa and gone to Chorzów, then part of Silesia, to work underground as a coal miner. My father and my aunts decided it would be safer to return to German-occupied territory. They thought that life and survival under the Nazis would be easier than under Soviet occupation.

Soon after occupying Polish territory, the Nazis established a Judenrat, a Jewish community council, in each major community. The Nazis selected members and the leader to the council from among the most prominent people in the community. In Sosnowiec, Moshe, or Moniek, Merin was not the most respected person by far, but he nevertheless appointed himself as head to the Judenrat and the Germans confirmed him. Moniek Merin was considered a hero by some and a villain by most. People said he lived in luxury, behaved like a king, was arrogant, corrupt and thought he was invincible.

Shortly after my father's arrival in Sosnowiec, the Nazis demanded that the Judenrat provide four hundred men to be sent to a labour camp, to work on highway construction. Moniek Merin knew my father through family connections and knew that he was respected in the community. He appealed to my father to volunteer, as this would encourage others to do the same. My father agreed, and there was no trouble putting together the work force of four hundred men. The camp was in Lower Silesia and known as Gross Strehlitz. It was an enclosed camp but the workers were allowed to leave the camp after work and go into town. My father traded with the locals and sent parcels home to us. In addition to that, they received pay, so it seemed like a good job. After three months, the camp was dissolved and the men were shipped back.

A couple of weeks later, the Judenrat informed the community that the Nazis required two thousand men. My father volunteered again, as did many people, since their previous work camp experience had been fine. Nonetheless, the Judenrat could not get the required quota, so the Nazis set up checkpoints on the street, and anyone without a work card was immediately picked up to fill the labour quota. This time, however, the men were sent to a camp that was entirely different. It was an enclosed slave labour camp with a barbed wire fence, and no one was allowed to leave.

The enlistment of new recruits to other labour camps continued but the Judenrat was not able to supply the numbers quickly enough. People without work papers, or even with work papers, if they had soft hands, were verbally abused as shirkers and taken on the spot to a waiting truck and ferried away. Families, including those of my friends, did not know what had happened to their men. They just disappeared. Women and children were left without means of support. If the man resisted he was beaten or even shot. People were afraid to venture into the street.

With my father away again, this time to a slave labour camp, conditions deteriorated for our family. My mother's supply of wool ran out and she knitted for people who could either supply their own wool or give her an old sweater or dress to rip and knit a new dress from. Food was now difficult to get even if we had the money to buy it, and with our ration cards, the food we could get was insufficient. People had to line up for hours and the supply was not always there. As hunger and starvation increased, the Judenrat established soup kitchens. Because my father was in a slave labour camp, we qualified to receive soup kitchen meal tickets. The meals – individual dishes such as soup, potatoes, small pieces of meat and vegetables – became our main daily meal and it was my responsibility to fetch it. There were long lineups and people congregated around the kitchen, trying to buy meal tickets or begging for food. We carried the food in a *menażka*, a canteen of metal containers stacked one above the other and held together with a metal band. Each portion required a ticket and we had four tickets but the food was not plentiful.

My friends and I had a scheme going. We would line up together, put our tickets on the serving table in front of us and then, as the girl serving took our containers and turned to fill them, one of us would put our hand over one set of tickets and cause a commotion by pushing each other. The girl would get distracted and not remember if she had taken both sets of tickets. We shared the extra tickets and this allowed us to get a bit more food or sell the tickets on the black market. If we had been caught we would have been arrested and sent away. This worked for a short time until the girls at the counter got wise to our scheme.

~

By the summer of 1940, the Judenrat had become more powerful, complying with orders to supply labour not only to slave labour camps but also to local industries in Sosnowiec that produced all manner of goods for the German army and war machinery. With the need of skilled workers growing, the Judenrat persuaded the Germans to allow the creation of trade schools. The enrolment age was fourteen but my mother was anxious to get me off the street, so she registered me even though I was only twelve. I enrolled in a six-month electrician apprentice course. I had been interested in electricity ever since our apartment in Chorzów was converted to electric lights. I was amazed that a wall switch turned on the light on the ceiling. I loved the coursework and studied hard. My mother was surprised with my success. To her amazement, I passed two exams without trouble and graduated as an electrician-apprentice.

I soon received a job with an electrician's helper; my task was to chisel channels in brick walls for the installation of electrical tubing in a multi-storey building. Most of the work had to be done on tall ladders, sometimes next to an open stairwell. It was hard and dangerous work – the hammer was heavy and if I missed the chisel, my hand received the blow. My hands were full of bruises. I was only a few weeks on the job when I lost my balance and fell off a ladder in a stairwell. I got hurt quite badly and the other apprentices carried me home on top of a ladder made into a stretcher. That was the end of my employment with that company.

By December 1940, three months before my bar mitzvah, my father was still in a camp so my grandfather took me to a Hebrew teacher to prepare me to read from the Torah. My Hebrew was practically non-existent, but my grandfather was very intent on my having a bar mitzvah; I think, with my father being away, he felt duty bound. Of course, no one at that time knew of such a thing as a learning disability, and everyone assumed that I was just plain dumb or lazy. My grandfather did not know about my obstacles in reading not only Hebrew, but also Polish. I knew what my parents thought about my academic ability because I often overheard them say that I did not have the ability to learn and would end up as a shoemaker or a tailor, which did not require book learning.

The teacher gave me a reading test and let out a deep sigh – I could tell he was disappointed. A month later he summoned my grandfather and told him, in my presence, that all he would be able to teach me in the time available was to recite the blessings for the reading of the Torah. With great conviction, he said that I would not be able to learn to chant or even to read from the Torah, as was the custom. He also confirmed that I had no head for learning. I never did learn to read Hebrew fluently. I partially memorized the two required blessings before and after the Torah readings.

In 1941, my bar mitzvah fell on March 7. By then, all prayer groups had to meet clandestinely in small rooms or in basements because the Nazis prohibited, under the penalty of death, the assembly of any group of men. On the day of my bar mitzvah my grandfather took me to a small room in a basement where ten men were assembled. The Torah reader, who was my teacher, put his *tallit*, prayer shawl, over my head, helped me say the blessings and then read my designated Torah portion. My grandfather managed to get a cake, some vodka and a bottle of wine to make a Kiddush, the blessing over the wine.

～

The Nazis selected the Jewish holidays to inflict the most pain on us. In the spring of 1941, during Passover, a holiday celebrating freedom from slavery, they evicted the Jews from the town of Oświęcim (later called Auschwitz) and surrounding towns, where Jews had lived for hundreds of years, and most of the Jews were resettled in our city. They arrived on horse-drawn carts and were deposited in the centre of the old city, staying there in the open for days. The influx of thousands of people caused more congestion in our already crowded section of the city. The lineups at the soup kitchen grew longer and the amount of food distributed diminished.

By the summer of 1941, more deportations to labour camps took place. Those taken were usually young men and women. More people from adjoining communities were transferred into Sosnowiec, and it was harder to get food and almost impossible to get a job in the city. Through my grandfather's efforts, and his connections to the Judenrat establishment, I obtained a job as an electrician in a shoe factory that repaired footwear for the mining industry. I was quite proud that, as an apprentice, I could work independently without an electrician's supervision. I did some wiring for outlets and lights but when the work was finished I was afraid I would lose my job so I tried to make myself useful by sweeping the floors and dusting off the shelves in the little supply room where the boss's father was in charge. As I did, I noticed that the boxes containing different items were very disorganized. I started to line them up and I labelled each box so that it was easy to find the various items. I combined half-empty boxes and removed the empty ones, and I made inventory lists to help him see what needed to be reordered. The old man appreciated the work and allowed me to help him in the morning to hand out the material to the shoemakers. Each shoemaker had to fill out a requisition sheet for the material needed to make repairs, and I helped fill out this form. At the end of the shift, the workers had to come back with the finished shoes. If the repair was not complete, they had to hand over the shoes and the unused materials.

Shoe leather was scarce and very much in demand, commanding a high price on the black market. Every night, the workers were searched for any stolen material. Through my work with the old man, I gained the trust of his son, the big boss. One of my jobs was to search the shoemakers as they were leaving the factory. I hated the job because I had to act as a policeman. On one occasion, the boss was observing me in the search and my hand must have slowed when I felt some material under one boy's clothing. I knew that if I removed whatever was hidden in his jacket, the boy would be punished for stealing and fired on the spot. A job in the factory meant life for a whole family. After I let the boy through, the boss stopped him and pulled out a pair of soles from his inside pocket. He turned to me and hit me over the head – my glasses went flying – and he kicked me. I thought that would be the end of me and that he would fire me or report me to the police. But when I came in the next morning he wasn't there, and the old man didn't mention anything to me. However, he fired the young shoemaker, without reporting him to the police.

The boss was a *Volksdeutsche* and a member of the Nazi Party. He had been appointed *Treuhänder*, trustee, of the factory after it was confiscated from its Jewish owners. The Jewish owners weren't allowed into the factory. The boss's father, who I worked for, had no use for the Nazis, but he would not tell this to his son, who would have had him arrested for not supporting the Party. Secretly, he was very sympathetic to me. He liked the way I kept myself busy. He treated me as a human being, and I thought he was fond of me. The old man would bring me a stale loaf of bread and occasionally a piece of salami and other food items, which was a great bonus for my family. He would ask me to go and fetch him some good pipe tobacco, available only on the black market, and pay me with German Reichsmark. I made a profit on the tobacco and on the currency exchange. We became very friendly, especially when his son was out of the factory, which was often.

After the initial morning rush and clean-up, I still had lots of time on my hands so I went into the shop and helped the workers to grind, polish and wax the soles. The men who had been hired were not shoemakers, and they did shabby work. They didn't know how to fit the leather pieces properly together and left a lot of holes. Also, the wax filled the voids between the layers of leather but fell out when the shoes got wet. This caused a major blowout when the shoes came back with a complaint from the mining authorities, and a lot of people lost their jobs.

As time went on, by carefully watching the old man, I learned how to lay out and cut top leather for various parts of shoes. I liked the job; it was like working out a jigsaw puzzle. A template was used to trace out the various shoe parts so as to have as little waste as possible. I could visualize the layout and became very good at getting the maximum pieces out of a hide. The next step was to cut the leather, which was tricky, as a slip of the knife could ruin part of the hide. At first, he let me cut a small hide. After a while, he saw that I was very careful and meticulous and actually cut it more exactly than he did. My next challenge was to cut the thick sole leather. Cutting the heavy leather hide required a lot of strength. The only way I could do it was to wedge the stiff hide against my chest and pull the curved knife hard toward my chest. Many days I went home with pain in my chest but I was happy. The old man smiled at me approvingly when I finished carving up a hide.

After promising to keep it secret from his son, I convinced him to allow me to make a pair of shoes for myself provided I did it in the plant after hours. Working in the storeroom and giving out the work, I was in a position to do favours for the shoemakers. I chose one and convinced him to help me make my shoes. He guided me through every step. Each step was challenging, but it was fun as the shoe started to take shape. Sewing on the soles was the trickiest part but in the end I made a pair of shoes and thus became a shoemaker – my parents' prediction had come true.

My workplace was in the Jewish area and across the street from the factory were some large apartment buildings where my friends lived. We congregated after work and had a lot of fun fooling around, playing games. We spent most of our free time on the street and in the gateways of the apartment building because our homes were all overcrowded. I liked one girl and she apparently liked me, but one of my friends lied to her that I had boasted of kissing her, and she became very angry and wouldn't talk to me. I was hurt. I was thirteen and that was the second crush I had on a girl.

In the summer of 1941, my grandfather Shimon had a stroke that disabled him and took his speech. I was devastated; it hurt me deeply seeing him incapacitated, in bed, not able to move or speak. I loved him very much and tried to help my mother look after him by feeding him, giving him water and adjusting his bed. After a few weeks his condition worsened and he had to be taken to a hospital. He died a few days later, with my mother at his bedside. She was forever thankful that he died before the first deportation. The death was painful for our family. My grandfather had been the patriarch of my mother's family and instrumental in getting us through the first months of the war, especially with the absences of my father. My mother arranged his funeral but for reasons unknown to us, we were not allowed to go. He just disappeared from our lives, which made it harder for us to accept. We did not have an opportunity to say goodbye. I mourned his loss, missing his cheerful and jovial disposition. Without him, our house seemed empty.

~

My sister was sixteen years old, and her friends and various boyfriends sometimes gathered in our home. Her friends would bribe me to leave, but I managed to overhear some of their conversations. They talked about the war in the Soviet Union, although I had little concept as to where that was. Her boyfriends were older and belonged to Jewish youth organizations that were strictly forbidden. One day I had quite a surprise when I arrived home and saw my sister sitting on the couch with a German soldier; he was the eldest son of Mrs. Ullmann, who had kept our wool. I was very upset to see him with my sister but my mother told me to leave them alone. My sister must have written letters to his sister; I had no idea how he would have found us otherwise. She told us that he had been drafted and was on his way to the front. I was worried that my friends would see him in my home and would accuse me of collaborating with the Nazis. I think he was as uncomfortable being in a Jewish home as my sister was sitting next to him in his German uniform.

Around this time, the Nazis seemed to have a greater need for workers and they continued to send thousands of men out of our area, presumably to labour camps. After months in the second forced labour camp, my father could not stand it any longer and started looking for a way to get out. To escape from the camp was almost impossible. When my father found out that the sick or injured were shipped back to Sosnowiec for treatment because there were no medical services at the camp, he complained of a bad pain in his back and was sent back; however, in Sosnowiec, the examining doctor didn't believe him and declared him fit for work. He was taken to the Jewish community police hall to await a transport back to the camp. My father then escaped by jumping out of the second floor window, suffering only a sprained ankle. He hid with acquaintances and friends, not daring to go home.

Moniek Merin, the head of the Judenrat, sent a message to my father that he knew his whereabouts and that he had one of two choices – either surrender and join the Jewish police force, or be found and arrested. If arrested, he would be sent back to the camp to receive punishment at the hands of the SS and our family would be deported "to the east." The Jewish police had to enforce the Judenrat orders and some went beyond the call of duty and were brutal in carrying them out. Others abused their power by accepting bribes or intimidating women to provide sexual favours. Most people did not trust the police and considered them collaborators, and some didn't want to join the police force for fear of having to do things that were against their principles. Consequently, it was not easy for the Judenrat to get new recruits. But my father really had no choice but to surrender and join.

My mother hated the idea. I thought my father looked rather dapper in his peaked white hat and double-breasted brown jacket. He was a handsome man and women had always been attracted to him. He was immaculate in his attire, his boots or shoes always shined and pants always pressed. His being a member of the police would apparently give us some advantages, such as better living quarters and, we thought, protection from deportation or having to go to labour camps. We were never made aware of any wrongdoings by my father, either during or after the war.

Nonetheless, in the fall of 1941, we were ordered by the Judenrat to leave our home on Prosta Street. The bathroom was the hardest to lose – bathing in a full-length bathtub instead of a metal washtub was a luxury hard to come by. This move changed my life – not only did I lose my friends, who were sent to different parts of the ghetto, but

my environment was also shattered. The area into which we were required to relocate was small and congested. We were able to transfer
into a building much better maintained than most others, but moving into a single room on Towarowa Street was a disappointment to
us all. Even so, the single room was actually larger than what most
people received, and it had room for two single metal beds, a table
and a wardrobe, as well as a kitchen counter, a shelving unit and a
sink with running water. Linka and I had to share a bed. The washroom, which was shared with other rooms on the floor, was in the
hallway and did not have a shower or bathtub. This was the best that
my father could get, even with his position as a policeman.

I kept on working in the shoe factory. I made new friends in the
apartment building and after a while we adjusted to the new conditions. Some of the people there were better off than us, but we shared
whatever we could scrounge in food and sweets.

In the summer of 1942, at the beginning of August, the Judenrat
issued a decree requiring all Jews to report to a large park, which Jews
were usually forbidden to enter, to get our food ration cards stamped.
We started out with joy and enthusiasm; it was a beautiful summer
day with full sun and a cool breeze. There were a lot of people, approximately 30,000, in the park, which was completely fenced in. We
were all gathered in one end of the park and the kids were running
around and having a great time; mothers brought out snacks and it
was very pleasant.

Suddenly, all fell silent; it was as if someone had turned off the
sound on a radio. We were ordered to pass between tables manned
by Nazi officers. Everyone had to produce their documents and work
papers. Those with at least one member employed in a factory were
allowed to leave. Older people and children were separated from
their families. Young people between the ages of eighteen and thirty
were segregated; thousands of people were detained. Our family was
allowed to go home. When we arrived home, we were ordered by the
Judenrat to pack a suitcase for each person and vacate the premises

in two hours. We had to find temporary accommodations with other members of our family or friends. We packed all of the belongings that we could not take with us into our wardrobe and sealed it as best we could. Then we had to leave.

Those detained were moved from the park into a group of connected buildings, including ours, and kept there for a week. Terrible scenes ensued as members of families not taken tried to have their family members released. I was told people offered a lot of money and much bribery went on, especially with the senior Judenrat members and Moniek Merin himself. My mother's aunt Helen, Yehoshua's wife, was among those detained. Moniek Merin was related to her, and her family appealed to him to let her out, but he refused to use his influence to release her. He wanted to show that his family members would not be treated differently. He kept assuring us that nothing bad would happen to these people and that they were only going to be "resettled." Helen's family blamed my father for not rescuing her, although he tried. They never forgave him and never spoke to him again.

When they finally took the people out of the building and walked them to the railway siding not far away, a group of us followed them and watched in horror and disbelief as the Nazis loaded the people into boxcars. The Nazis were quite brutal, shoving people and even tossing infants into the boxcar as if they were sacks of potatoes. We had no inkling where they were being sent, but we did not hear from them again. It was rumoured that some postcards came from the deportees saying they were well and awaiting the arrival of their families. Years later, we found out that this was the first major transport from our area to Auschwitz.

After the people were deported, we were allowed to return to our apartment. The sight and stink was unbearable. All the furniture that we left behind had been moved, some into other apartments. The wardrobe stood open and all the items were gone. Pots and pans were on the floor and it appeared that they had been used as toilets.

Our bed sheets, pillows and towels were all gone as well. The mattress was soiled and unusable. The Judenrat hired a sanitation company to clean and fumigate the building. Two weeks later, when we moved back in, we had to start from scratch. The strong disinfectant smell was horrendous and lingered for weeks. Friends gave us cooking utensils, spare bedding, towels and other essentials. Even though my father was a policeman, we had a hard time acquiring used mattresses.

In the fall of 1942, we were ordered to move to Środula, a small village located on the outskirts of Sosnowiec. The village was on a hilltop, surrounded by fields. Polish farmers had been forced to vacate their homes and the Jews moved in. My father managed to get a place at the far end of this new ghetto, where it was less congested, with a backyard, a garden and a huge pear tree in the middle. We were allocated a room in a two-room apartment on the second floor of a two-storey building. This room was a quarter the size of our previous room and there was no inside washroom or running water; the water well was hundreds of metres away, down a steep hill. Uncle Yehoshua and three of his daughters occupied the second room. A curtain divided our room into two; the front part was used as a corridor and our kitchen, which had a dry washstand, a commode and iron stove. Our two beds were behind the curtain to give us some privacy. Linka and I again slept in the same bed, which was embarrassing to both of us, as I would sometimes have an erection. We slept head to toe, which was uncomfortable, but less embarrassing. Our parents slept in the same room, our beds separated by a table. The beds also served as benches. Our living space was non-existent. Our life in the new ghetto was much more difficult, but we were together as a family and that was what mattered. Although I had a long walk to my job in the shoe factory, my life in Środula had some advantages. I had a garden and a girlfriend, Mania, although we kept our relationship secret. Mania and her family lived in the apartment next to ours, which had a large room and a kitchen. Her father must have been a member of the Judenrat to obtain a whole apartment for just his immediate family.

There was talk among my sister's friends that an underground resistance movement was being formed. I thought that maybe I should leave the ghetto and join them so, as a first step, I decided to dye my hair blond. I got hold of some peroxide and poured half a bottle into a bucket with some water. I applied this mixture to my hair and instead of turning it blond, it became yellow/orange. It was a disaster. I looked comical and my mother said, "You look even more Jewish." She cut my hair and gave me a lecture that should I be found outside the ghetto, the whole family would suffer terrible consequences. She did not elaborate. I knew what she meant.

There were uprising attempts in most large ghettos, including Sosnowiec. Moniek Merin was against any resistance group and would have turned them in if he had known who they were. He believed that as long as we went along with the wishes of the Nazis and were useful in the war economy, the ghetto would be saved.

After the war, I heard it said, like an accusation, that the Jews "went as sheep to slaughter," but this could not have been further from the truth. The Nazis kept their intentions secret and proceeded slowly and methodically, one step at a time. The penalty for running away was death not only for the person caught, but for the whole family. To run away or join the underground was a very big risk and responsibility. If our Polish neighbours were caught hiding a Jew, they too would be executed, sometimes right on the spot, to make an example.

Within the Środula ghetto we were free to go anywhere and on Sundays, my day off work, I explored various sections with some friends. I also did some electrical work for a wealthy German-Jewish family who lived in a big house. They must have paid a huge bribe to Moniek Merin for it. I installed additional lights and plugs in some of the rooms. They had a severely disabled daughter who was confined to a wheelchair. One day, while I worked in the house, two Jewish policemen drove up in a truck with the SS and told her parents that they were there to pick up their daughter and take her to an institution. We all knew what that meant. Moniek Merin had to deliver a certain number of people to the Nazis for deportation; it was no secret that he intended to keep the healthy people and sacrifice the elderly, disabled and sick. The scene was heart-wrenching. The parents protested without effect, and the police went into the house and picked up the panic-stricken daughter in her chair while the parents screamed and cried. As they drove away, everyone was in tears. I didn't want to show any emotion but the tears were streaming down my face, too. The parents paid me for what I had done and told me my work was done.

The threat of deportation was constant and we were always stressed. We never knew exactly when it might take place, but it was usually during the day when most of the able-bodied men and women were at work in the city. Since my father was in the police, we thought we were exempt from deportation, but that was not always the case. Some officers' families were deported when their family member was out of town rounding up people in outlying areas. As I worked in Sosnowiec, I only found out if there had been a deportation on my return to the ghetto. I never knew if my sister and mother would be home when I arrived. I would always run at top speed up the hill to our apartment at the far end of the ghetto, slowing down only to catch my breath and relieve the sharp pain in my side.

Beginning of the End

One day, after coming home and seeing that yet another deportation had taken place, my friends and I decided to build a hiding place. We divided part of the basement of our building by bricking over a doorway. We plastered over the bricks, sprinkled coal dust and chipped the wall to make it look old. Next, we made a small opening in the corner and closed off the opening with a coal bin. We mounted wheels under the coal bin so we could pull the bin against the wall from inside. I was involved in all aspects of the construction and I was proud of my contribution. We celebrated our success by entering the room with candles and sitting around until, unexpectedly, the candles went out. We suddenly recognized we had failed to provide an adequate supply of fresh air. This was a major setback. How could we create an opening to the outside without revealing the location of the bunker?

Fortunately, some bushes grew along one wall of the bunker. We punched through a hole, covered it with a heavy wire mesh and hoped for the best. This hole, in addition to providing more air, also provided a bit of daylight. The next day, I proudly showed it to my father. He looked at the new wall and the coal bin and said something to the effect that he would rather be deported than crawl like a rat to hide. He walked away. I was hurt but not surprised. I could never gain his approval, no matter what I did and how hard I tried.

We realized the basement bunker was too small to house the thirty residents of our building, so we examined possibilities for a second hiding place. Adjoining our two-storey building was a single-storey building that shared a common wall. There was no entryway into the roof space. We decided to see if we could punch an opening from the mid-stair landing of our building into this roof space. We punched through a pilot hole and, indeed, it worked. We made an access hole and then constructed a box slightly larger than the opening and filled it with sand. It looked good and not out of place, since each stairway had a sandbox for fire fighting. The only problem was that the box was too heavy to move against the opening from inside the hiding place. We came up with the idea of putting a false bottom in the box and filling the upper half with sand, leaving the bottom part empty. Little did we know that this would be our Achilles heel.

In this staircase, at the entrance to the hideout, Mania and I spent wonderful moments in the dark away from the others. Mania was my first girlfriend and I was very much in love with her. At fifteen, it was a new and very intense feeling to embrace each other and explore our bodies. She was my age and the same height, with long, blond, slightly wavy hair, held back in braids most of the time. During the day, to avoid teasing by the kids, we never showed that we were intimate. She would flirt and talk to other boys in our yard, which made me extremely jealous. To keep our secret I had to pretend not to notice or care, but it was burning me up. In the centre of the yard stood a huge pear tree with thick branches from which hung a swing. This was our gathering place, not only for kids from our building but also from surrounding areas. We would stand at the tree and talk and joke late into the evening.

The landing outside our apartment was my workshop, where a wooden chest contained my invaluable tools and stamp album. This landing was another hangout for my friends and me. On my return home, I loved being greeted by the younger kids and Mania. One day, coming home after a long, hot day at the shoe factory, I made the mistake of asking them not to make such a fuss. They stopped and I forever regretted making that remark. Soon after that, I was heartbroken because my wooden chest disappeared. I played detective, trying to find a clue as to who may have stolen it. It was the second time that I had lost my precious stamp album. During the early days in Sosnowiec I spent much of my hard-earned money on the stamps, which I painstakingly catalogued and mounted. Later, when we were preparing to go into hiding, all this seemed trivial.

During the beautiful summer days of 1943, I was always carrying buckets of water from the well to the apartment building. No matter who needed water, whether for the kitchen or the laundry, I was always asked to fetch it. My refrain was always, "Why me?" There were others in the house. At first, carrying water with an over-the-shoulder wooden carrier was fun. The boys in the area challenged each other to see who could carry the most water and who could get to the top of the hill faster without spilling any. The women encouraged the race, especially on a washday. The reward was a piece of a baked good or a rare candy.

When we moved into the ghetto, the weather was cold and I had worn a jacket with shoulder pads. However, when the weather grew warmer and it was too hot to wear a jacket, the wooden carrier pressed on my bones and was very painful. I got some old felt hats and other felt-type material and after hours of fitting it out, the carrier fit snugly over my skinny shoulders.

I never minded getting water for my garden, which was in the courtyard and had been left by the previous occupants. No one else in the building was interested in doing the hard work needed to restore the garden, nor in hauling the water from the well. The garden was about two metres wide and ten metres long. I dug up the soil, raked it and made numerous beds. I obtained seeds from my boss's father at work and planted radishes, carrots, lettuce, beans, peas, beets and even tomatoes. My hard work was finally starting to show some results, and we had already enjoyed some radishes and lettuce. The problem was that my neighbours would help themselves and it was a race to harvest the produce before they did.

Once, during the spring, I had been at the well when I spotted my father with a woman. He called me over and swore me to secrecy. I resented that he made me part of his deceit, although I wouldn't have told my mother anyway because I didn't want to hurt her. I figured she knew but was not in a position to do anything about it. He claimed the woman was supporting him with cigarettes and money. This behaviour was not new to me; family members had told me about his prior infidelities – he had even had an affair with the wife of one of his brothers – and my mother knew as well. They had had confrontations about it. But at that time, I felt my mother was vulnerable and I did not want her to know. It was a terrible time for all of us and the moral attitude of many was, "What the hell, who knows what tomorrow will bring."

~

On July 31, 1943, a Saturday evening, my sister and her friends gathered whatever food they could scrounge from their parents, which was not much, and organized a birthday party for one of their friends. We usually waited up for Linka to come home but that night she warned us that she would be very late. Linka arrived home at two o'clock in the morning. She woke us up without turning on the lights, and in hushed tones told us that something was happening at the SS headquarters. Over the past few weeks, the air had been filled with expectation. We had been hearing that other areas were being liquidated, with everyone deported east for resettlement, but we never thought it would actually happen to this ghetto. None of us wanted to think about it. Moniek Merin had assured us that we were safe because we were doing essential work for the Germans.

It was still dark outside and my sister and father were sitting at the table, talking in low voices. I had always envied their special rapport. My father respected Linka's opinion and often confided in her. While my father and sister continued their discussion, my mother was preparing meals with the remnants of whatever we had left. I was glad that I had brought up two pails of water the night before. It would be dangerous to go to the well now. My family tried to assess the situation; my father had not heard anything about this deportation. Normally, the Jewish police would be assembled to keep order before the SS arrived. We did not know if this would be a partial or total deportation. We assumed it was a partial one and that hiding would save us. If it were a total and final deportation, hiding would do no good.

My mother inquired about the birthday party. According to my sister it was a great success. Her friend's parents had brought out every bit of food in the house and each friend contributed something. Linka was glad the party had taken place. If something drastic was to happen, this was the last time they would be together in the ghetto. While dressing, we moved around our tiny space. My father retrieved a small suitcase from under the bed and started to pack, which was simple because there was not much to pack. All of our items of value had already been sold for food. My mother put the food in a hamper. We were all busy doing something, without conversation. The sky began to lighten. We were packed and sitting on the beds, trying to decide what our next move should be.

On Sundays, no work details went into the city, which meant that if anything were to happen, such as a final deportation, it would happen on a Sunday, when all the people were in the ghetto. The residents of our building had stationed lookouts on our rooftop, and since our building stood on a hill overlooking the entire area of the ghetto, they could also see the Gestapo headquarters. Šrodula was a ghetto without walls or barbed wire enclosures, but the village was surrounded by farmers' fields, as was typical in Europe. The Nazis could surround the village with a few dozen soldiers and all of us would be trapped.

The lookouts noticed that Gestapo headquarters had been awash with light for hours – this meant the Nazis were preparing for an "action," a euphemism for deportation. At five a.m., the lookouts informed us that the village was surrounded and the SS had set up machine guns at strategic points. Trucks with loudspeakers drove down the streets announcing, "We're going to resettle you. You're allowed to take whatever you can carry. Take warm clothes; you're going to be resettled in the east. Come voluntarily! If we have to come and get you, you're going to be punished and you're not going to be allowed to take anything with you." Many people volunteered. They took their suitcases and walked out to be escorted away.

My family decided to hide in the basement, but by the time we got there it was full. When we argued that it was our hiding place, people yelled at us, indignant, saying their lives were as precious as ours and there was no more room. We had to go to the roof hiding place that I knew was not as secure, but we had no choice. It hurt me to see my parents crawl on all fours and squeeze into the hiding place. Even though my father had previously said he would not hide like a rat, he did not protest – he helped my mother through the opening. Just before the opening was closed off, a woman came and asked to be admitted. She had a baby in her arms. I heard the men at the opening arguing with her that she could not come in because the baby's cry would give us away. She assured the men that it would not happen and was admitted. She settled in the far corner of the roof space.

Each family huddled together. The heat in the attic space was stifling and people crowded at the air vent to catch as much air as possible. We all held our breath when we heard the soldiers go upstairs and search through every room, moving furniture and banging on walls in search of hiding places. Finally, they went back down, shouting to someone that there was no one there. A long time after, when we could not hear the movement of soldiers, the men at the entryway pushed back the sand box and we came out, relieved to not have been discovered. Suddenly we heard a terrible, heart-wrenching cry coming from the woman with the baby. Apparently, someone near her, during the search, had suffocated the child. She left the building, alone and sobbing. I never saw her again. I did not know who she was or where she came from. It is something that is etched in my mind and to this day I can still hear her.

The tragedy of this occurrence did not sink in right away. At the time, the sacrifice of a child's life to save the lives of thirty people seemed reasonable. In the end, though, we all were found and most went to their death. Years later, it struck me that the tragedy was that we were made to commit murder, to take the life of a child, so that we might live possibly another day or a few weeks. The Nazis not only murdered us; they also perverted our moral values.

We came out of the oppressive heat and returned to our home and had some food and water. We thought that the deportation was over but we did not dare leave the building or make any noise. It was a beautiful summer day and it was getting hotter. My uncle Yehoshua boisterously announced that he had found the best hiding place – he had lain down in the gazebo at the end of my garden and they did not find him.

Our reprieve was short-lived. In the afternoon, at the height of the day's heat, we had to go back into hiding. The soldiers were seen coming back, this time armed with axes and ladders. After the morning's experience, my parents refused to go back into the roof hiding place. We didn't even try to use the basement hideout. My parents and my girlfriend's parents opted instead to hide in the attic space above the second floor. The attic was accessible through a pull-down panel in the stairway's ceiling with a ladder attached to it. Mania and I had often hidden in the attic to get away from the other kids. The attic was high and clotheslines were strung between the rafters. It was used to dry clothes during rainy days. The soldiers had not discovered the attic on the first search and my father considered it safe.

The heat in the attic was unbearable. Sweat was pouring down our faces and our shirts were soaked. My mother sat next to my father, talking quietly. For the first time in my life I saw my father perturbed, not in control of the situation. This frightened me more than anything else. It hurt me to see them cooped up like this. My mother wore a light summer dress. Her skin was tanned but thin; I could almost see every bone in her body and face. The hardship of the last few years was visible, but her youthful beauty was still there. No matter what, she was a graceful lady.

The Nazi soldiers came upstairs and again did a thorough search, turning over any furniture that stood against walls. As they tapped the walls, looking for concealed spaces, we held our breath and did not move. Some of the footsteps started to recede, and I thought we were safe. Then we heard one soldier order, "Look in the attic." We heard the motion of a table being pulled into the hallway, and the access panel was pulled down. We were ordered out. We came out to blows from the butts of guns and abusive language. Because we had been hiding, we were not allowed to take anything from our apartment.

As we passed the landing-hiding place, the gun of one of the last soldiers struck the bottom of the sandbox concealing the opening and a hollow sound was emitted. He punched his bayonet into the sand and realized that it had a false bottom. He called back to some of his comrades and they proceeded to pry away the box from the wall, shooting into the opening. Some twenty-five people came out and those who lingered were threatened with death. They were pushed down the stairs and joined us on the street. Uncle Yehoshua, who had hidden in the gazebo, was also caught in this more thorough search, and he was with us as well. From there, surrounded by SS men, we were marched off as a group to the assembly place at the ghetto gate.

We arrived to chaos. Kids, abandoned or separated from their parents, were running, crying and desperately searching for them. Mothers separated from their children were frantic. Some others bundled their infants and left them by the curb. I could not understand what desperation would lead a mother to abandon her child. Even the guards were amazed and ordered random women to pick up the bundles. Some women picked up the stray children voluntarily and tried to comfort them as best they could, not realizing it would cost them their lives.

After a while we were marched out. We did not know where we were being taken. As we walked through the streets Polish people gathered on both sides of us. Some women bystanders cried and wrung their hands while others, especially the young boys, jeered at us and spewed out obscenities. We tried to stay together as a family group, but people were pushing and jostling for position to be with their own families.

It was almost dark when we arrived at the railway station in Będzin, the sister ghetto to Sosnowiec. The SS officers were selecting young people to be sent to labour camps, and some of my cousins volunteered. My father suggested to my sister that she go with them to the labour camp but my sister refused. She didn't want to leave my mother, and she wanted to stay together as a family. At that point a woman, elegantly dressed in suit and hat, ran from the line toward us. An SS officer shouted, "Halt!" She did not heed his command. He removed his side arm and shot her. Beads of blood appeared on her legs, her legs collapsed under her and she fell next to us. The Nazi walked over to her and shot her in the head.

We lay down on the bare ground. Our family group included my parents, my sister, my second cousins and Uncle Yehoshua. As night and darkness engulfed us, people became restless. Mothers tried to quiet their children, softly assuring them that all would be well by the morning. The children continued to cry and ask, "Mommy, when are we going home?" I knew the mothers had no answers. My stomach was growling from hunger, and I was thirsty. Our family sat together, leaning and lying on each other, not speaking. Everyone was engrossed in his or her own speculations as to what would happen next. The night felt long and no matter how I sat or lay, I couldn't find any comfort. I must have fallen asleep though, because I woke suddenly as a freight train entered the station. Suddenly, chaos erupted – kids were crying and family members separated during the night were searching for each other, shouting out names. The sound was deafening. The Nazi guards, who were not noticeable before, appeared and started to shove people toward the open doors of the freight cars. They pushed us in, shut the door, and the lock clanged in place.

We had no idea where we were being shipped. We huddled together; there was hardly any room to move. People were crying, sobbing and moaning, or embracing, forlorn and silent. Each group was in its own world. Most of these worlds, somehow, I knew, would end shortly. One of my sister's boyfriends was standing at the small barred window, trying to see what direction we were travelling, and was shot by a guard through the wall of the boxcar. He sustained a flesh wound under his arm and was bleeding profusely. I was scared and could not think. The pounding of my heart synchronized with the clang of the wheels. I did not know what the next few hours would bring but I did know that something catastrophic was about to happen.

All around, people pressed against us. We were oblivious to them; all that mattered was that we were still together. We all sensed this could be our last time together. With her arm around our shoulders, Mother said to us, "Take care; look after yourselves. If we get separated, we will meet after the war at grandmother Elka's neighbour." To avoid thinking, I repeated the words, "After the war." The words stuck in my mind like a mantra. After the war. The words blended into the clang of the wheels. Would there ever be an end to the war? It did not seem possible. I could hardly remember when there was no war. The words suppressed other thoughts more awesome and ugly. There were rumours about our destination, but no one knew the truth.

My father handed out the last of his money. He told us that he had been tempted to use the money many times in the last few months, but had kept it as a last resort. He told us most likely we would be separated. "Hide it on you," he suggested. Where should I hide it? I had only a shirt and a pair of pants on. I kept the money clenched in my fist. We had no luggage, but it did not matter, we were still together. My mother had repeated this anxiously in the last few months – whatever we had did not matter; we had each other. We were one of the few families who were still together, and this was only because of my father's position. My thoughts were interrupted by squealing wheels as the train suddenly slowed down. We gripped each other tightly; people behind us pushed against us. Our eyes were downcast, as if to look at each other would bring on panic and tears. The train stopped with a jerk and the crowd stood up in unison as if lifted with an unseen force. The car door slid open with a bang. "Alle raus, Alle raus!" (Everyone out!) was the command.

We jumped down onto a platform in the middle of nowhere.

Days of Grey

Men in striped uniforms and SS men confronted us. Anyone who had managed to bring something with them was ordered to drop their bags. SS men were shouting in German, "Men to the left, women to the right!" There was bedlam, people rushing here and there. The men in striped uniforms were everywhere, tearing people apart. Husbands didn't want to leave their wives and mothers were clinging to their sons and daughters. I was standing with my mother and sister when my father grabbed my arm and pulled me to him. The prisoners shouted in Polish, "Men to the left, women to the right!" but no one was paying attention. Somehow, order was restored and two columns of people were formed: men and boys over the age of twelve and women and children – boys and girls – under twelve.

I did not say goodbye to my mother. I did not say goodbye to my sister.

In the men's column, my father and I found ourselves facing an SS officer in green uniform and white gloves. He pointed to my father and commanded he approach; he spoke to him for a few seconds and sent him to his right. (I later found out that the SS man instructed my father to line up the men he sent to him in rows of five and march them off. This was unusual, as the prisoners on the ramp usually did that.) The officer looked at me, not quite catching my eye, and motioned to me over his shoulder. I moved as directed and found myself in the first row of another column. This column was composed of boys of my age and younger and Uncle Yehoshua. I turned around to assess my situation. I saw my father busy lining up the young. My mother and sister were in a column with young people. I reasoned to myself that my mother, my sister and father would most likely go to Germany to a work camp. Our group, I thought, would stay in this place, whatever this place was. For years in the ghetto and even before that, we were told people would be resettled somewhere and this must be it. I was not worried. I had a trade. I was an electrician. I would make myself useful, no matter where I was to be sent. I certainly had no fear or inkling that someone would want to kill me.

In the meantime, trucks arrived and the older women, women with children and young girls were being loaded onto the trucks. I saw my girlfriend helping some older women onto the truck. Our eyes met, but we did not acknowledge each other otherwise. We were in a strange place, and strange things were happening to us. I hadn't realized how much she had developed physically in the last few months. She had the figure of a young woman.

Our column moved up and I lost sight of my father. Just then, I heard someone calling my name. At first I did not realize that it was me who was being called. Suddenly, I recognized my father's voice. I jumped out of the column to see him standing with an SS soldier. He said, "This is my son. He is seventeen years old and has worked as an electrician's apprentice for three years." The soldier looked at me and said, "He looks very small for seventeen." My father explained that I was small due to lack of proper food in the ghetto. The soldier asked me a few questions about my work as an electrician. Then he paused, and after a few seconds of thought he said, "Take him and make it fast." We ran over to the other lineup and my father placed me in the centre of the column to be less conspicuous. Another boy my age, who looked older than me, ran after us and made it across as well.

Then the soldier beat back any other person who tried to change from one line to the other. A few minutes later, we were marched off.

We went past a long building with an observation tower. All we could see were an endless number of low buildings and barbed wire fences with guard towers between them. As we marched, I concentrated on the man before me so as not to falter and attract attention.

When we arrived at a large barrack, we were told to put anything of value, including money, rings and watches, in our palms. I held my money out dutifully as an official-looking prisoner in a striped uniform went between the rows with a basket and collected all the items. One man had trouble removing his ring; as he struggled with it, the prisoner told him he had better take it off or he would lose his finger. He also warned that anyone hiding anything in any body cavity would be severely punished. We had to strip off our clothes and were lined up naked, and all our body hair was shaved with a straight razor. The shaved areas were swabbed with disinfectant, which burned. I winced but did not cry out. After a thorough body search, we were tattooed. My number was 133628; my father stood behind me and his number was 133629. We were issued a pair of pants, a rope for a belt and a jacket marked with the large letters "KZ" in white paint on the back. No shoes. We dressed quickly. My father's pants were too short and his jacket too tight. My clothes were terribly large; we exchanged our clothes quickly and mine fit him a bit better. My jacket was still much too large and could fit around me twice; obviously, boys had not been expected. When I put on the pants and pulled them up, the top went to my armpits and when I put them down to my waist the crotch was at my knees. I tucked my jacket inside my pants, tied the rope around my waist and rolled up the pants and sleeves. My appearance was comical. No one laughed.

We lined up again and were told the rules of the camp. "This is a concentration camp, not a sanatorium; you'll do as you are told, or else. Your life expectancy is four months and there are two choices: you may be selected to go to work or you may be sent to the gas chamber where your family members are now being 'processed.'" No explanation was needed; we all knew what processed meant. My mind went blank in horror and fright. My mind felt paralyzed. After a moment, I regained my senses. I still could not believe what I had just heard. I looked at my father; he nodded lightly as if to say, "You heard right." We were considered the lucky ones, to still be alive. There were no more secrets, no more deceptions and no more mystery as to the fate of those who had been "resettled." How long before we went the same route? I did not dare to think about it. Our lives depended on the whim of others, who would decide how long we would live. We had been reduced from humans to animals, and were expected to follow orders. "Left face, forward march!" was the command.

We were marched out of the reception area. The road was stony and covered with loose gravel. The stones cut into my soft soles. Some men stumbled and fell out of step. The irritated guards responded with verbal abuse and rifle butts. With tears in my eyes and clenched teeth, I suffered the pain. I did not dare call attention to myself. We walked along a barbed wire fence – behind the fence stretched long barracks as far as I could see. We entered the last enclosure, which we found out later was the quarantine camp.

In rows of five, we were marched past guards with writing pads, counting us as we entered. We lined up in front of a barrack in the centre of the camp; there were barracks on either side of us. A prisoner in striped uniform barked out orders: "Stretch out your right arm on the man in front of you and your left arm on the shoulder of the man next to you." Men were confused and moved in all directions. Most did not understand the orders. He used his club to hurry up the process. "Now, listen to me, you swine dogs," shouted the man, who turned out to be our *Stubenälteste*, a room-leader who was also called our kapo, "you are in a concentration camp, not a sanatorium!" We heard that line over and over again. "You better learn how to behave quickly and snap to it, you swine dogs." After a shuffling of feet and pushing, and more blows to some, we were lined up to his satisfaction. We were ordered to stand at attention and were counted and recounted as if we were the most precious commodities. We used to joke that they counted us like gold and treated us like dirt. The heat of the afternoon was now abating, but the long day and hours of standing took its toll and some men fainted. I shifted from leg to leg to ease my discomfort.

After a while, soup kettles were brought and we were given a metal bowl and dished out a portion of soup. No spoon. We did not need one, since the soup was thin and we could drink it. We used our fingers to shove some solid pieces of potatoes into our mouths. We were to keep the bowls. Next, we were herded into the barracks. The barracks were long buildings with a low brick structure in the centre that was connected to a fireplace and a chimney at each end. On each side of it stood three-tiered bunks. My father and I got a middle bunk, second-last from the end.

As we sat on the bunk together, my initial shock passed and I was trembling with fear and anger, tears streaming down my face. The full impact of what we were told about people being gassed to death hit me. I had never heard about that in the ghetto. There was talk about people being killed but no one mentioned how. And why? My tears ran uncontrollably. I was still shaking when my father asked what was the matter with me. He told me to pull myself together. I asked him how they could kill a train full of people by gassing. Why, what had they done to deserve to be killed? He did not move or look at me; he just stared into space.

I told him I had seen Linka and Mother standing together with the young people. I asked whether he thought they were sent to be killed. He told me he thought they went into the camp. He had seen them as well. I asked him what had happened during the selection. He told me that while he was lining up the men, he was looking around to see where I was and how he could get me out of the lineup when a guard walked up to him and started a conversation with, "Don't I know you from somewhere?" My father tried hard to recall his face. Could he be an acquaintance of his from Chorzów, our hometown? The face did not look familiar. Could the uniform make it difficult to recognize him? My father took a stab. "Are you from Silesia?" my father asked. He shook his head, no. He took another blind stab. "I was a foreman in a uniform factory." The guard replied, "Yes, that must be where I saw you. I inspected many factories." Having solved the riddle, the soldier lost interest in him and began to turn away. That was when my father grasped the opportunity to ask if I could join his column. The guard looked around and said, "Where is he?" My father said he shouted three times before I responded. By the time he called, the column had moved up. He frantically searched for me. He saw the trucks pulling up and being loaded. He thought it was too late, and then I finally heard him and jumped out and stood at attention.

This was the longest conversation I had ever had with him. It was really the first time that I remembered being alone with him, without my mother or sister or other members of my family. I was afraid that I would mess up somehow, or say something he would consider stupid and that he would turn away. But he did not; he put his hand on mine and said, "We have to try to stay together."

I lay down, painfully aware of the hardness of the bare bunk bed that I shared with seven others. We used the metal bowls as pillows. The intermittent snoring kept me awake. I was stuck between my father and another man, and there was no room to turn. My mind raced over the events of the last twenty-four hours. Was it possible that in such a short time so much could happen? For the moment, we were safe. Here we were in a concentration camp, deprived of our clothes, our names and our identities. My arm was swollen and burning from the tattoo. The number 133628 was burning itself into my memory. It became my new name, my birth certificate, my identity card. Later, any time we entered the barracks, no name would be asked for. "Roll up your sleeve and show your number," was the command. That is all that mattered here, the number. In the darkness, I found my father's hand. I pressed it against my cheek. It was soft and warm and I was happy to be with him.

The morning came fast. The *Stubenälteste* and the barrack scribe came down the aisles banging their clubs against the bunks. We were chased out of the barrack and lined up in rows of five on the *Appellplatz*, roll call place, and were counted. After that, we were ordered to turn right so we all faced the barrack, five-people deep. The first row was ordered to take three steps forward, the next one two steps. We all stood in long rows, spaced apart. The kapo and scribe told us that this was the procedure for examination and we had better be quick in lining up, or else. They selected a prisoner who was not standing up straight and beat him just to make a point. Another prisoner tried to help and he also received a beating. We were told that we were in the quarantine camp, Auschwitz ɪɪ, also known as Birkenau, Block Bɪɪa. After the *Appell*, roll call, we were ordered back into the barrack, where we lined up and each received tea in our metal bowls, along with a chunk of bread. Then we were released and permitted to go to the latrine at the end of the camp.

We were a sorry-looking group. I looked like a scarecrow in my oversized clothes hanging loosely around my thin body. It was awful to see my father in these mismatched clothes. He had always been elegantly dressed and meticulously groomed. Even during the last few months in the ghetto, when all clothes were old and repaired a number of times, he was wearing properly fitted clothes, clean and neatly pressed pants with a sharp crease. His shirts were always without wrinkles and I marvelled at how he kept his shoes polished even in the dust and mud of the ghetto.

We were not required to go to work but every so often we were assembled, counted and exercised. The exercise consisted of marching around the grounds and doing push-ups or frog jumping. The kapo beat anyone who fell out of step or faltered. Our barrack kapo was a French Jew who was strict but, compared to other kapos, he was not too bad. The scribe was more humane and compassionate. Most of the day was spent sitting around outside the barracks because we were not allowed into the barrack during the day. The days seemed endless. August that year was hot and dry. We sat against the walls of the barracks to gain some shade and relief from the sun. However, when the sun was high there was little shade. Every day, new transports went past our camp. We now knew that the new arrivals were sent to their deaths by gassing.

We often sat by the barracks crying and praying for a miracle. We could not understand how a civilized nation could commit a crime of such magnitude. My father said the world did not know what was happening to us, that otherwise people would have done something. But he was wrong. We were constantly thinking about the lives we had in the ghetto, how no matter how bad it was, even if we were crowded and had little food, we were together with family. Was it possible that life was over for us? In the ghetto, we thought things were tough, but no one could have imagined this.

Our camp was separated from other similar camps with barbed wire fence. To the south were the brick buildings of the women's camp and to the west were rows of barracks, the so-called Kanada camp, which stored various goods confiscated from prisoners, and the gas chambers and crematoria. The barracks we were in were long, single-storey structures with peaked roofs and no windows. They were actually horse stables.

The *Appellplatz* was in front and a deep ditch and coiled barbed wire separated us from an electrified fence. There was another fence four metres from the electrified fence with guard towers in between. We soon found out that the guards played deadly games to entertain themselves. They would throw something into the camp and call to an unsuspecting prisoner to retrieve it. If the prisoner obeyed his order, he would shoot him. If the prisoner refused, the guard would threaten to shoot him anyways, although they never did. The guards played this game every time a new group of prisoners arrived.

The kapo selected a few individuals to do *Stubendienst*, barrack-duty, which consisted of sweeping the floor and keeping order, fetching soup kettles from the kitchen and assisting with the roll call. My father was one among other strong men selected to fetch the kettles of soup from the kitchen located at the far end near the entrance to the camp. He ladled out the soup each evening, which made him a privileged person in the barrack, and he was also allowed to enter the barrack during part of the day. My father tried to be fair and stirred the soup often so each person got his share of the bit of solid food. But if an acquaintance came up, he was sure to dip the ladle deep into the kettle to get some of the thicker soup, as he did for his friend Dr. Zabramski. The other boy who had run over with me from the lineup at the selection site (whose name I do not remember) and I were the first to get an extra portion if there was any surplus.

The next morning, the boy was standing near the *Stubenälteste's* and scribe's sleeping area, so my father told me to join him to see if we could do something for them. The boy was very indignant and tried to shoo me away. I ignored him and stood there, not knowing what to expect. I thought that the kapo would chase us away, but instead he motioned us to approach. He took us to the back of the barrack where, on the top bunk, curtained off with blankets, were stacked loaves of bread. He told us to cut the loaves into quarters and if a loaf was longer than the rest we were to take a slice of bread out of the middle. He told us that if we stole any we would be punished. We nevertheless ate our fill as we sliced the bread, and I passed some on to my father.

The kapo collected the slices and gave them to selected individuals instead of the quarter loaves. Thus some whole loaves were left over, which the kapo collected from us and took to his space. We did that every evening, in preparation for the distribution in the morning. We also slept on those bunks and guarded the bread. One night a prisoner sneaked up and scared me, trying to grab a loaf. I caught his hand, and he pleaded with me not to make a fuss, as he would be severely punished. I let him go without incident.

One day the scribe came by to see how we were doing and asked why we were cutting slices out of the middle of some loaves. We told him that the kapo had ordered us to do so. He got angry and said that by giving the inmates a smaller slice we were killing them, as the amount of food given out was the minimum for survival. He walked away and had it out with the kapo. That was the last time we were asked to cut a slice out of any loaf of bread. We continued to do our job each day and we did not lack bread. It seemed that when a prisoner died, his ration still came for days after.

My job was mostly with the scribe, who was in charge of recording the number of prisoners in the block and keeping up to date the list of names and prisoner numbers. I made his bed and shined his shoes. The other kid looked after the kapo. These jobs were a great advantage, allowing us to stay out of the relentless sun, which was relieved only by thunderstorms. After a thunderstorm, water would collect in puddles and some prisoners drank it. Soon after, they became sick and were taken away at the next selection. My sister's friend, the one shot in the train, still had the wound, which started festering, and he developed a fever. I gave him some extra bread to help him but he was taken away shortly after. I think he was among those of my sister's friends who had been involved in the unsuccessful underground movement in the ghetto.

Being inside the camp did not offer us a reprieve from selections to the gas chamber. After only a few weeks in the August heat and sun, without water, men started to get sick, sunburned and dehydrated. Every week, SS soldiers would select prisoners who exhibited any signs of weakness or sickness. Many people developed swollen hands and feet, and were taken away. I was sure that if I was seen during a selection, I would be taken away, too. I was small and skinny and wore thick glasses; with my bald head my ears stuck out even more. Our barrack was in the middle of the camp and I noticed that they did not count the prisoners prior to lining them up for the selection. I decided to hide for the duration of a selection. My father, not wanting to let me out of his sight, decided to hide with me. We hid mostly by mingling with prisoners of other barracks or in the latrine barrack by entering it at one end and exiting at the other. We had to be careful not to attract the attention of the supervising kapo.

One day when we were hiding in the latrine, we returned late to our *Appellplatz* and the kapo noticed us. He got very angry with my father and me, but he punished only my father. The barracks had brick heating ovens at each end, which were never used for heating but as a punishment rack. My father was ordered to put his hands and upper torso into the oven, which exposed his backside. The kapo grabbed a shovel and used it to hit my father over his backside. I was ordered to watch. I cried and tried to stop him by grabbing his hands. He pushed me off. Someone held me back while the kapo gave my father ten hits. My father yelled out but did not move. He realized that if he moved he would be hit on some of his internal organs and that would be his death. His bottom was black and blue and he could not sit for days. We continued to hide, but we were more careful about getting back on time.

～

The continuous flow of transports and the knowledge that unsuspecting people were being marched to their deaths in the gas chambers was unbearable. On some days, the smoke from the crematoria obscured the sun, creating a continuous dull grey transition from day to night. We watched as transport after transport arrived and people were marched or transported by trucks to the gas chambers. The smell of coal dust, mixed with the distinctive smell of the burning of human flesh, permeated the whole area. It was a horrible realization that the Nazis intended to kill us all. Young and old, secular or pious, our destiny was death. Our days were numbered and we knew it. I knew that I had to put it out of my mind and after a while, I learned to ignore what was happening outside our camp. The daily fight for survival occupied all my senses.

After a time, the rigorous routine of lineups, daily exercises, make-work projects and weekly selections created a strange sense of order in spite of total insecurity. The newcomers, unfamiliar with camp life, suffered more. For us, the seasoned prisoners, hunger, discomfort, resignation and despair were old companions. I accepted the inevitable weekly selections, knowing that sooner or later my father's destiny and mine would be determined by a flick of the wrist. Living in this camp gave us only a temporary extension of a miserable existence.

I asked my father, "How are we going to behave if they select us for the gas chamber? Are we going to lie down and let the kapo beat us to death or the dogs tear us apart?" "No," Father said. "No, we will march with our heads held high in defiance and we will say the first line of the Shema over and over again." He made me repeat it after him until I knew it by heart.

I thought a lot about God. I had a very simple understanding of the nature of God – I was told that if you were good, God would reward you, and if you were bad, you would be punished. I was taught that God is all-seeing and all-knowing; therefore, God must know what was being done to us. Why was God not punishing the Nazis and not saving the good people? What sins had the babies committed, to be sent to their deaths? How did pious men and women sin? I knew my understanding of our religion and of our God was basic, but what I did know made no sense. There was talk of God giving men the power to do good or bad and men were therefore responsible for what they did. Justice would come, I was told, and the sinners would burn in eternal hell. All this did not diminish my anger and anguish. Nor did it give me solace. I would certainly not resign myself to fate.

One day, a young SS man came into the camp and found me and the other boy. I thought our time was up. However, he was only looking for some sadistic diversion, and he made us his whipping boys. He used a long cane whip; the game was to see which of the two of us could withstand more pain without whimpering or crying out. He also ordered one of us to punch the other and see who could inflict greater pain; if we did not hit hard enough, he whipped us. We had welts on our legs and arms for days.

No matter what occurred, we could not lose hope of getting out alive; hope was the only thing that sustained us and made us fight to survive each day. When my father heard that the men who went to work had a passing contact with the women in the camp, he was determined to let my mother know that I was alive; the last time she had seen me was in the line destined for the gas chambers and she may not have seen that I had run over to the other line. Knowing that I was alive would give her renewed hope. My father decided to volunteer for work. He left in the morning and I felt alone, making it a very long day for me. As the sky grew overcast and the light of day gave way to darkness, he had not come back. I stood in the yard, tears steaming over my cheeks, my mind numb with fear. I feared the worst – that he had been taken straight to the gas chamber. At the far end of the camp, the flames and smoke that shot out of the stubby chimneys of the crematoria illuminated the sky in crimson red. I imagined the soul of my dear father, floating to the sky.

It was late in the evening when he finally returned, with a bundle under his arm. I asked, "What happened? Did you see Mother or Linka?" He told me that after work, they would be taken near the Kanada warehouse for showers and he did not know whether the showerheads produced water or gas. It was rumoured that the gas chambers were disguised as showers. After the showers, the head of the tailor shop in Kanada recognized my father from Chorzów and came up to him. My father told me he used this opportunity to ask him for some good clothes for himself and for me. The kapo took my father to the warehouse and my father picked out the clothes. For me he picked up a pair of riding boots, breeches and a nice jacket. In those clothes I looked more like a human being than a scarecrow. But I didn't find out what really transpired until many years later, when my father was telling the story to our friends. The kapo had actually said to my father, "Jacob, I can save you! Come, I'll take you into the tailor shop and you will have an easier time and possibly survive the war." My father told him that he had a fifteen-year-old son in the transition camp, that I was very handy, and that I had learned to sew in a shoe factory. To this the kapo replied, "I'm sure that he can learn to sew but I cannot get him out of the transition camp." He said, "You are here and I can save you. Forget your son. It is not a question of if, but a question of when, he will be found. Forget him, save yourself." My father refused the offer and told him that he was going to go back to stay with me as long as he could.

~

Fall came, and with it, rain. When it rained, the sun-baked clay of the hot summer turned into a sea of endless mud. Our feet sank in the mud, restraining each step and producing an unreal slow-motion effect, which was in keeping with our thought process. Each step, like each day, was a prolonged struggle. It seemed that the elements conspired with our tormentors. The treeless, man-made landscape of barbed wire fences, of chimneys and horse barns in which no horse ever lived, reinforced our feeling of being abandoned and forgotten by the world.

Near the end of September another selection, one of a different type, gave rise to confusion and unrealistic hope. As we were wondering what to do, whether to report or to hide, we noticed that young and strong people were being selected. Stories were told of selections in which people were sent to work in Germany, to food factories, sugar refineries or farms. Perhaps today was such a selection, but no one knew for sure until it was too late. On the other hand, maybe it was just another trick, another way to reduce the camp population.

Yet, there was hope that this selection would be a life-saving one for a few. We lined up. My father told me to stand behind some smaller individuals to de-emphasize my small frame. He stood a few places behind me. We stood in line for a long time and in my nervousness I soiled myself. I was terribly embarrassed to appear in that condition before the doctor. As part of the examination we were required to turn around, bend over and show the doctor our behind. Naked, with my clothes under my arm, I approached the doctor and explained my accident but he insisted I turn around. He berated me and quickly dismissed me with a flick of his finger over his left shoulder. My father was sent in the other direction.

It was the opposite of what we wanted to happen. We wanted to get out of Auschwitz together. If I were to be left in Auschwitz, alone, my chances of survival would be slim. Panic-stricken, I dressed quickly and ran around to the front of the barrack. The selection was still in progress and an SS officer was walking up and down, supervising this procedure. My father was standing with the selected transport group, which was guarded and separated from the rest of us. I saw him and he waved to me. My father approached one of the kapos and told him he wanted to talk to the officer. The kapo got agitated and pushed him back, and my father sidestepped and tried again; the kapo raised his voice and restrained my father. My father was taking a massive risk – people were shot for less than that. The officer saw the scuffle and wanted to know what the trouble was. The kapo now stood holding my father back and said, "This man wants to talk to you." To the kapo's surprise, the officer nodded to him to let my father through. "What is it, what is it that you want?" he said indignantly, visually irritated by my father's chutzpah, forwardness. My father pointed to me and told him that I was his seventeen-year-old son and that I was an electrician. He asked that I be allowed to go with him. The officer became angry and shouted, "Don't you know there is a war on? Families are separated. My wife is in Germany and I have to be here. I would like to have my son with me, but he is on the eastern front."

He looked at my father in contemplative silence, as if reflecting on the words he had just spoken. He then said, "Where is he?" and my father motioned to me to come. I ran to the Nazi officer, stretched myself as high as I could, clicked my boots together and stood at attention. He asked me a number of questions as to where I had worked and what I had done. I told him, in flawless German, that I worked as an electrician in a shoe factory. He asked me where I learned to speak German, and in what year I was born. I had memorized the correct birthdate of 1926. After another few questions he said, "Wait here." Another boy ran up and stood beside me and said, "My father is also here," pointing to the selected men. The officer looked at us, turned and walked away. I was angry with the boy, thinking he was diminishing my chances of being allowed to join my father. As the selection proceeded, I spent the next half hour in agony; it felt like an eternity. My life was in this man's hands. This man was going to determine if I would live or die. As long as I was with my father, there was hope. I thought to myself how stupid it was of us to report for the selection, and that we should have hidden, as before. Now we would be separated and all would be lost. I was happy for my father; at least he would get out of this hellhole. I watched the officer as he, in his highly polished boots and immaculate uniform, strode back and forth. Would he agree to let me go? Would he be my saviour or my executioner? The doctor conducting the selection nodded to him. The selection was over. My heart sank. Suddenly the officer turned and said to both me and the other boy. "Give the doctor your numbers." I later found out that I was number 601 in a 600-man transport. The other boy was number 602. They took forty-eight extra men from whom to draw should anyone get sick or die.

We were told that we were being kept in a two-week quarantine to make sure everyone was healthy. My life was tied to the misfortune of one of these men. During the days, it was easier to push my worries into the subconscious. We were kept busy marching, exercising and getting ready. After hours of practice of endless commands – line-ups, left face, right face, forward march, attention, hats off, hats on – they made us do push-ups, frog jumps and other energy-sapping exercises. For hours, we practised the "hats off, hats on" routine until the slap of the hats against our bodies became a single slap. We became like a military unit, performing the commands with precision and speed. No one let down his guard for fear of making a mistake. A mistake could end up in a beating and injury, which would mean being removed from the transport. At night, I lay on the bunk sleepless, counting seconds to keep back unwanted thoughts. My destiny was suspended between life and death. In this factory of death, where the gas chambers and crematoria were operating day and night, we were just raw material waiting to be processed. It was only a matter of time before we would be condemned. Waiting; waiting for the day of execution or death through disease. Now that we were selected for work, there was hope.

Our destination was a secret, but no one cared – as long as we left Auschwitz, there was potential for life. My sentence had been commuted for two weeks. My eyes constantly searched through the crowd to detect a weakened or sickly person. However, there was no sign; everybody took strength from the hope for life. People even joked and laughed, their spirits soaring as they speculated about the future. Would it be a food-packing house, a sugar refinery or an armament factory? Winter was coming and it would be good to work inside. I dared not dream such dreams. My father and I did not talk about such things. We made no plans. The nights dragged on while the days flew by.

Finally, the numbers were called out and counted off. I was still number 601. We were separated from the selected transport. My father approached the scribe prisoner in charge of the list and asked him to change his number, 133629, to my number, 133628. He argued that it was easy to change the nine into an eight and let me go in his place. The scribe pushed him away and told him that he would not risk his life to do this – besides, there were many lists and he would not get away with it. The other prisoners became agitated and angry; a disturbance of any kind could endanger all. Just then, an SS officer entered. Everyone snapped to attention as he proclaimed, "All will be going." I ran up to my father and we embraced; my face was wet with tears of happiness. We had to dress once again in striped uniforms, have our hair closely clipped, and a stripe was shaved from our foreheads to the napes of our necks. The next day, we were marched to a train station. Our exit from the hellhole of Auschwitz-Birkenau had become a reality after all.

Kleiner

We still did not know where we were being transported. The trip took two days, some of which we spent waiting on the railway sidings, for hours at a time. The transport was travelling in open-roofed boxcars and there were approximately sixty or sixty-five men in each car, just enough room for us to stand or sit very tightly together. My father had secured space for us, which provided a measure of security and comfort for the trip. Before we left Auschwitz, we were each given a double ration of bread. My father suggested we ration our bread, even though we would have liked to eat it all at once. Some prisoners did just that. After the first day of travel, when most prisoners did not have anything to eat, we had to eat our bread quickly and secretly.

Two SS guards were in each car, sitting on bales of straw at one end. One made eye contact with me. I took that as an encouragement and I moved closer to him. I could tell he was bored and would welcome some distraction so we started a conversation. He told me he was Hungarian, of German descent. We made small talk on various subjects. He wouldn't let any other prisoner approach him, but I guess he didn't consider me a threat. Over the two days, we had quite a few conversations.

Some weeks later, while we were marching to work, the same SS officer approached me. "How are you, Kleiner? [Small one]" he inquired. "Do you have enough to eat?" "Oh yes, sir," I said. "Listen

Kleiner, you can trust me; I know what it is like. I was once a prisoner also. I can help you with food and a better job, if you tell me who is trying to escape or see something suspicious or see someone doing sabotage. You tell me and I will reward you and protect you." Yes, I thought, fat chance; no way would I become a stool pigeon for the SS. The next time I saw him, I avoided him. Even just by talking to an SS man I could be accused of squealing on someone and end up dead.

We had arrived in Fünfteichen, about thirty kilometres from Breslau in lower Silesia; it was mid-October 1943. It was a new camp, not completely finished. We learned that it was a sub-camp of the Gross-Rosen concentration camp. We were issued two printed cloth number tags; one was for the chest and one for the left side of our pants. My father's number was 48516 and mine was 48517. The insignia next to our number consisted of two triangles, a red one facing downward, designating a political prisoner, and a yellow one facing upward, designating a Jewish prisoner. The two triangles superimposed on each other made a Star of David.

The camp was completely different from Birkenau except for the double fences and guard towers. The inner fence was electrified and large coils of barbed wire lay in front of it. The barracks, instead of being horse barns, were single-storey long buildings with many windows and two sets of doors, leading into a dining-common room that separated the two bedroom wings. Each bedroom housed a hundred men. We were ordered into the barracks and assigned bunks. My father and I got the bunks near the door to the dining room. He took the lower bunk and I took the one above him.

Fünfteichen had been established by the SS administration to provide slave labour for the industrial giant Krupp. Krupp had factories in the west of Germany and wanted a plant in the east to produce cannons for ships and tanks, torpedo tubes and heavy boilerplates for tanks. The plant was called Friedrich Krupp-Bertha Werke, in honour of his wife, Bertha.

The camp had been built by prisoners from Gross-Rosen. Those prisoners, long since established, held all the privileged positions, such as *Stubenälteste*, in charge of each barrack, and *Stubenschreibe*, room scribe. The kitchen staff – from the chief cook to all other kitchen workers – were Polish or German prisoners, as was the majority of the infirmary staff. All the positions were full-time jobs except the room scribe, which was part-time, and his duties were after work. The *Lagerälteste*, who was in charge of all the prisoners, was a German criminal who had already spent years in a concentration camp, and he behaved as the king of his domain. He had a special uniform, made to measure, with high boots and riding pants. He strutted through the camp with a riding switch and was quick to use it when someone attracted his attention by not lining up straight or stepping out of line.

Early on the first morning, we were lined up before each barrack. The *Stubenälteste*, room kapo, impressed on us that he was the boss. He hit anyone not lined up properly or not standing up straight and at attention; we were used to this routine from Birkenau. He was a small and skinny man, but he had a deadly fist. He could bring a man down with one clenched fist to the head. He took us through "cap-off" and "cap-on" routines until he was satisfied that we did this in unison. The scribe shouted for carpenters, electricians, doctors and medical personnel to step forward. I stepped forward as an electrician. My father's acquaintance Dr. Zabramski stepped forth as a doctor and some others did so as carpenters. The scribe took my name and number and told me that I would be working in the camp to complete its construction.

After that, we were ordered to go to the main *Appellplatz* to be counted. Again, the same procedure and more beating took place. As we were new arrivals, the kapos tried to assert their authority. The Nazi officers counted us and recounted. Those designated for camp work were ordered to come forward while the others were told to close the ranks and were marched off to the factory three kilometres away.

Camp life in Fünfteichen was easier and less stressful than in Birkenau. For one thing, there was no gas chamber, so we were not in constant threat of being selected to die. In my assigned work in the camp, with a prisoner electrician as my boss, my main task was to be a gofer, getting material and tools, holding his ladder and doing whatever he ordered me to do. Wiring the building was not very challenging and I knew much more than I was required to. Whenever I was sent somewhere, I moved quickly, usually on the run. The kapos and supervisors liked that. They would say to the other prisoners, "Look at the Kleiner, he always moves quickly." The prisoners did not like that, but it was just my way of moving. I could never move slowly or sit still, and when I saw that my supervisors liked me, I used it to my advantage.

Those working in the camp were required to get the soup kettles from the kitchen after work and before the men came back from the plant. The kettles were heavy and I had trouble carrying them, so I avoided being selected for this. Working inside the camp, I was able to meet most of the important functionaries in the camp – the prisoner establishment and the administration. The prisoners ran the camp almost entirely; the SS men entered only to count us and to punish us. Some SS men looked for excuses to beat up prisoners, usually with the help of a kapo. I witnessed some of these incidents. If a prisoner's attention was distracted somehow and he lingered too long, the kapo would jump on him with his truncheon and the Nazi soldier would look on, laugh and usually help in the beating.

The camp was small in comparison to the camp at Birkenau; when we arrived, the camp had only 1,500 men. I soon learned the layout of the barracks, the kitchen, the infirmary compound, and the many empty barracks. Obviously more prisoners were expected, and shortly thereafter, they arrived. The original Jewish prisoner population soon started to dwindle, especially those that were designated to work on the construction site at the Krupp factory. The work was hard, with twelve-hour days, and there were large losses of life due to starvation, exhaustion and the cruelty of some of the kapos. The losses were even higher in the winter months, due to harsh conditions and improper clothing.

Some of the prisoners inside the plant worked directly for Krupp and others worked for various contractors and subcontractors. The bosses and overseers were civilians. There was a whole hierarchy. My father worked for Krupp whereas the outside construction crews worked for the general contractor. Whom you worked for made a huge difference. The skilled workers were generally better treated because the plant had taken time to train them and were invested in them, whereas the supply of unskilled construction workers was almost unlimited. Krupp and the contractors paid the SS for every prisoner and each day they worked. Krupp, more than the contractors, was quite anxious to make sure that we were treated well because absence from work caused interruptions in production. Although those of us working in the plant were much less exposed to brutal beatings by the kapos or guards, anyone caught committing a serious crime, such as sabotage or attempted escape, was punished on return to the camp. Some prisoners suffered from malnutrition and illnesses and could not return to work.

Janek, the *Stubenälteste*, soon set up a single bed against the wall next to the entrance to the dining room. He told me that since I worked in the camp, I would sleep there. I was surprised and happy, as this gave me a special privilege and respect from the other prisoners. During the next few days the kapo was very kind to me, talking to me quietly; in addressing other prisoners, he always shouted. He would call me first to receive an extra portion of soup and after that he would give out the extra soup to other prisoners that he favoured. A few days later, I found out why he had asked me to sleep there. In the middle of the night, he came to my bed, placed his hand on my mouth and whispered, "If you as much as let out a peep, I will kill you." He forced himself between my legs and after a few thrusts, he ejaculated over my legs and bed. As kids in the ghetto, we would pretend to have intercourse, but since none of us had reached puberty, no semen was ejected. The sticky mess dried by the morning and I made sure that my father did not notice it. I was embarrassed and felt guilty. I did not tell anyone about it, not even my father. Homosexual activities were strictly prohibited and severely punished by the SS guards.

Some Polish prisoners in our barrack had arrived from Gross-Rosen with Janek and were his friends. Most of them had jobs inside the camp or were kapos on the job site. They had friends in the kitchen and were in a position to organize extra food not available to the rest of the prisoners. They would congregate in our barrack most evenings and on Sunday to eat together and play cards. I was required to cook and serve them and clean up the pans and dishes. Their favourite food was salami with eggs and I became an expert in frying them. For my services they would allow me to have some of the leftover food, which I would share with my father.

In the camp jargon, I was known as a "pipel." The Polish prisoners suspected that Janek used me. They would tell stories that were meant for my ears. I pretended not to understand. They recounted an incident where a boy who was used as a woman conceived a child. I did not worry about it, as up to this point he had not entered me. I also knew that to be impossible, but it still bothered me.

One day, I came into the barrack before the men arrived from work. The kapo took me to the bedroom and tried to force me to perform oral sex. I resisted. He then told me to drop my pants and tried to enter me from behind but could not. He told me not to move, rushed into the dining room and returned with a square of margarine, which he applied to himself, and then he forced himself into me. It was an embarrassing and painful experience.

As soon as I got away from him, I rushed into the washroom to remove as much semen as possible. Even though I knew the stories of conception were false, at some level it had me frightened. When we were in the ghetto, we inherited the library from my aunts and there were books on female physiology and childbirth. I understood enough about sex to believe that the men suspected my relationship with the kapo and were trying to frighten me.

I tried hard not to expose myself to such a situation again by never entering the barracks ahead of the men. But there was nothing I could do about the nights. He could still take advantage of me. I was afraid and embarrassed to tell my father. Afraid because I believed there would be a confrontation between him and Janek, which could be catastrophic for us both. On the other hand, had I told my father and he dismissed it out of hand as one of the things one does to survive, I would have been angry and disappointed. I have always wondered if my father knew, but he never asked and I never talked to him about it, not even after the war. It was one of the secrets one carries through life. It took me many years to admit it to myself and to accept it. For years, I wondered if these events would affect my life, and whether I would end up with some homosexual tendencies. It was only after sports personalities and native residential school survivors came forward and disclosed their sexual abuse by their trainers and superiors that I had the courage to speak about my experiences. Up to that point, I felt the abuse was somehow my fault and I was terribly ashamed to disclose it.

The relationship with the kapo was not without benefit. The prisoners who were aware of it afforded me respect and did not bother me. I liked these special privileges. Janek, as I mentioned, was a friend of one of the cooks and occasionally he sent me to the kitchen to get special items such as salami, eggs and cheese that were available only to the guards. The camp establishment was a closely-knit group and some of the privileged prisoners were working in SS houses, cleaning and doing repairs. These men could get all kinds of goods, such as chocolate and cigarettes. The tobacco ration the prisoners received was *machorka*, very rough tobacco consisting mainly of the leaf stems. Paper was at a premium and most prisoners, including my father, used newsprint. Using my tobacco as payment, I was able to obtain from the supply house a new uniform that the tailor shop altered to fit me. In my new, clean and fitted uniform, the prisoner establishment people did not bother me, as they did not know whose favourite I was.

My work inside the camp lasted only a few weeks. When the camp buildings were finished, I was sent to work in the Krupp-Bertha Werke armament factory. The first time I was marched into the plant a German civilian approached me and asked, "So, Kleiner, what are you in prison for? Did you shoot at the soldiers or kill your mother?" "Neither," I replied, "I am here because I am a Jew." He looked at me askance and said, "I guess Hitler knows what he is doing," and turned away.

My day started long before dawn. We were woken up by one of the kapos banging on the bed boards with a stick. Anyone taking too long to dress or make his bed was subject to a beating. Then there was a mad rush to get into the washroom. I was lucky that I could hold it and avoid using the washroom in the camp. Washrooms were always overcrowded and the kapos were busy using their clubs to hurry the prisoners out. I managed to wait until we got to the factory, where the washrooms were much larger and less crowded.

I had to get to the *Appellplatz* on time or I was treated like all other stragglers, whipped by the kapo on duty. We lined up to be counted, formed into work groups and then marched off on the three-kilometre trek to the plant. We arrived at the plant at 5:30 a.m. to start work at 6:00. Even though I had much easier work than most, the day was long. At noon we were assembled and counted, but no food was issued. Our morning ration consisted of about a quarter of a loaf of bread, some two hundred grams, a square of margarine and, once or twice a week, a teaspoon of jam. Those of us who could not resist eating the whole bread ration from the morning had nothing to eat for lunch. I usually kept a piece of bread for lunch.

At the end of our twelve-hour shift, we had to assemble to be counted again. Officially, we finished work at 6:00 p.m. and marched off at 7:00, but that rarely happened. If the SS guards made a mistake in the count, thinking that someone was missing, we would have to stand on the *Appellplatz* until they were satisfied that we were all there. We often stood for hours while they counted and recounted us. The SS seemed to have a contest as to who could make a prisoner fall with one hit to the head. The prisoner, usually for a small infraction, such as talking or not standing at attention, would be called out of the line. The Nazi would order the man to stand at attention and hit him with his closed fist. If the prisoner did not fall, another soldier would approach him and repeat the process. After a while, we all knew to fall down on the first blow.

For me, the day did not end on entry into the barrack. I had to do whatever the kapo had laid out. I ate the bowl of soup as quickly as possible and then was available to look after his needs. He usually supervised the distribution of the soup and could be very rough with the prisoners. Anyone pushing or with his uniform in disarray would be hit with his stick or strap. He made sure the food distributers were fair in dishing out the soup. Prisoners would try to position themselves to avoid being in the line at the time a new kettle was started, since that meant they would receive a thinner portion of soup. If the kapo found someone manoeuvring for a better spot, he would receive blows and have to move to the back of the line. If there was not enough soup, he would be out of luck.

The prisoner's day was not finished after receiving his soup. The block kapo would find something for him to do. His favourite pastime was to make the prisoners shave the benches and tables with broken pieces of glass so that no mark was visible and they looked new. In the summer, when daylight was longer, the prisoners were sent out to do some exercises, which most prisoners could not do due to exhaustion. This gave the kapo yet another excuse to hit the poor souls with a stick or rubber hose.

In the Krupp factory, my father's supervisor was an elderly German civilian who treated him well. My father was assigned to work on a router/drill press, machining the intricate parts of the firing mechanism or "lock" for the guns. My father learned quickly and made few mistakes. Mistakes were very serious, especially at the end of the process, after a lot of time had been spent on the piece. He was told directly that spoiling work would be considered sabotage and punishable with death. I do not know if it ever happened, but the threat was enough and no one doubted that it would be carried out.

I was assigned to an electrical crew that was wiring machinery. The crew worked for a private German civilian contracting firm under a civilian foreman. My supervisor turned out to be my barrack scribe, Staszek. The work wasn't hard and I had freedom to move around the plant with tools and materials. I learned a lot about electrical work on the job, such as wiring motor controls and reading circuit diagrams, and I really liked it. However, "working" for Janek after work and late into the evening, I was always tired and looked for an opportunity to get some sleep. As we worked in the new and still unoccupied part of the plant, I could hide in the wiring trenches by crawling under the wooden covers. I got about a half hour of sleep there, and I paid off a co-worker with some bread or tobacco to keep watch so I would not be discovered. I had to make sure that I didn't come out when others were present, especially the German civilian supervisor. It was imperative that I not miss a roll call because anyone absent from the roll call was automatically assumed to be an escapee and would be punished as such, which usually meant death by beating or hanging.

I worked with German and Czechoslovak civilians, which meant there was a possibility of obtaining some extra food. Although the civilians were afraid of the adult prisoners, since they had been told that most were hardened criminals and could not be trusted, I, looking like a child, did not fit that image, which resulted in some expressions of sympathy. At noon, the civilian workers received soup from the factory kitchen. The soup was not very good and many of them did not eat it. They could not give it to anyone, but they just left it a distance from where they sat. They were forbidden to have any contact with us but they nodded their heads or winked when they saw me approach. I had bartered a canteen from one of the sheet metal workers in the plant and was able to transfer the soup quickly from their bowl into the canteen. If someone saw me take the soup, the civilian would say that I took it without his permission. If caught, both of us would be in trouble. I shared the extra food with my father.

A tense situation occurred when one of the Czech civilians was caught with a letter addressed to someone in Poland. He had the letter in his back pocket and it fell out as he was walking. An SS guard noticed and picked it up, but before giving it to him, he glanced at it. He became suspicious and asked why he was sending mail to Poland, and then arrested him on the spot. Under interrogation, the civilian admitted that he was mailing a letter for a Polish prisoner. The following week, the SS had a platform built in the centre of the plant and assembled all civilians. The Czech was brought up on the platform, was made to put on prisoner's clothes, and then his hair was clipped and a streak shaved. This was to serve as an example of the consequences of fraternizing with prisoners. For a few weeks after that, it was impossible to make contact with any of the civilians. I never found out what happened to the Polish prisoner who wrote the letter, but most likely he was severely punished and sent back to Gross-Rosen.

A few months after I started to work in the plant, my father was placed on a night shift and the only contact we had was when we saw each other walking in and out of the plant. We both arranged to be on the outside of the column of men so we could see each other. On occasion, I would throw him my bread ration, hoping to get some food during the day. However, there were days when I was unable to get any food from the civilians, which meant I had a long day of fasting.

The seasoned prisoner knew the basic rules of survival – keep clean and avoid punishment. Punishment, even a small beating, could cause injury and disability. On Sundays, the factory was closed and we had a day off. This was our time to wash our uniforms and have our hair clipped and the streak shaved. If you were lucky, you would not be cut. Some prisoners, including my father, performed barber duties in exchange for extra soup rations. This was also the day we were allowed to shower. Showers started out with warm water but it would quickly run out and the last prisoners into the showers had to bathe under cold water. At first, my father and I lived in the same barrack, luckily located across from the wash barrack. This was especially fortunate in the winter when we had to run from the barrack to the showers naked. In the summer, when the weather was hot, we could wash our uniforms and dry them in the sun, but in the winter that was impossible.

The showers were overcrowded and fights would break out to gain access to a showerhead. Here, everyone was for himself and, being small, I would be pushed away. One rather cold day, I decided to take my coat with me into the shower barrack so I could put it over me on my way back. Our uniforms were permeated with cutting oil and dust from the machines, and to my chagrin, when I removed my coat I was covered in oil and dust and I had to go back to shower again. By this time there was little of the stone-like soap left, and the water was ice cold. I had a hard time getting the oil and dust off me. That was a hard lesson.

On Sundays, unless it was raining, we weren't allowed to stay in the barrack. And, if we were in the barrack, we weren't allowed to sit around. The kapo would find jobs for us, such as cleaning the tables and benches or oiling the floors, or cleaning up the bedrooms and turning over and shaking up the straw mattresses.

Fünfteichen, like other work camps, had various categories of prisoners of different nationalities. Most of the non-Jewish prisoners were political prisoners, saboteurs, partisans or accused of unspecified crimes. The infirmary's chief doctor was a German national who was serving a sentence of several years, apparently for performing illegal abortions. A Russian POW in our camp was there because he had been accused of planning an escape; his presence was unusual, as most escapees were shot on the spot. One of my co-workers in the electrical group was young Ukrainian boy, not much older than me. He had been sent to Germany as a farm worker. He claimed that the farmer's daughter falsely accused him of animal buggery after he rebuffed her advances. These prisoners had a chance of being released after the end of their sentences. The Jews, on the other hand, were sentenced for life. The only way we could get out with our lives was with the defeat of the Nazis. Our daily struggle was to survive the day and to outlast the war.

One day, one of the prisoners in our block who was a suspected member of the Polish underground was called to the SS office, issued a clean uniform and told he would be sent to Gross-Rosen the next day. That evening, he ran against the electrified fence and died. He must have known that the interrogation he would have faced in Gross-Rosen would have been severe. Prisoners sent to Gross-Rosen for interrogation came back with horror stories of their torture. The most common torture was to hang the prisoner by their hands for hours at a time and beat them. One of the prisoners in my barrack was left with permanent painful injuries to his shoulders and wrists, and had no feeling in the skin of his hands. He swore that he would rather commit suicide than endure another interrogation. The Polish prisoner's friends thought that he committed suicide not because of the pain of torture but in order to protect the others prisoners in our camp who were his accomplices. We knew there were underground groups but we didn't know who they were or whether they were communists or Polish nationalists.

Suicide was actually rare in the camps – living was a form of resistance, defiance and triumph over the Nazis. The death toll of prisoners in our barrack was not high, but some prisoners died of exhaustion, disease or severe punishment. Some prisoners were transferred back to Gross-Rosen. The most life-threatening diseases were tuberculosis, infections due to injuries sustained on the job site or boils erupting from poor hygiene.

Early in 1944, with a group of new arrivals, a young boy about two years older than me was assigned to our barrack. He almost immediately became Janek's favourite and took my position, and I was relegated to mundane jobs of cleaning and running errands. It also meant that my privileges were curtailed and I had less access to extra food. One evening the boy was doing the dishes and when he went to empty the porcelain basin, it slipped out of his hands and broke. The kapo got very angry and blamed me for it happening. He took a fire poker and hit me over my shoulder, impaling the hook in my shoulder blade. I knew that my time as favourite was now totally up, which I somewhat regretted – it meant the kapo would not abuse me any longer, but it also meant that he withheld his affection. I was actually jealous of the other boy.

A few days after the incident, my wound became infected. I went to the infirmary and lied that I had injured myself on the job. If I had told the truth, it could have led to severe consequences for Janek and me. Although the camp establishment often knew what was going on, reporting it would involve the SS guards, and the Germans considered homosexual activities a crime even if they happened in the camp. Punishment was always severe. I had to let the incident pass.

Now that I was no longer Janek's favourite, Staszek the scribe took a special interest in me. He was my electrical supervising kapo and was in a position to assign better work to me. He gave me more responsible and less physically taxing work. His position in the barrack also meant he could ensure that I got an extra portion of soup, but he did not have access to more bread rations.

So my life in the camp continued. As an electrician, I had the run of the plant and could go to visit my father whenever he worked on the day shift. I usually carried some pipe or wire with me to look as though I was on an errand. One day after visiting my father, on my return to my workplace, I stopped at the huge lathe that was turning a ten-metre long steel muzzle of the big Bertha cannon. Usually I walked quickly, as the kapos and SS men liked us to, so as to not attract their attention. I had never allowed myself to linger, but I was always fascinated with machinery. I must have stood too long, for an SS guard spotted me and came over to me. I of course stood at attention and removed my hat, as was the required protocol. I started to tell him I was making a delivery, but he interrupted me by hitting my face with his fist. I hit the ground hard. As I lay there, dazed for a few seconds, too long for his liking, he kicked me in the chest with his army boot. I thought I was going to die. I lay breathless, sweeping the ground around me with my hands for my glasses; being very short-sighted, I was not able to see them. He stood over me and suddenly burst out laughing. He then kicked the glasses to me, but unfortunately, one lens was broken. I got up and again stood at attention while he wrote down the number on my jacket. I was sure this episode was not over. He walked off and I proceeded to my workplace. I didn't tell anyone about the incident. I taped pieces of the broken glass together but after a few days, the pieces fell out and I was left with no glass over my left eye. My vision was distorted and I lost depth perception but after a while, my eyes adjusted.

Shortly after, I was working in an electrical pipe trench, installing conduit into terminal boxes. I knew that the exposed terminals were live and I had to be very careful not to touch them, since the 360 volts could result in electrocution. I removed a knockout in the side of the terminal box but the knockout did not break away clean, leaving a piece of metal that prevented installing the conduit. I fetched a file to file out the spur. I saw a huge flash and the next thing I knew, I was lying down on the floor. My file must have touched one of the live terminals – the file had burned in half, my face was burnt and I was temporarily blinded in the eye that had no lens. I was ordered out of the factory and confined in the camp for a few days. My father was not allowed to see me. According to Staszek, the SS guards were accusing me of sabotage because a number of machines had shut down due to the short circuit. The civilian boss reported that it was not my fault. He told them I didn't know the terminal was live. I was sure that I would be punished severely. I expected to be thrown out of the plant to work on the construction site. Winter was coming and working outside during the winter was very hard; people died each day from exhaustion and cold.

The guards believed my boss and I was allowed to return to the factory, but I was not allowed to work with tools. Instead, the German boss assigned me to work in the warehouse, which was enclosed in a wire cage so the workers could be watched all the time by the guards and our boss. I had thought the accident would end in catastrophe, but it actually placed me in a better situation. Staszek was still my supervisor and treated me well. I again had the ability to walk all over the plant delivering material. I paid more attention and did not linger. My face healed, without a mark, although the sight in my left eye deteriorated, partly due to the lack of a lens and partly due to the flash.

Staszek took advantage of me in the warehouse and made me masturbate him behind stacks of material. This was a regular occurrence. He would lean back with his eyes closed, apparently enjoying the procedure, even though he never had an orgasm. I learned to be flexible and adjust to the conditions as best as I could. This was one of the conditions of survival.

⁓

In order to reduce the number of guards needed to supervise our daily march from camp to the factory and back, the Nazis erected a three-kilometre wire mesh fence. The fence kept us in and prevented prisoners from darting out of line under the cover of darkness. Every few nights, some prisoners had tried to get away, only to be found and dragged back or shot on the spot. Rumours were that the local farmers complained about the dogs and guards running through their fields in pursuit of attempted escapees. The fence also kept the civilian population from staring at us as we marched by. During the march, I would hang on to my father's arm or to another prisoner if my father was on night shift and not with me, and I would sleepwalk. I would only wake up when I tripped on the feet of the prisoner ahead of me. I became quite adept at this.

I continued to work for the scribe at night and was constantly sleepy, so I devised a hiding place inside the warehouse in a small desk. In the afternoons, when the demand for material was lowest, I would crawl into the desk and go to sleep for an hour. I paid the other worker in the warehouse with some bread or tobacco to be my lookout and warn me if the German civilian boss or the kapo was approaching. One day, the German boss came from behind a pile of material and my lookout could not warn me in time. I heard the German ask, "Where is the Kleiner?" The co-worker told him I had gone to deliver some material, so he sat on top of the desk where I was hiding and waited. I was afraid to breathe, hidden in the desk. I dared not come out lest he fire me for loafing or accuse me of trying to escape. Some prisoners who attempted to escape had hidden in the plant and waited until the search party left.

After a while, he left, and I crawled out of the desk and made myself busy. Shortly thereafter, he returned and asked me where I was when he came looking for me. I told him I'd gone to deliver material to a job site. "Which one?" he asked. I chose the wrong one. He had just come from there and knew they had not requested any material, and that I was not there all day. He lifted his hand as if to strike me, but he did not; he called me a liar and ungrateful. This is when he told me that he had testified on my behalf to the SS after the electrical accident. He said that I had endangered him, and this was how I was paying him back? He told me he would have to report to the SS that I was absent and possibly trying to escape, and ordered me to follow him. I walked beside him crying and begging for my life. They would hang me for sure. Then I told him that I was sleeping in the desk that he had been sitting on. He stopped and looked at me. He shouted at me that I was a barefaced liar – no way could I fit into the desk. I cried and begged him to come back so I could show him. Reluctantly, and angrily, he turned. I walked quickly ahead of him, afraid that he might change his mind. The desk had a roll-down front on one side and shallow drawers on the other side. I lay down on the ground and pushed my legs behind the drawers, then hoisted my body into the desk and pushed up from inside on the rolled-up front until it was closed. He looked at me in disbelief and burst out laughing, then said he would fire me.

I had always feared being thrown out of the plant to the construction site, where prisoners died weekly from exposure, hunger, exhaustion and disease. So, even before I knew for sure I'd be sent out, I had been preparing. In the warehouse, I had access to coils of electrical wires that came wrapped in long streams of crepe paper. These made excellent insulation bandages for feet and arms. The paper was in great demand and I traded it for tobacco, food or cement bag paper. The cement bags were multilayered and the inside layers were clean and could be used for insulation under one's jacket. I cut out openings for my neck and arms and used it as an undershirt. It provided protection from wind and was very warm, but the paper was stiff and didn't cling to the body, so the jacket would puff out. The SS guards soon became aware of this practice and whenever they saw someone's jacket bulging out, they would tap him with a little cane and the stiffness of the paper would produce a hollow sound. The SS would pull the prisoner out of the line, make him undress and beat him severely. To avoid this, I crumpled the paper until it became soft and clung to my body. Even if they tapped me, they would not detect it. I accumulated paper bags and rolls of crepe paper under my mattress. I also managed to get a good pair of wooden-soled shoes. I was well set for the winter.

The Race Against Death

I thought my boss had forgotten the desk episode, but I was mistaken. He was a decent man, and he waited until the winter ended before firing me and sending me to the construction site. It must have been late March or early April of 1944; the days were warmer but the mornings were bitter cold. It was around this same time that more than two thousand prisoners were brought into our camp from the adjoining labour camp at Markstadt. They were working on the construction site at the Krupp factory. We would see them working in civilian clothes, wearing a yellow star. With the addition of the Markstadt prisoners, for the first time the Jewish population in the camp was the majority.

The new Jewish prisoners were not used to the rigorous discipline of a concentration camp. They were more defiant and walked around with their heads high, and they didn't look as emaciated and bedraggled as the older inmates did. On entry into our camp, they received clean, new uniforms. They were housed in a different part of the camp, in the new, clean barracks, with new straw mattresses. They even had their own kapos and *Lagerälteste*, camp kapo, who were not as brutal as ours. The old camp administration kapos proceeded to change the situation and impose stricter discipline and rules of behaviour. They subjected the new group to exercises and drills. Some SS guards encouraged the kapos to beat prisoners for no apparent reason. They beat many Jewish prisoners to death.

For us, the former inmates, the new arrivals provided an opportunity to seek relatives and to speak Yiddish, but it was also a very traumatic time for both groups. The Markstadt prisoners had been taken to labour camps prior to the final deportations from their towns in Poland. For the last eighteen months, they had stopped receiving mail from home, and although they had thought that something terrible was happening, they did not know what. When we told them that we came from Auschwitz, and told them what was happening to the Jewish people, they were devastated.

Their Jewish *Lagerälteste* became an assistant *Hauptkapo*. Both strutted around the camp like cocks – like good cop, bad cop. The German *Hauptkapo* was fierce, while the Jewish assistant *Hauptkapo* tried to intervene on behalf of the Jewish prisoners as much as possible and had the respect and cooperation of his people. The two *Hauptkapos* became good friends. One day, they devised a foolproof escape plan and made their break. We quietly cheered for them and hoped that they would be successful. The odds were against them. In all previous cases, the escapees were caught and brought back to camp. On Sundays, all prisoners would be assembled and forced to witness their execution. The SS always gave us a long lecture and tortured the escapees, trying to find out who had helped them, before proceeding with the hanging. This process lasted hours, and we had to stand at attention the entire time.

Our elation at the possibility of a successful escape did not last long. The next Sunday morning, when we were usually allowed to stay in bed a bit longer, the SS guards entered our barracks with sticks and rubber truncheons, hitting the beds and us as we tried to get up. They assembled us on the *Appellplatz*, made us stand at attention and told us, "You will stand here until we find them." The guards passed between columns and beat anyone not standing straight. When prisoners became faint and fell, they were dragged out of the line and severely beaten. Many died that day on the *Appellplatz*. After hours of this punishment, we cursed the two kapos and wished they would be caught quickly. We stood through Sunday and late into the night. When we went back to work the next day, we were relieved, if not happy, that they had succeeded. The rumours were that they bribed some guards to help them escape, that the guards provided them with civilian clothes and transportation. The SS never found them.

At the construction site, my civilian boss turned out to be a large Bavarian man with a huge stomach and enormous hands. I could see, from the corner of my eye, that he watched me closely. I had to be very careful, not knowing what kind of man he was. I had to establish myself in this new environment. I worked hard and did not take too many breaks. I rested only when his back was turned to me. I was much more fit than the other prisoners who had worked on the construction site longer and had had no extra food, as I had had earlier. I moved quickly whenever I was ordered to do something and I could see the boss liked this.

Our job was to construct railway tracks for mine carts to transport sand and gravel from the gravel pit to various construction sites within the huge Krupp enterprise site. I worked shoving sand under the railway ties with a wooden paddle. This was a job I could readily do and it was not too taxing. Now that my food supply had diminished, it was important to save my strength as much as possible. Along with five others, we had to push the mine carts from the pits to the construction site. I tried to push hard but the guard was not satisfied – he booted me in my behind and I went flying. My boss just laughed. Then, when I had to work with nine men to carry rails on our shoulders, I was too short and my shoulder was about fifteen centimetres below the rail, so I put up my hands to push up. The boss came over to me and asked, "Kleiner, are you pushing up or hanging on? You better stay with me and carry my briefcase." Our guard saw that my boss took a liking to me and stopped pursuing me. From that point on, whenever we went from one place to another, I would carry his briefcase. I soon found out that the only thing he carried in his official-looking briefcase was his lunch. As time passed, I became his helper and gofer within our immediate workplace. It was a dangerous situation, as I had to be on my guard not to go too far from our work area; if another SS guard found me away from my group I could be taken away, and my boss would not be able to save me. The guards for our group were used to seeing me help him and did not bother me. I think he bribed them with food that he brought from home. I believe he lived on a farm in the area of the plant. In the early fall, my boss brought raw potatoes in his suitcase and asked me to make a fire and roast them. He would share those with the SS guard and I was allowed to have one or two.

During the warm weather, I removed my shoes and walked barefoot so as not to wear them out. They were a good pair, and I would not be able to replace them. Unfortunately, one day I stepped on a twisted piece of rusted wire, which penetrated into the soft part of my arch. It felt like the wire went almost all the way through my foot. I yanked it out with all my strength and it started to bleed heavily. I ripped a piece of my shirt and wrapped it around my foot, but the pain was intense and I knew I was in trouble. An injury like this could cost me my life.

I hobbled the three kilometres to the camp. The kapo examined my injury and allowed me to go to the infirmary, which was a separate area fenced off from the rest of the camp. Dr. Zabramski, who had been with us in Auschwitz, saw to me and recognized me from Birkenau. My father used to give him an extra bowl of soup and they had become friends. Some weeks before, my father developed a carbuncle under his arm and Zabramski operated on him, giving him anaesthetics, which most prisoners did not get. It was a huge carbuncle and he underestimated the time it would take to remove it. My father woke up in the middle of the operation and started to scream. Instead of giving him some painkillers, he knocked him out with his fist. My father never forgave him for that.

The doctor cleaned my puncture wound, inserted some gauze with medication and admitted me to the infirmary. After the first two days, my foot stopped hurting and I could walk on the heel. It was not in my nature to sit around, and I knew that I had to work out some angle to either work inside in the camp or get back to the factory. To spend the next winter on the *Baustelle*, the construction site, would be terrible. Most casualties and deaths were on the construction site, especially in the winter. We had inadequate clothing, not enough food, and if you got wet you stayed wet and died from exposure. Each night, wagons with dead prisoners were brought back to the camp.

I started to look around the infirmary for things to do. The barrack had a small kitchen and a few prisoners were distributing meals to the hospital inmates. I picked up a broom, started to sweep the floor, and washed some kettles, which always had some food left in them. The prisoners in charge of the infirmary wing liked me doing things, but I was on my feet most of the day. At the end of the week, my foot was inflamed and swollen. Dr. Zabramski examined me and could not understand why my foot was still inflamed. He asked me if I was walking on it and I of course denied it. He warned me to stay off my foot and gave me one more week before he would discharge me, even if the foot was not healed. I complied as much as possible, but I just could not sit still. At the end of the week, my foot hadn't healed and the doctor, true to his word, discharged me. He wouldn't listen to my begging. He just waved me away and I was taken out of the infirmary to the clothing barrack.

When I had entered the infirmary, they gave me a different uniform and I lost all the good clothing I had accumulated. I was also transferred out of my barrack and lost my bed and all that was under my mattress. All I had now was a used, threadbare uniform, a thin coat, wooden clogs and no socks. I was miserable and I thought I would die. It was a rainy, cold morning the day I was released and it never warmed up. I became wet on the way to the job site and stayed wet all day, shivering, with my teeth chattering, and very uncomfortable. I was assigned to a different job site and my former boss was no-where near. All day, I suffered from the pain in my foot. I tried to go to the infirmary that evening but they wouldn't let me in. In my new barrack, I did not know anybody. I couldn't even find my father; he may have been on a night shift. I went to sleep wet and hungry and got up in the morning still wet and still hungry.

By morning, my foot was getting even worse. I convinced the kapo to let me go to the infirmary. I was lucky to get to see Dr. Zabramski, and I pleaded with him to re-admit me. After he looked at my foot, he agreed, but with a stern warning that I had one week only. I real-ized I was playing with my life and I stayed in bed most of the time. At the end of the week, my foot was still not healed; pus was oozing out of the wound. I begged the doctor to see if I could get a job in the infirmary compound. I reminded him that my father helped him in Birkenau with extra food and that if he sent me back to the building site I would not survive a week. He agreed to speak to the hospital's head kapo to get me a job.

During the next examination, he informed me that I would work in the infirmary laundry. I was elated, and thanked him profusely. Another near disaster was averted and in the end, it turned out better than I expected, even though the work in the laundry was not easy. We stood in water all day and had to scrub infirmary prisoners' uni-forms on a scrubbing board. However, it was indoors and we received more food than we would have on the outside. At the end of the shift, we were allowed to change our wet clothes for dry ones. The soap we used was very harsh, and by the end of the day my skin was raw up to my knuckles. I couldn't immerse my hands in the wash water with-out severe pain. I went to the doctor again, and as he examined my hands, I was afraid he would fire me. To my surprise, he said I could work for him as his cabin boy and help in the infirmary. I suspected that he would abuse me, as all my other supervisors had; however, at this point it was a life-and-death situation and anything was better than going back to the *Baustelle*. I cleaned his room, which he shared with another doctor, a prominent German Jew; I made their beds and washed their dishes. He never attempted to abuse me.

Usually the doctors didn't eat the camp food and instead had special food brought from the kitchen. I took their soup ration daily and gave much of it to my father. In addition to working for the doctors, I worked in the infirmary cutting off prisoners' old bandages, exposing the wound for the doctor to see. After he applied some paste, it was my job to apply fresh bandages. Although the smell of decaying flesh nauseated me, I was good at applying bandages and after a few days, the doctor allowed me to do most without supervision. It was also my job to clean up utensils, clean floors and do anything that needed to be done. To me this job was the best I ever had in any camp.

The dirtiest and most dreaded task was oiling the floors in the entire infirmary. It was a hard and exacting process. On my knees, I had to spread a uniformly thin film of black oil. Too much oil would make the floor slippery and not enough would expose the bare boards. Once, I was on all fours when the *Hauptkapo* of the infirmary approached. I had been going over the same spot a few times to make sure that it was evenly spread, and he thought I was not working fast enough. He yelled, applied his boot to my behind, and sent me flying over the freshly oiled floor. My uniform was black with oil and Dr. Zabramski was very angry with me. I had to finish the job before I was allowed to change my clothes. My bottom hurt terribly, and I could not walk properly for days.

The infirmary was mostly filled with non-Jewish prisoners because Jewish prisoners did not last in the infirmary very long. If Jews became sick with a serious illness that could not be cured within a couple of weeks, or were emaciated to the point of no return and unable to work, they were sent to Auschwitz. The Polish, Soviet and German non-Jewish prisoners were treated much better than the Jews and had a better chance of recovery. Some suffered from tuberculosis and had high fevers. I was assigned to haul pails of ice cubes and fill their bathtubs to cool them down.

Dr. Zabramski had the terrible responsibility of deciding who was beyond the point of recovery and not able to work. It was assumed that those he selected would be sent directly to the gas chamber at Auschwitz. It happened once that one of the sick prisoners was Dr. Zabramski's relative and he felt he had no choice but to select him for the transport. Apparently, he felt his relative didn't have a chance of recovery, and he did not want to show any favouritism.

Polish prisoners were allowed to receive parcels from home, especially around holidays, some of which contained things like chocolate, salami, tobacco and other scarcities. The SS guards confiscated many of the goods. Some contained white bread, and by the time the parcels arrived at the camp the bread was mouldy. Some prisoners would cut off the green mould and throw it away; other prisoners picked it up, ate it and became deathly sick. Their stomachs had to be pumped. The doctor would insert the hose through the patient's nose into the stomach and then I took over the procedure, which was a smelly and sickening job.

Working in the infirmary meant I could sleep in the barrack designated for privileged inmates, which gave me a special status A few days after I was transferred to this barrack, I ran a high fever. I had convulsions and shivers. The young man who was the chief cook's *pipel* looked after me and brought me some aspirins and cold water. It took me two days to recover, and we became friends. He eventually made advances to me to become his *pipel* but fortunately for me he was not violent and, when I resisted, he didn't pursue me further. I soon befriended the warehouse personnel and I was able to acquire a good uniform, leather boots, underwear and even a sweater, not only for myself but also for my father. My father couldn't enter the infirmary compound but I could pass him food and clothing through the barbed wire fence. I was able to pass him some soup and occasionally bread and he gained some weight. When he had more food than he could eat, he shared the extra with a fellow he befriended from Sosnowiec.

The infirmary had a commodity that was in high demand by the prisoner establishment: alcohol. My favourite job was to go to the main kitchen with a bottle of medical alcohol under my jacket and bring back eggs and salami. I made sure to have a homemade (illegal) knife on me and the salami always shrank on the way back to the infirmary. I would always save a small piece for my father's next package. Our physical condition continued to improve and we were optimistic that we might survive the war.

Through the civilians working with my father we received information about the war and knew that it was going badly for the Germans. The Soviets were advancing through Poland and the American forces were advancing from the west. We heard explosions and constant bombardment, so we knew the front must be near. There was an air raid practically every night. The Soviets bombed the Krupp factory from great heights and as a result, were inaccurate and ineffective. The bombs ended up in the nearby fields and the only damage sustained by the plant was blown-out windows.

By December 1944, the air raids became much more frequent and we could hear the roar of cannons. The question on everyone's mind was what would happen to us. Would the Germans kill us before the Soviet army got to us? Our speculations ended on January 21, 1945, when we were evacuated. We were assembled early in the morning on the *Appellplatz*. As usual, we stood for hours at attention, motionless. The weaker ones, those that fell or even wavered, were immediately removed. The SS encouraged those who felt sickly or weak to step forward. Very few volunteered. Everyone tried his best to appear healthy and strong.

Although I lived in the infirmary compound, I was ordered to leave as well. The hospital medical staff was allowed to stay. We wondered what would happen to those in the hospital. Before leaving, I got a large piece of salami and some bread from Dr. Zabramski. Finally, we were given a double ration of bread and were marched out of the camp. We looked back at those in the infirmary and were glad not to be among them. We marched with determination in straight lines, in rows of five, and were counted as we left the gate. The line stretched behind us and in front of us beyond the line of sight. For about two hours, we all made progress and maintained our positions. After that, the lines deteriorated and people started to fall back.

The stronger ones surged ahead. My father and I were in better shape than most Jewish prisoners because of my position in the hospital for the previous three months. Our leather shoes, which we had procured at a high price, proved to be a disadvantage because unlike the wooden clogs, they got soaked quickly as the snow under our feet turned into slush and wet mud. The spaces between the lines got longer and the guards shouted and beat us with their gun butts to close up the ranks.

By late afternoon, most of the prisoners had devoured their double ration of bread. The food from Zabramski had sustained my father and me, and we divided each bread ration into four and ate only one portion; we hid the rest in our clothing. By nightfall, we reached what we thought was our destination. We estimated that we had marched about forty kilometres. We were herded into huge barns with straw on the ground and were told to bed down. We were practically lying on top of each other. Some prisoners climbed the rafters and found more space but were in danger of falling off. Apparently, not all could be shoved into the barn and about a third of the prisoners had to sleep outside in the snow.

We received no food or water. We ate another portion of our ration secretly, fearing the prisoners around us might attack us if they found out that we still had bread. One of the men on the rafters had diarrhea and let loose, spraying us below. In the morning, we were roused at dawn and had to wait until the guards completed the search for prisoners hidden in the straw. We used snow to wash off the feces, but the smell stayed with us. Finally, we were driven out onto the road, again without receiving any food or water.

The second day our progress was much slower. We walked mechanically, in disarray, trying to keep up. Without realizing it, my father and I drifted to the end of the line and suddenly found ourselves at the rear of the column. The guards encouraged any stragglers to sit down at the side of the road. Those who did were left behind. A few metres behind us, we heard shooting and we could see the SS guards putting two people's heads together and shooting them through their heads to preserve bullets. Their bodies were left by the road. Seeing this, we gathered our strength and pulled each other along. We struggled to get closer to the front of the line but our strength ebbed and we fell back again. We repeated this procedure over and over again. Whenever we could, we gathered snow to quench our thirst. The day seemed endless.

We eventually arrived at the place designated for our overnight stay. This time we bedded down outside, in the open, on straw spread on the snow. Again we received no food or drink. We estimated that we had walked about thirty kilometres that day. We gathered snow and ate it. After darkness engulfed us, we ate some of our food secretly. My father and I huddled together to keep warm. All through the night we heard shooting as prisoners desperately tried to run away under the cover of darkness. Few succeeded. In the morning, all around us were frozen bodies. Still no food or drink. We lined up and while the guards searched for prisoners in hiding, we manoeuvred our way to the front of the column. This would allow us to slow down occasionally, regain our strength and give us a degree of safety from falling too far behind.

Our march slowed down to a crawl. Even the guards were slowing down. They selected stronger-looking prisoners and made them carry their backpacks. Our last piece of bread was tempting us but we struggled with our hunger and resisted, not knowing how long it would be before we received more food. It was our only hope for survival. Exhaustion and hunger took their toll. People fell down while still walking. Some became delirious and started walking backwards, stumbling and falling. We stepped over their bodies and continued, not knowing for how long. At first, the guards didn't bother to pick up the bodies, but as we moved further away from the front and through populated areas, they collected the bodies on wagons and carted them away. We estimated that we had travelled only twenty kilometres the third day. The fourth day, our progress was even slower.

When I was working in the infirmary, my father would share his extra food with a friend. On the fourth day, we were very thirsty and there was little snow to quench our thirst. My father noticed that his friend still had water in his canteen. He approached him and asked, "Give my son a little bit of water?" to which the man replied, "What do you think, I run after you with a balia [washtub] of water?" He would not give me a drink. My father did not speak to him again.

By the fourth day my father and I were marching arm in arm and leaning on each other. If I weakened, he would pull me, and when I got a spurt of energy, I would pull him. By nightfall of the fourth day we were met by wagons with lukewarm watery soup and different guards. We were told that our destination was only a few kilometres away. By this time, our numbers were reduced. That day, we reached the much-feared concentration camp of Gross-Rosen. We were told that, over the four days of our march, we had lost one-third of the men.

At Gross-Rosen, our kapos and prisoner officials were received as old friends by the camp establishment. They got good jobs again and continued to control us. We knew from the original Gross-Rosen inmates at Fünfteichen that it was a brutal, terrible camp. The camp operated a stone quarry and had predominantly Polish gentile prisoners, many of whom belonged to the partisans' underground movement. We were told that thousands of Polish prisoners had lost their lives there. Fortunately for us, we were not required to work in the quarry, but because we did not work, our rations were reduced.

The camp was overcrowded, as, in addition to us, other prisoners from surrounding areas had also been transported there. We were assigned to a new, empty barrack. We slept on the floor, on just a little straw. We were infested with lice – a shake of our clothes and we would see the lice fall out like sand. When we squeezed the lice between thumbnails, we saw our own blood squirt out. Getting sleep was difficult; the lice sucked our blood and our strength. Many people contracted typhus fever.

Each morning, people were selected to carry the dead out of the barracks and place them on pyres for burning because the crematoria could not handle the number of dead each day. When I was selected, I resented the fact that I had to carry these dead bodies and use up my strength. There were three of us to one body – two of us had one arm each and the third had to carry the legs. The mouths of the corpses were open, as if their souls had escaped with a scream on their last breath. The head bounced on the ground, emitting a hollow sound that I will remember forever.

After two weeks without showers and washing facilities, we were lined up, issued a loaf of bread and marched to a waiting train. It was snowing and bitterly cold. We were loaded eighty men to an open boxcar, a part of which was taken by the SS guards perched on bales of straw. There was not enough space for all of us to sit down, so we had to take turns standing. My father cut the bread into six slices, reasoning that the SS would not suddenly become more generous; he anticipated that we would not get any food for at least four or five days. As it happened, it was six days. We hid our bread and ate one piece of our self-imposed ration each day. Most people, again, devoured their bread in the first one or two days. The temptation to satisfy hunger was tremendous, but those of us who withstood it had a much higher chance of survival. After two days, my father and I realized that only a few still had something to eat. We didn't dare eat during the day, within view of starving men. We again ate only after everyone around us was asleep.

The weather was snowy and cold enough that the snow on our clothing did not melt right away. The snow soon covered us totally and we ate the snow from our clothing. After three days, more and more prisoners fell where they stood or crouched, and died. My father and I secured spots against the wall of the boxcar, giving us some support and safety. We were not allowed to dispose of the bodies. We lined them along the perimeter of the boxcar, covered them with straw and sat on them, as on a bench. Every day, more men died from exhaustion, hunger and lack of water. The SS guarding us were old men or soldiers who had been wounded in action and had now recovered. It was in their interests to keep us alive so as to keep their jobs guarding us; otherwise, they would have to go to the front again. They did not want to talk to us or even make eye contact.

The railway ended about two kilometres from what we learned was our destination: the Flossenbürg concentration camp. The camp was high up in the mountains and the beauty of the scenery could not be ignored, but it only contributed to our misery. We walked to the camp up a steep incline and, not used to the high altitude, we quickly felt out of breath. We kept pulling each other up, step by step. The guards were impatient and started to shout and beat us to hurry up. The climb was difficult and I thought we would not make it. The beautiful surrounding mountains and forests made the situation seem unreal.

When we finally reached the camp it was late afternoon. We were led into a shower room and stripped of our lice-infested clothes, which we did not mind. We had to spend the night, naked, in the shower room, one huge space with partitions and no windows. Since we didn't know what a gas chamber looked like, we were afraid that this might be our end. Since leaving Fünfteichen I had lost weight; I was now skin and bones. No matter how I sat or lay, I was terribly uncomfortable. I couldn't sleep because every few minutes my bones ached and I had to shift. Most of the time, I stood or leaned against a wall. Some of the spouts dripped water and I tried to catch a few drops. Other prisoners had the same idea and since I was smaller, they easily pushed me aside. The night was very long. Eventually, the water came on and we surmised that it must be morning. After shaving and delousing, we were issued uniforms and assigned to barracks.

The former Gross-Rosen kapos tried to get a privileged status in Flossenbürg but this camp had no connection with Gross-Rosen and the Flossenbürg kapos did not want to share their authority with any new arrivals. Flossenbürg kapos, having heard of the brutality perpetrated by the kapos in Gross-Rosen, isolated them and beat them up with the help of the mistreated Gross-Rosen prisoners; some of the most brutal kapos were so badly beaten that they eventually died.

The barracks were similar to those in Fünfteichen – two wings for sleeping with a dining room in between, with large windows. In this camp, we were allowed to sit during the day in the bright dining room. As only some were selected to go to work, the others, including me, had a lot of time during the day to talk. The camp provided labour for a quarry, as in Gross-Rosen. We were a real mixture of prisoners; many were from the Soviet Union, but there were prisoners from almost all the countries of Europe. Jews were in the minority, but we were not as likely to be killed without reason, as had been the case in Auschwitz-Birkenau. I met a Russian who was very interested in educating me about the way things were done in the Soviet Union. He told me that the secret police had come to arrest his father for political reasons but since his father was not home, they arrested him instead and sent him to a Siberian labour camp. When the war with Germany broke out, he volunteered to go into the military and since he had some education before his arrest, they sent him to be trained as a pilot. His plane was shot down over German-occupied Polish territory and he managed to parachute down with his crew. They hid among Polish peasants but shortly thereafter were discovered and arrested. For that, instead of being put in a prisoner-of-war camp, they were sent to a concentration camp. He told me that if he survived he would not return to the Soviet Union. He felt that the Soviet Union was as brutal as Germany. Of course, he was not talking about what was happening to the Jews.

Each day we had to line up on the *Appellplatz* to be counted; some were selected to go to work and those who remained in camp had to do exercises. One day, my father was selected. On his way back from work, he walked past a truck that was carrying carrots and saw one just sticking out from the side of the truck. He leaned over and grabbed it. An SS guard saw him and almost killed him for that one carrot. Luckily, he survived the beating and none of his bones were broken, but his body was covered with black and blue marks. It had been a stupid thing to do.

Flossenbürg, like Gross-Rosen, did not have a gas chamber, but it did have a crematorium. The hardest job was to drag bodies out of the barracks, load them onto wagons and take them to a ramp that led down to the crematorium. When the kapos were looking for people to do heavy work, my father would invariably be picked – even though he was thin and half-starved, his large frame made him look big and strong.

After the war, having witnessed so much death, I was asked what my feelings were about death and what effect it had on me when someone I knew died. In fact, I had no fear of dead bodies. As I mentioned, I resented the fact that I had to use up my precious strength to carry them. For a long time after the war, I had difficulty feeling empathy for people who died in bed at an old age. I wished my family members could have lived a full life and died at the age of seventy or eighty. However, that started to change when members of my own family started to die. One of the reasons I started writing this memoir, at the age of eighty-four, was the fear of not knowing when my time will come. There were many questions I had wanted to ask my father before his death, but it was never the right time, and I had not expected him to die at such an early age.

We kept hearing that the war was going badly for the Germans. American troops were fast advancing and Germany was retreating as the Allied forces closed in. We still feared that the SS would finish us off rather than let us go. After about two weeks in Flossenbürg, near the end of February, we were told that a transport of mechanics would be going to another camp. We didn't know whether or not to volunteer. Flossenbürg had no gas chamber, but the quarry work was dangerous and many people died from the hard labour. Whether we should register or not was a serious decision.

We eventually decided that it would be best to leave Flossenbürg. My father registered as a mechanic and I registered as an electrician. We were lined up in rows and the SS men walked between the rows to take out the weak ones. I was terribly afraid that I would be separated from my father. I still looked like a kid, small and skinny, and I was trembling with fear, which made me even more vulnerable to be selected. I tried to make myself as tall as I could, and I stood next to some shorter people so that my height would not be as noticeable. I breathed a sigh of relief when the SS guard passed me.

The next day we received a two-day bread ration and we were marched out of the camp. This time it was downhill and we were in better spirits. The train ride, in a closed boxcar this time, took a few days and we had no additional food or water, but we were nonetheless more upbeat. The train moved much faster, as if there was urgency to get us where we were going. We had no idea where that was.

We arrived in the small town of Leonberg at the beginning of March. We didn't know where in Germany we were, but because it was warm already we thought we must be somewhere in the west. We marched from the train station to the camp through streets lined with houses. The German people looked away as we went past, as if we were monsters. The camp looked relatively new, with two-storey buildings with large windows and two-tier high bunks. The weather was beautiful, sunny and warm with trees sprouting leaves and the birds singing. It felt surreal. I even experienced a wave of hope and allowed myself to take a deep breath. I was with my father and I almost felt happy.

The camp was situated on a road that led to a factory, a road lined with single-family houses. My window overlooked the camp's double fences and the distance between the fences and the houses couldn't have been more than one hundred metres. We could practically see into the white curtained windows with flower boxes on their sills. Boys and girls congregated on the street, leaning on bicycles and having a good time horsing around. I almost forgot that there was life beyond the barbed wires and sentry towers. I had forgotten that people were living normal lives even though the war was still on. I was envious and wished I could change places with them. I wondered why my fate was so different from theirs just because I was born Jewish. I would have gladly renounced my religion if it meant I could be on the other side of the fence. My fate still hung by the thinnest of threads and I wished with all my might to be freed from this hellish place. Although Leonberg was better than the camps I had been in previously, it was still a concentration camp and my life depended on the whim of the SS. There were no gas chambers or crematoria here. Being so close to the civilian residences, I felt more secure. This camp had a large number of prisoners from various European countries, although the Polish prisoners still constituted a majority and we Jews a minority.

On the other side of our barracks was the *Appellplatz* and beyond that were anti-aircraft trenches. The next day we were separated into groups according to our work experience; my father was selected for a different group and barrack. My father's group was marched off to the aircraft plant and we stayed behind. The next morning my rather small group was marched to the plant, which was located inside an Autobahn (motorway) tunnel, running through a low mountain. The plant was a huge, cavernous place that had been carved out of the rock. I walked right past my father, who was working as a riveter on an aircraft wing. The next thing I knew, I was lying on the ground; apparently I had fainted. I came to shortly after. The following day, I was relieved from the workforce and confined to a barrack with other weak and sickly-looking prisoners. Out of the 150 people in the barrack, only two or three had a fever. The rest of us felt well. I didn't know why I had fainted. I had only an infected finger, from biting my nails, which throbbed and was terribly painful. I managed to break the skin and suck out the pus until blood came. Over the next couple of days I kept sucking my finger to make sure no pus accumulated; eventually it started to heal, though I lost the nail in the process.

It was only a couple of days later that we experienced an air raid by American fighter planes. The air raid sirens came on and we were ordered to lie face down in the trenches. I could not resist looking at the sky. The aircraft attacked the parts storage building next to our camp. Not even one live bullet landed in our trenches, only the spent shells. I was frightened but happy to see the American fighter planes. We heard the anti-aircraft guns, but no planes were hit. The prisoners rejoiced. We were told by some of the prisoners that were taken to clean up the damage that almost all of the aircraft parts were destroyed and the roof of the warehouses looked like a sieve. The Americans bombed the entrance to the factory but were unable to damage the factory itself.

Unfortunately for me, some prisoners in my barrack broke out with typhus fever. Rumour had it that we would be shipped out of the camp. My father, wanting to take me out of that barrack, went to the SS camp commander and asked him to let me out or to let him join me. The commander, my father told me, looked at him as if he was insane. The commander said, "You must be out of your mind; they are being shipped to another camp. These prisoners have developed typhus and we are not able to deal with them here." Then he asked if he had been in contact with me. My father said, "Yes, I saw him today." The commandant started to shout and ordered my father out of his office, demanding that he join me.

The prisoners of our barrack were put in trucks, taken to a train station and put into closed boxcars. We were only seventy or eighty people per car. There was a bucket in one corner and many had diarrhea, including me. Fortunately, I could control my diarrhea and did not soil myself. Most people did not make it to the bucket in time and went where they stood. The stench was unbearable. One prisoner took charge of the boxcar and organized the prisoners into two groups in the car: a clean side and a dirty side. My father and I stayed on the clean side.

After a couple of days, people started to die and we could not get rid of the bodies so we had to stack them in the dirty part of the car. The guards were not with us in the car; they were stationed on a platform overlooking the roofs of the cars. We travelled across Germany, moving slowly, being bombarded. We were often shunted onto railway sidings in stations between various tracks, going back and forth, changing directions. It appeared to us that the Allies were bombing the rail lines and sometimes we had to stand on a siding for hours. Those tall enough to look through the small barred windows would tell us where we were if they could recognize the passing towns. The weather was getting cooler and we knew we were travelling east.

Three or four days after leaving Leonberg, we got to the Munich railway yard, which was being constantly bombed. We thought our cars would jump off the tracks. The train stopped and we were sealed in. Whenever the train stood for a while, the SS would get off the train and watch us, with machine guns aimed at the cars. It was the third week of March when we arrived at Mühldorf am Inn, a small town with a huge railway yard that had been badly bombed only a couple of days earlier. Approximately half of the people in our boxcar were still alive on arrival. We left the bodies in the car and were marched to a camp, where we were lined up in front of a single-storey barrack with big open windows, similar to those in Fünfteichen. I could see double bunks inside, with white linens on them, and I could not wait to be able to lie down on those beds. I was exhausted from the trip and my diarrhea. An SS guard stood in front of us and asked if anyone was sick or feverish. He told us that, if so, we should report to the infirmary and after a few days of care, we could rejoin the workers. I was about to step forward when my father put his hand on my shoulder and said, "You are not sick, you don't want to go." He was right – the next day some of the prisoners from our group had to go into the forest and bury all those who had said they were sick. Apparently, they had been taken to the forest and shot.

A Hollow Victory

Mühldorf was a sub-camp of Dachau. The area was in the foothills of the Alps, in Bavaria. When we got there the weather was warm, as spring had come early that year. I was selected for work in the kitchen, a premium job, which was most welcome as I was depleted and could do with a bit of extra food. I was quite happy sorting the leftover potatoes from the winter, even though most of them were partly frozen and starting to rot, smelling terribly. The SS got the good potatoes and the prisoners got what was left – a hat full of cooked and partly disintegrating potatoes. My father and I were very careful not to eat rotten potatoes. Notwithstanding the smell, many prisoners ate them and became sick.

My main job in the kitchen was peeling the good potatoes for the SS. The kitchen kapo shouted at me for leaving some of the eyes on the potatoes. After that, I peeled them quite thick to remove all the eyes. It was dangerous to steal potatoes, but that was the only way I could help my father. I stole a few small ones, which were easier to hide in my shirt and quicker to cook. We tried to cook them on our stove in the barracks but unfortunately, we could not get the fire going because we didn't have any dry kindling or wood. In the end, we were going to throw them away but some prisoners took them and ate them raw.

My father went to work in the village, cleaning up the debris left from the Allied bombing. He worked hard but could scrounge some food on the site. He was not allowed to bring anything into the camp. After a week working in the kitchen, with a little bit more food, I regained some strength. It is interesting how quickly the body can recuperate with some food. We were there for about two weeks and were very disappointed when we were told that some of us had to go into another camp known as Waldlager, the forest camp. My father was one of them. Giving up the kitchen job was hard but there was no way that I would be separated from my father. I volunteered to go with him and I was accepted.

Spring had come early to Bavaria, but in this camp, no grass grew. The camp was deep in a dense forest. Here, nature had to struggle hard against the destructive forces of man. On the barren ground only a few blades of grass sprung up around the barracks. Overhead, the trees sprouted their light green leaves as if to cover up in shame the horror and suffering that lay below.

The forest camp was very different from anything we had seen before. All the sleeping barracks or, rather, sleeping rooms, were half buried in the ground. An excavated trench formed the walkway, which was the only place we could stand up. On either side of the trench were platforms with wooden planks on which straw bags were laid. Over this was an A-shaped roof covered with earth and grass in order not to be easily detected from the air as a camp. From above, all that could be seen were mounds of earth. Each hut must have accommodated one hundred prisoners. We slept with our heads at the walkway; our feet were in the low end, where the space was only a few centimetres high.

The next day we were marched to a construction site that consisted of an above-ground huge archway of poured concrete that was part of the plan for an underground aircraft factory. I was amazed that with the war almost over, the Allied troops advancing on all fronts, they were building this massive archway for a factory. I was assigned to unload cement bags from a truck. As a bag was placed on my back,

I collapsed under its weight. Fortunately for me, the bag did not break open as it fell on top of me. The SS man laughed at this and the kapo got very angry and yelled, "Get out of here and don't come back!"

After that, I was allowed to stay in the camp and was assigned to kitchen duty. It seemed that another near disaster had turned out for the better. However, it was not what I expected – there was no work in the kitchen for me. I was assigned to a five-man work detail, accompanied by an SS guard, that had to go to the farmers' fields and gather nettles, which apparently were a good source of protein. Touching any part of the plant would cause burns and blisters; I soon learned from the other prisoners that I had to dig my fingers into the ground beside the plant, grab the root and pull it up and out of the ground. The next trick was to shove them into the bag we were required to fill without touching the leaves. On our way to the fields, we passed farmers' houses, and when we noticed food put out for the dogs, we broke out of the line to grab it. The guard chased after us and beat us with his gun butt. We could see the farmer looking on in horror. The residents around the camp had been told that we were all hardened criminals and murderers and that they should not have any contact with us. I guess the farmer was amazed to see a young boy like myself, hardly a hardened criminal.

Fünfteichen felt like so long ago. My physical condition was now on the decline again. I still had diarrhea and, with so little food, I lost a lot of my flesh and muscle. Collecting nettles all day long was getting harder and I was getting weaker and weaker. At the end of April, no one went to work; we were told that we would be evacuated from the camp.

Over the past few months, we knew that the Allies had advanced on all fronts, and they could not be stopped. This had caused the Nazis to move prisoners from one camp to another; no one knew the fate of those left behind. We had hope that as long as the Nazis needed our skilled labour, they would keep transferring us from one camp to the next. The movement always went in the same direction:

away from the front to the interior of Germany. I felt time was against us. In the past three months, we had moved four times. Each transfer meant a loss of lives. Lack of food and water, coupled with exhaustion and random killing, had taken hundreds and thousands of lives. With each trip, our desperation increased and our hope for survival diminished.

Survival depended on the will to live. For my father and me, survival depended on staying together; we had to sustain the will to live for each another. Once you gave up hope, you were lost. Now, for the first time, I did not care. I knew I could not go on another death march; I knew it would be my death march. I said to my father, "You go on. I will stay here and whatever will be, will be. I cannot go." I urged him to go. My father was surprised by my decision and responded angrily, "I will not hear of this, and I will not leave you. We did not give up before and you must not give up now. You will come with me even if I have to carry you." I knew that he was right. To give up was like committing suicide. We knew that the front was near – all day and throughout the night we could hear artillery fire. There were rumours that the SS would destroy the camp and murder all who remained. Still, I did not care. I was so weak and tired that I knew I could not walk for any distance. I saw what happened to those who couldn't maintain the pace. I would rather take the consequences of staying behind than face a certain death by exhaustion or a bullet to my head on the road.

The order to leave the camp was issued to all except those in the infirmary. I suggested we hide, but everywhere we looked was occupied. The only good places one could hide would be under the boards inside the barracks or between the roof overhang and the ground, but when we tried, there was not enough space. We tried to lift the platform boards, which some prisoners had managed to crawl under, but the boards were nailed fast. Hiding did not appear to be an option.

All who could walk were assembled, lined up in rows of five, waiting to be marched off to the trains a few kilometres away. My father and I were hanging back at the end of the line. The camp comman-dant stood at the gate observing the evacuation. I broke out of the line and approached him, my father following. I told him that I didn't have the strength to go on the march and asked for permission to stay in the camp infirmary. I looked more like a twelve-year-old now, even though I was seventeen. He took one look at me and said, "You can stay." I told him that I wanted my father to stay with me to take care of me. "No, he looks strong enough, he has to go." My father said, "Sir, we have been together all through these years, please let us stay together now that the end is near." The commandant demanded my father join the marchers. I wouldn't stay without my father, so we started toward the gate, my father half-carrying me. Suddenly, as if it was an afterthought, the commandant turned and shouted with a smirk on his face, "Hey you, you can both stay." We didn't know what that smirk implied. Why had he changed his mind? Could it be that some ray of humanity entered his soul? Or did he think that no mat-ter what, we were doomed either on the road or in camp? I didn't care, as long as I was with my father.

We went to the infirmary, an above-ground building with win-dows and double bunks. No one seemed to be in charge. We took two lower bunks and settled in. All we could do was wait and see what would happen. Decades later, I was telling this story to a friend of mine in Toronto, Michael Mason, and he said, "I was in that camp and I was put on that train." The people were marched to the railway and put in boxcars. The Allies didn't know it was a train with prison-ers and they attacked it, killing many people. The SS stationed them-selves outside the train with machine-guns and as prisoners started to run they opened fire, and most of the ones who ran out were killed. Eventually, the Americans came and liberated them.

Staying in the infirmary was much better than living in the dug-outs. We got some food, which meant that kitchen staff remained in the camp. This gave us some hope. About two days later, the com-mandant came to the infirmary and stood at the door. I noticed that his SS insignia and rank markings had been removed from his uniform. He waved a letter at us and said he had been ordered to destroy the camp and evacuate the rest of the prisoners. He informed us that since he did not have vehicles to transport us, he was ignoring the order, and planned to deliver the camp intact to the Allies. No one cheered. I don't think anyone believed him.

We weren't in a position to do anything except wait and hope. From the constant, loud bombardments, we knew the front must be near. In hushed tones, we talked about the possibility of Germany's imminent defeat, but time dragged on and we feared the Allies wouldn't get to us in time.

May 2, 1945. A heavy, overcast sky fit the mood of the inmates in the infirmary. The air stunk with decay and death. The last evacuation transport had left the camp five days earlier. Only two guards and the commandant stayed guarding us. The end was surely near, but would liberation come in time? My father, one of the few still able to walk, shuffled among the bunks helping others with a cup of water, or shifting their bodies on the wooden bunks and thin straw mattresses. The daily soup, usually lukewarm and thin, had not yet arrived.

Suddenly, the door burst open and a shout penetrated the putrid air. "The Americans are here! We are free! We are free!" No one moved; the long awaited words were now incomprehensible to our minds. They promised life and freedom to people who knew only hunger, despair and death. Could it be true, or was it a trick? After a few seconds, the realization came upon us simultaneously. As a rupture in a dam, floods of emotion so long suppressed – joy, tears and laughter – were uncontrollably released. My father and I embraced, danced, laughed, and cried with joy. We survived. We survived! Unnatural strength entered my body as I rushed with others to greet our liberators. My father stayed behind. "Get some food!" he cried out after me. An American tank with a white star dominated the scene. Behind it stood American soldiers guarding a few SS men. I was startled. Those Nazis, who only a few minutes earlier were the "master race," with their shiny boots, pressed uniforms and their high peaked hats, had looked invincible. Now they stood there with their jackets open, hatless, their hair dishevelled, and fear in their eyes. Gone was their superiority. They looked like ordinary, frightened men. Some of the prisoners could have torn them to shreds with their bare hands. We stared at the SS, throwing rocks and obscenities at them, while the Americans shot into the air to warn us that they wouldn't tolerate any attacks on their prisoners. In disgust, we turned away.

The crowd moved through the camp, looking for food and looting and breaking everything in their path. By the time I reached the warehouse, everything was gone. I stumbled through mounds of empty broken cartons. I ran from room to room in panic. All the food was gone. I was too late. However, I was determined not to go hungry on the first day of my deliverance, not to return to my father empty-handed. I had to find something.

A group of men tore at the flesh of a dead horse. My pulse quickened as I dashed over to the carcass, but the sight turned my stomach. I moved on. In the last storage building, under a pile of paper, I found a sack of flour. With a piece of broken glass, I ripped open the sack and carried away my precious loot in a broken cardboard box. Back in the barrack, we mixed the flour with water and baked our own bread of redemption, matzah, on top of the wood-fired stove.

Our liberation had occurred on that day thanks to a couple of Soviet POWs from an adjoining camp. On seeing the reduced number of guards, they ran out, stole a motorcycle and drove to the nearest village, where they met up with the Americans. The Allies didn't know of the existence of our camp and weren't eager to advance further that day. They were also suspicious of mines and booby traps. The Russians convinced them of the urgency, that lives were at stake, and agreed to drive ahead of them into the forest. The Americans followed the motorcycle from a safe distance and arrived at our camp in the late afternoon. They came with one tank and a personnel carrier; the SS commandant and the few guards surrendered without a fight.

That evening, some of the prisoners from the kitchen butchered the horse that had been shot that day and made a soup for the inmates. A thick layer of fat floated on top of it. Many men, after gobbling up the soup, suffered severe stomach pains and got sick. My father took some of the soup and put it onto our matzah. Our stomachs were incapable of absorbing this rich food.

The next morning the Americans brought a whole troop of soldiers and photographers who looked at us, in our emaciated state and in rags, in disbelief. They photographed the camp and asked me to open my shirt so they could take pictures of my skeletal body. I felt like a freak, exposing my emaciated body, but I complied as I was eager to be part of the documentation. I am sure there is a picture of me in some American's photo album. Then they helped us onto their trucks and took us to the nearest hospital.

The hospital was located in a beautiful convent operated by nuns, who were nurses. It was very strange to sleep in a bed with a regular mattress and clean linens. The nuns treated us with respect and as human beings, addressing me as Mr. Leipciger instead of "Speckdeckel" or "Schweinehund." I had difficulty adjusting to a world I thought no longer existed. The convent, known as Ecksberg, which means on the corner of a mountain, was set among gently rolling hills at the foothills of the Alps, overlooking the river valley. This world existed only a few kilometres from our former camp. The incongruity was unbelievable. Everyone claimed they had no knowledge of the camp, no knowledge of prisoners being murdered daily through starvations or beatings and shootings.

The scene was serene and peaceful. It was the beginning of May, the valley was green and the trees were covered in beautifully coloured blossoms. This was paradise; the large willow trees with their branches overhanging the river reminded me of women with long hair, lamenting over our condition. The beauty of our surroundings contradicted my troubled mind, preoccupied with the fate of my family. I thought of my sister, my mother, and her two sisters. I thought of my father's parents, and his two brothers, four sisters, their spouses and their children, who I knew had been in the Częstochowa ghetto.

The Americans summoned the mayors of the nearest town, which was Mühldorf am Inn, and ordered them to collect clothing from the population to replace our tattered striped uniforms. The civilian clothes gave me a human look, which I hadn't had for so long. We had no ration cards, nor money, so we had to ask people in the town to help us. My father made friends with the owner of a butcher shop, who supplied us with salami and other ready-to-eat meat products. However, my diarrhea did not allow me to retain much of the nourishment, and I remained very thin.

Five days later, on May 8, 1945, the war was over and Victory in Europe Day was declared. We celebrated by going for a walk outside the hospital. It was a simple but unbelievable experience to be free, to go for a walk wherever we desired. But it was a low-key celebration, a hollow victory. We realized that many of our family members might not have survived. We feared that we no longer had families, homes or even a country to return to. Although I was with my father, I felt utterly alone. The happiness of our liberation and the joy of the moment were overshadowed by the question of who had survived. We had high hopes that my mother and sister had survived Birkenau, as we knew they were taken into the camp.

Most of the inmates with us in the hospital were very sick and truly alone. Some died within the next few days. Some of the Soviet POWs, intent on celebrating the end of the war, went on a quest in search for vodka, found a barrel of alcohol and proceeded to get drunk. Unfortunately, the alcohol was methyl and most got violently sick, some went blind and others died. The hospital was not equipped to handle these cases. Other POWs found arms and went on a search for former guards in the adjoining forest, seeking revenge. If they found any is hard to say. One thing was certain: they did not bring back any prisoners. A few days later, Soviet trucks pulled up to the hospital and forcibly collected all the Soviet POWs. Some of the Russian men had anticipated this and had already disappeared into the countryside.

On May 10, my father and I went for a walk and talked about what we should do next. He sat down on the grass but I felt tired and had to lie down. I felt chills and hot at the same time. My father helped me walk back to the hospital. I was diagnosed with typhus fever. Even though the war had ended and the Americans were with us, no medication was made available to me. (The Americans had penicillin but were not allowed to share it with the civilian population.) I was put into an isolation ward with other typhus cases. My strength was gone and I could hardly pull myself to the upper bunk I had been assigned. My father remained in his room on the second floor.

That night, I woke up from a deep sleep disoriented, slid off the bed and walked through the corridors looking for my father's room. I could not remember the room number. An orderly found me wandering aimlessly and took me back to bed. The next day my father arranged for me to get a lower bunk and, at the risk of contracting typhus himself, took the bunk next to mine. From that point on, he looked after me. I didn't even have the strength to lift my head from the pillow. The only medication was two aspirins every four hours. My chances of surviving were slim.

One of the nuns, Sister Josephine, became my nurse and took charge. She put cold compresses on my head to relieve my fever. My body was but skin and bones, and she worried that my organs were damaged. She fed me little multicoloured pills; I had no idea what they were or where she had obtained them. Whenever I came to, I saw Sister Josephine kneeling by my bed, praying.

Most of the time, I was unconscious or delirious. During my few lucid moments, I argued with God, "Why now? What have I done to deserve this punishment, now that I have tasted freedom? I have seen the most horrible tragedies, the cruellest side of humanity and suffered all these years, only to be taken now? Why was I spared from the gas chamber? Only to die now, now that I know no one is trying to kill me?" I pleaded with God to save me. I asked Him to forgive whatever sins I had committed.

Typhus fever can last for days, and usually after three or four days either the fever breaks or the patient dies. On the fifth day, my intense fever suddenly dropped and I was in a deep sleep. I was told that Sister Josephine came to my bedside, put her hand on my head and found it cold and clammy; in her panic, she could not find my pulse. She thought that I was dying and immediately summoned the priest to administer the last rites. My father arrived, saw the priest in his vestments and asked what the matter was. The sister, in tears, said she thought I had passed away and had called the priest. My father, also in panic, started to shout at the priest that I was a Jew and that he would look after me. This commotion woke me up. Sister Josephine was convinced that my survival was a miracle in response to her prayers.

My recovery was slow and painful. As is usually the case with typhus, some complications ensued. I developed a skin disease, with itchy blisters. Scratching only made the situation worse, as the blisters broke and became infected. My joints ached and my entire body was covered with blisters and sores. Especially painful were the areas between my fingers and toes. Even my genitals were covered first with blisters and then with scabs; urinating was terribly painful. In addition to my malaise, I still had diarrhea and could eat few things. The doctor gave me transfusions of blood plasma to help my recovery and advised my father to get some eggs and let me eat them raw. My father went begging to the local farmers and mixed the egg yolks with sugar; this was my main nourishment. My discomfort was so great that on most nights I cried myself to sleep. I somehow felt that I was being punished for some unknown sins.

To lift my spirits and help me regain my strength, Sister Josephine spent a lot of time with me; she took me on short walks and as I recovered, the walks became longer. Sister Josephine was a slight woman, even shorter than I, her thin face peeking out of her head covering. It looked to me like she was thirty but she told me that she was older. She moved with energy and walked briskly, as if in a hurry. Walking slowly with me was uncharacteristic and it seemed an effort for her. When she spoke to me, she avoided eye contact.

I tried to tell her my story, and she showed interest and sympathy, but I felt she either did not believe me or that it was beyond her understanding that such a thing could happen. She told me that everyone was under the impression that the prisoners in the concentration camps were convicts and murderers. She was visibly shocked to find out that we were there because we were Jewish. Of course, in her self-imposed isolation, she had not had contact with Jews and probably did not know what was happening to us.

~

The city of Mühldorf am Inn issued us identity cards and we could assume any name, nationality or age that we wanted, as there were no records and we had no papers. My father suggested that I make myself two years younger since I did not look my age anyways. Armed with identity papers, we could travel. By the end of June I was well enough to take day trips and we hitchhiked with army vehicles to some of the nearest Displaced Persons (DP) camps in search of records of our family and to register our names in case relatives were looking for us. Our minds and conversations were totally absorbed with how to go about finding out what had happened to our families and who had survived. On occasion, walking the streets of whatever city or town we visited, I would run after any woman who vaguely resembled my mother, shouting her name. The disappointment was painful, but my hopes were not diminished.

When we left Auschwitz-Birkenau, we both had a feeling that my mother and my sister were alive. The question of who in our family had survived was constantly on our minds. The other question burning in our minds was what to do next. Should we remain in Germany or return to Poland? Was it possible to reconstruct our lives? At this point, we had nothing but hopes.

We felt that the only way to find out who had survived was to travel to Poland and go to the last known addresses of our family members. The last time we were together as a family, in the boxcar to Auschwitz, my mother had said that if we got separated, no matter what happened, we would meet at her mother's next-door neighbour's and leave word of our whereabouts. For years after, I speculated whether my mother knew what was coming or if she had a premonition.

Getting back "home" was now our greatest priority. We decided to travel to the Tracing Office in Munich to gain some information. We didn't find any news there, and we left for Poland two days later. In the railway station of Munich we joined thousands of refugees trying to get home or to some other place. No one had money and there were no passenger trains available. We hopped on the next freight train and sat on top of a boxcar with dozens of others. Neither the railway authorities nor the Allies stopped us. The weather was warm, but the wind made us cold as we sat or lay down to avoid the bridges and overpasses. We huddled together and held on to each other for security. We travelled like that for several hours and arrived in the town of Bamberg, about sixty kilometres north of Nuremberg. That was as far as the train was going and we were ordered off.

It was late in the afternoon and we had nowhere to sleep. We asked a military police officer at the railway station where we could find lodging, and he directed us to the social services office. From the other people lined up we found out about a DP camp in Bamberg in an old military compound but we decided to stay in line and see what the Department of Housing, run by German civilians, had to offer us. Since we had lived in Chorzów, an area annexed by the German regime during the war, we were considered German nationals; as former inmates of Nazi concentration camps, we were entitled to receive welfare, food ration cards and lodging. Lodging was extremely sparse, as the centre of Bamberg had been badly ruined by bombing. The city was also inundated by thousands of refugees from east Germany and other parts of the country, including former prisoners of concentration and labour camps. The Allies ordered the German population to make any spare room available for the newcomers.

We were assigned one room in the home of an elderly German couple on the fourth floor of a walk-up apartment at Schrottenberggasse 8. The room had a separate entrance and was spacious, with a large double bed and a commode with a washing bowl and water jug. It also had a sofa and two chairs with a small table and most importantly, it had a small iron stove, for cooking and our sole source of heat. We were thrilled that we could make our home here for a short while before moving on to Poland. The rent included a change of linens and towels once every two weeks. The elderly couple were hospitable and sympathetic. They knew that we were former concentration camp inmates and we tried to convince them our crime was that we were Jewish. They seemed surprised yet said they never gave it a thought when the Jewish population of pre-war Bamberg was deported. The lack of knowledge they claimed about the fate of their town's Jews was something that we were used to hearing by now.

Living in one room with my father caused me to recollect the circumstances of our life in the ghetto, when we had also shared one room. This was a time of terrible emotional pain, combined with the desire to establish a new life. After living in barracks, incarcerated behind barbed wire fences, living in a private home was beyond comprehension. I could go out and come back at any time and do as I wished. Looking out of the fourth-floor window over the red-tiled roofs and at the horizon beyond gave me a sense of limitless possibilities. I knew how to organize things in an abnormal world but how would I function in a world of freedom, law and endless opportunities without an education? I lived an aimless existence. It became clear that my first priority would be to get an education.

We registered with the local United Nations Relief and Rehabilitation Administration (UNRRA) office and received rations of corn flour, sugar, canned meats, an army blanket and cigarettes. I tried smoking but after a few attempts and a lot of choking, I gave up on the idea. The cigarettes were like a currency, which meant my allocation could be traded at the local butcher shop for fresh meat. That usually meant horsemeat, but we seldom cooked and mostly ate dinner at the local tavern. We settled in and made plans for travel to Poland. We decided that my father would go alone while I stayed in Bamberg to try to regain more strength and get rid of my diarrhea. The doctors couldn't find the cause of my illness and tried various remedies, including charcoal pills and opium, but nothing worked.

We went shopping for a backpack, a change of clothes and utensils for my father, and while we were at it, I bought my first pair of new ankle-high boots. My father packed his bag, including the American Army blanket, and we set off for the highway leading to the border of the American Occupied Zone of Germany and Czechoslovakia. I wasn't happy with this separation but I rationalized that it would be easier for him to travel alone, since he had to traverse various borders and occupied countries. I now had an apartment and money, and I was not worried about living on my own. I actually looked forward to it, as a young man of seventeen without parental supervision, even though my relationship with my father was more like that of brothers. I had been robbed of my adolescent years and freedom; I needed to catch up. I was not frightened of anything now that we were free. I was excited at the prospect of being on my own.

On our way to the highway, we met a group of Jews returning from Poland. After exchanging information about where we were coming from and whether any of us had met anyone we might have known, we told them that my father was on his way to Poland in search of our family. They told us that Poland was occupied by the Soviets, who were forcefully enlisting anyone of military age and sending them to the Soviet-Japanese front. They looked at me and said, "Send him."

On my papers, I was fifteen, and I still looked even younger. Suddenly, my father took off the backpack and placed it on me. I had no time to think about the implications of this decision, and it didn't even occur to me that the bag contained his clothing.

There was no mail system in place yet, and no public telephones, so we decided that if I didn't return within four weeks, my father would come join me in Poland. He gave me a list of his relatives and their names, some of which I knew. I parted from my father after a bear hug and handshake. He gave me twenty American dollars he had purchased on the black market for the journey. This all happened so fast that I had no time to consider what it meant and how I would manage to travel on my own through unknown territories.

The first part of the trip was on top of a large open truck and was rather pleasant. After two hours we were dropped off at a point near the Czech border. Most people on the truck were intending to travel to Poland. I followed the group, as they seemed to know the way to a forest pathway supposedly leading to the border. The walk through the woods was both frightening and exhilarating, and it took me out of my depression. It seemed like an eternity since I had last walked through a forest, yet it was only six years. I had spent most summers in the countryside and a lot of time in forests, but this was nothing like those carefree and happy summers – now I was returning home through strange lands with trepidation about what I would find at the end of the journey. The woods were dense with underbrush and I imagined soldiers jumping out at any minute and shooting at us. We walked in total silence on the worn but narrow paths, the stillness of the woods filled only with birdcalls and our footsteps. I did not pay much attention to where we walked, hoping someone knew where we were going, and I had no idea what direction we were going in.

The woods seemed endless. After hours of walking, I felt a sharp pain in my feet. The new shoes were not broken in, and the stiff leather rubbed at my toes and ankles. I started to limp and tried to keep up with the group, paying as little attention to my pain as possible.

I knew I would be in trouble if I fell back and got separated from them. They paid no attention to me and since I didn't know any of them, they would not even miss me. We emerged from the forest and walked through open fields; the lead person spotted a farmer and tried to get directions to the border. It turned out we had lost our way and had to go back to a fork in the forest path where we had taken a wrong turn. By this time, it was late afternoon and we would not reach the border before dark.

The evening came up suddenly and keeping up with the group became more difficult as the darkness engulfed us. Suddenly, out of nowhere, a voice called out to us in Czech or German, I don't remember which, "Halt! Who goes there?" A flashlight beam blinded us. It was a Czechoslovakian border guard. After a short interrogation in broken German and Polish, we explained that we were on our way from a Nazi concentration camp to Poland. He politely asked us to follow him to a border post some way through the woods, where we were offered some bread and ersatz coffee and allowed to stay the night. When I removed my boots, the sock on my right foot was soaked with blood and stuck to my foot. The soldiers gave me some gauze.

The next morning the guards issued us temporary travel passes and directed us to a train that would take us to Plzeň (Pilzno in Polish) in the American Zone of Czechoslovakia. In Plzeň, I separated from the group and tried to find my way to the Polish Repatriation Office. I wandered through the city taking in all the wonderful buildings – unlike the cities in Germany, very little had been destroyed by bombs.

I stopped a person on the street to ask for directions to the Repatriation office. He took one look at me and guessed that I was returning from a concentration camp. He walked with me to the office, where I was issued a travel card that allowed me to travel on the railway through Czechoslovakia from Plzeň, through the Soviet zone to Prague, and on to Poland.

The train ride took hours. I kept thinking, how did this all start?

Who could have predicted this and how could we have prevented those tragic times and suffering? I asked myself this many times. The scenery passing by my window reminded me of our annual trip to the Carpathian Mountains and the different villages where we spent our summers. Now going back physically, I also had to go back mentally. I relived the last years of my innocent childhood. Sitting on the train going back to Poland and remembering those sweet moments was painful; I knew all that was gone, as was my childhood. The fields and the forests and villages flew past my window as the images flew past the windows of my mind.

What Was Lost

On August 28, 1945, late in the afternoon, I arrived at Dziedzice, the entry point into Poland. I arrived in my hometown of Chorzów the next day and immediately went to the home of my grandparents, Elka and Shimon Perciks, on Wolności 38. My grandmother's neighbour was a fine Christian woman and a very dear friend of my grandmother. I stood at the gate of the apartment building for a long time, unable to bring myself to enter. I was afraid of the truth. An invisible force stopped me from going through the gate into the yard.

I stood at the gate, looking around. Everything was the same. I saw my grandfather's glazer's workshop, the tall wall and the prison building behind it. A number of women were standing in the backyard of the prison trying to contact their husbands or sons through the wired and barred windows. The stairwell of the carpenter's shop where I had fallen down was still there and still unprotected. Garbage cans stood exactly how they had always stood in the corner near the gate.

Next to the gate was a photography store that used to throw out old glass photographic negatives. We would pick up used rolls of celluloid film and make stink bombs. I looked into the window, which once held pictures of familiar faces; now it displayed images of people I didn't know. A gentleman approached me and asked what I was looking for. I told him that my grandparents had lived in this courtyard.

On the street, people were walking without concern, rushing along to their chosen destinations as if nothing horrible had happened. The street looked the same. The apartment buildings looked the same. Everything was exactly how it always was, except for one striking difference: The synagogue across the street, where my entire family prayed on Shabbat and holidays, was gone. In its place was an empty lot.

Looking at the empty lot gave me a jab in my ribs. The world of my childhood had vanished, as had its people. Sweet memories entered my mind. I remembered the exciting moments of Simchat Torah, marching around the synagogue with decorated flags. I remembered the high holidays when my parents spent most of the day in synagogue, my friends and me running around the yard playing games and chasing each other. On Yom Kippur, the Day of Atonement, I loved visiting my mother in the women's section in the balcony, when she would let me smell the sweet fragrance of orange and cloves that she used to ease her fasting.

I had left this town as an eleven-year-old boy and returned six long years later as a broken teenager, feeling like an old man. How was this possible? In 1939, my future was bright and hopeful; I looked forward to finishing school and getting a trade. My whole life had been ahead of me. At this moment, it seemed that all was lost. I had no education, nowhere to go; now I was left praying to God that my mother and sister were alive.

I was still standing at the gate, biting my nails in deep thought. I must have been standing there for over an hour, delaying the inevitable. Whoever survived should have left word by now, two-and-a-half months after the war. I could no longer delay finding out the truth. I had the feeling that the next moments could destroy my hopes. I gathered up my courage, walked across the cobblestone yard to my grandmother's staircase, and walked up to the second floor. I knocked on the door of the neighbour whose name I did not recall. After a long while, I heard some movement inside; the door opened as far as the chain allowed and a voice asked, "Who is it?" I answered, "Elka's grandson." I heard a cry and the chain being removed, and the door was opened. A corpulent older woman threw her arms around me and we both sobbed. We finally settled down and she told me that my mother's sisters, Ruzia and Zosia, had come to see her soon after the Nazis left Poland. They hadn't left a forwarding address. They themselves did not know where they would find lodging; she thought that they had gone to Lodz, where my aunt Zosia lived before the war.

I was at a loss. What to do next? Where to find a place to sleep? It did not even occur to me to ask if I could stay the night with her, and she did not offer. I thought about Krysia, my sister's friend, and asked if she still lived across the yard. She nodded. I left the apartment, still hopeful that my mother and sister would come back. They could be sick or stuck somewhere in Germany or some other country. Travel was difficult and I convinced myself that this was the case. I could not fathom nor accept that they were not alive. I thought it was only a matter of time before they would come back.

Tears were streaming down my cheeks as I walked across the yard to Krysia's apartment. She was both surprised and happy to see me. "Thank God you survived," she said. By this time, most people knew what had happened to the Jews. She asked about Linka and when I told her that I had no information, for the first time it occurred to me that she might not be alive. I pushed the thought out of my mind. Krysia told me that her father, a high-ranking officer in the Polish army, had not come back and they feared the worst. As soon as the Nazis occupied Poland, they arrested all leaders in the community, including university professors, intellectuals, church leaders and military officers, and in many instances they arrested their children and spouses. Krysia was arrested in 1943 and sent to a farm in Germany as a slave labourer. She had just come back. Her brother was arrested as a Polish patriot and as a son of a Polish officer. She didn't know what had happened to him but she hadn't given up hope. It was only a few months since the end of the war, and things were still in flux.

Krysia and her mother lived alone now in a sparsely furnished apartment; her mother had sold everything to buy food during the war. She walked over to her dresser and came back with two photographs of my sister from the ghetto. The pictures were dated 1942. In 1942, we were in the open ghetto of Sosnowiec. I don't know how Krysia received these photos. It was dangerous for Christians to have any dealings with the Jews and it was remarkable and courageous for Krysia to have kept a picture of Linka with a Star of David on her clothes. We had lost everything, and to recover a photograph of a family member was especially poignant. They were the first photographs in my possession. The pictures brought back a flood of memories and tears, but I thought them to be a good omen. I still feel indebted to Krysia for these photos, and regret not keeping up a correspondence with her. But the time was so complicated and my feelings so raw. I was driven by a desire to get away from the past. The irony is that the more I tried, the less I succeeded.

It was late afternoon and I still didn't know where I would spend the night. I must have been in a daze, for I don't remember how I found my way to the Registration Centre. There, I found the names and addresses of cousins Cesia Leipciger, Roma and Genia Nadelberg and uncle Israel (Kurt) Nadelberg. My aunts' names were not there. I was not surprised that my aunts were still concealing their identity. Many people were afraid to register, especially with the Jewish community organizations, because of latent antisemitism.

I recognized the address as my Uncle Tobias's store, and ran through the familiar streets up a long stairway to the part of the city known as Hajduchy, past the silent steel mill and over the bridge overlooking the smelter yard where I used to spend hours watching the crane smash hot glowing slack with a huge ball. Now, I had no interest in it and rushed past.

I reached the apartment and rang the doorbell. My uncle opened the door; I knew him instantly but he did not recognize me. The last time he saw me, I was practically a little boy. Roma came to the door and let out a shriek. "Natek, Natek, kochany [dear]!" Cesia and Genia came running and we all embraced and cried and laughed at the same time. After a staccato of questions that I could not answer, they took me into the next room, the table set for dinner. A welcome sight for my eyes, as I had totally forgotten about food.

We spoke for hours on end and I found out that this was all that remained from my father's large family. From them, I found out that my father's parents, four sisters and two brothers, together with their spouses and nine children, had not come back. Most were shipped away to death camps during the final deportation from the Częstochowa ghetto in the fall of 1942. They did not know which one. Cesia, Roma, Genia and Uncle Kurt had been sent to a forced labour camp known as HASAG in Skarżysko-Kamienna. Uncle Tobias Leipciger had been sent to Auschwitz and did not return. Cesia's father, Leon Leipciger, had died on a death march in the last days before liberation.

My cousin Roma became engaged to Mietek Goldach a few weeks after her liberation in January 1945. Mietek was a handsome, dapper man who survived the war in the Soviet Union and came back to Poland in 1945 with a small fortune. In 1939, his whole family had voluntarily gone to the interior of the Soviet Union and he and his three brothers became truckers and were able to survive, and even prosper, by transporting black market goods. Roma's quick engagement was typical at that time. Most young women were left without family and were insecure and anxious to find a partner. Very few young, eligible men came back to Poland. Roma was swept off her feet by Mietek, and they married shortly after I left. Roma was a beautiful girl of twenty, full of life, intelligent and an excellent musician. Before the war, she had aspired to become a doctor.

After a couple of days in Chorzów, I started to get ready to travel to Lodz in search of my mother's sisters. I had great hopes that I would find them, as they had had Polish Christian papers. My aunt Ruzia, who was two years older than my mother, had married a Polish Christian, Antek Uziemblo, with whom she had lived for nine years but would not marry until after her mother's death. My aunt Zosia, two years younger than my mother, had been married to a Polish Christian and though she was divorced, I remembered that she had retained her married name of Balasinska. I still had the railway pass that allowed me to travel to any destination within a designated time. I arrived in Lodz that night and I went to a youth hostel. No sooner were the lights out than the bed bugs came out and attacked me with a vengeance. I chose a hard bench instead of the bed. In the morning, I went to the city hall and found my aunt Zosia Balasinska's address.

Before the war, Zosia had worked as a private secretary to the president of a Polish state-owned forest monopoly. A career woman, she had a university education and spoke fluent French and German. She was secular in her religious outlook and most of her friends, I had been told, were Christians. She was a jet-setter in the pre-war years and I had loved reading the postcards she sent to her parents. My interest in stamp collecting had come from these letters and postcards.

As fast as I could, I ran through the streets and upstairs to the third floor apartment, my heart pounding in my ears. The door was answered by Stasia, Zosia's housekeeper, who had worked for my grandmother for many years. She looked at me hesitantly, not recognizing me. The last time she saw me, I was a small boy. I told her I was Lutka's (Leah's) son, and she shrieked and started sobbing and hugging me. Zosia came out from the other room and shrieked as well. "Natek, Natek," she sobbed, "we gave up hope when you did not show up right away."

During the war, when Zosia and Ruzia had met up with my father in Soviet-occupied Poland, Zosia felt that there would be no problem in coming back to Lodz during the German occupation, as she was not politically active and had documents as a Polish Christian. However, when she arrived back in Lodz she found her apartment had been confiscated by the Germans. She was single and easily found work and lodging. Although she did not look Jewish or speak with a

Jewish accent, she didn't feel safe, and she moved to a smaller town where she was unknown and there was less of a chance of being found out. Eventually, she obtained a position in a local government office in Lublin. One evening, her director asked her to go for a walk and told her that one of her co-workers had confided in him, saying she suspected one of the women in the office was a Jew. He asked Zosia if she knew who that could be. She took the hint, went home, packed her bag and was on her way. She continued to move from city to city and eventually hid in a friend's apartment until the end of the war.

Zosia's apartment was located in a relatively new building that German officers had commandeered for their families. Immediately after the Germans left, she had returned to Lodz and found her apartment abandoned. Most Jewish families were not that lucky – on returning, they found their homes occupied by Poles and the authorities would not displace a Polish occupant in favour of a Jewish family.

After the war, Stasia had found Zosia and was living with her more as a friend than as a housekeeper. Stasia had loved my mother and cherished a photo she got from her in 1938. All through the war she kept the picture with her, wherever she was forced to move. She brought it out and showed it to me. I looked at the picture in utter surprise – I had never seen it before. She looked beautiful and my heart broke. The three of us had another cry. Stasia didn't want to part with the photo, but I convinced her to give it to me with the promise I would send her a copy, which I did. Zosia gave me Ruzia and her husband's address in Katowice, which was only six kilometres from my hometown. I returned to Chorzów the next day.

Ruzia, like Zosia, was a career woman with a university education. Ruzia, living so close to us, visited often and was closer to my mother and much more emotional than Zosia. When things were not so good between my parents, Ruzia would often come to our home and give my mother financial and moral support. My sister adored her and considered her a role model. In turn, Linka was Ruzia's protégé; Ruzia often brought Linka various books and invited her out for lunch or to a concert. In the last two years before the war, when our parents could not afford to send Linka to high school, both Ruzia and Zosia paid for my sister's tuition fees and for her books and school uniforms.

Early the next morning, I took the streetcar to Katowice. Finding my aunt and uncle was easy. Ruzia opened the door, recognized me immediately, and became speechless and burst out crying. She threw her arms around me and pulled me into the apartment and shut the door. My uncle Antek, a very formal man, waited until Ruzia let me out of her embrace to give me a warm handshake. He was embarrassed when I hugged him for some time.

Antek was the epitome of the Polish intelligentsia. He was a soft-spoken gentleman with soft eyes who wore frameless pince-nez glasses and had a full head of hair, and a full moustache. He came from a Polish aristocratic family, was a member of the Polish Legion and had been a professor at the Katowice Polytechnic. As soon as the Germans marched in, he went into hiding. The Nazis closed all Polish schools above Grade 6 and arrested most university personnel. Antek was in danger of persecution because of his background, renowned intellect and membership in the Polish Legion. He was a very patient man; he and my aunt Ruzia were engaged for nine years. He understood Ruzia could not marry him because this involved conversion to Catholicism, which she did not want to do as long as her mother was alive. My grandmother was devout, much more so than her husband and her daughters. After my grandmother's death in 1939, Ruzia converted but kept it a secret from the family and married Antek just before the war.

I told them what had happened to us since they had last seen us in Sosnowiec, which was just before my grandfather's death. Ruzia and Antek, under assumed identities, had obtained jobs with Polish companies that were supervised and run by Germans. It was always a wonderful occasion for us whenever they came to see us, but very dangerous for them. They brought bags of food, even candies. Once we were confined to the ghetto, they would not come. Even though it was an open ghetto, just being among Jews was sufficient reason to be detained. All was well for them living on Polish Christian documents until a Polish person pointed out Ruzia as a Jew and she was arrested. Shortly after this incident, my mother had received a letter from Antek asking my mother to search through her father's documents and look for Ruzia's adoption and conversion to Judaism papers. He also wrote that Ruzia was ill and in hospital, which was a code for being arrested. My mother understood that Ruzia had made up the story and anticipated that eventually she would be asked to verify it. A few days after the arrival of the letter, my mother was summoned to the Gestapo headquarters. Few people came out of a Gestapo interrogation unharmed; most were brutally beaten and left barely alive. One of our neighbours had been arrested, supposedly for black market activity, and died within two weeks of being interrogated. Another neighbour, when summoned by the Gestapo, had jumped out of her window, to her death, to avoid interrogation and torture. With this in mind, we were extremely worried when my mother decided to go to the Gestapo.

My mother was a well-educated, elegant woman but dressed very simply for this occasion and went by herself. My father was in the forced labour camp at this time. She summoned all her courage and tried not to show her fear. The Gestapo treated her with respect and were polite but firm. She told them, in perfect German, that she had no idea why she had been called there, and that her husband was in Germany working on the Reichsautobahn. She pretended to be surprised when asked about Ruzia. They asked if she had any of her sister's adoption documents. She explained that most of her father's and sister's papers were lost during our deportation from our hometown of Königshütte, the name the Germans used for Chorzów. Ruzia's adoption was a secret, she explained, but she remembered hearing about her parents' adoption of the child of an unmarried Christian house cleaner who worked for a Jewish family.

The Nazis didn't buy this story, and my aunt remained in jail for using false papers and impersonating a Polish person. When Ruzia and another convert to Christianity were being transported to another prison in a passenger train, they jumped out as the train slowed. They were fortunate that the ground sloped away sharply from the train tracks and they rolled and sustained only superficial injuries. They were hiding in a grove of bushes when a Polish farmer came upon them and agreed to hide them in his barn until they could get in touch with their husbands. For the rest of the war, Antek's family and friends arranged safe houses for them in various locations. They were always in danger of being discovered.

After the war, Zosia, Ruzia and Antek decided to stay in Poland and make a new life there. They were patriotic, and Antek didn't want to leave his extended family. Zosia also did not want to leave the man who had hidden her and saved her life. She eventually married him. However, they understood why I did not want to stay. I didn't know if I would see them again, but we promised to keep in touch.

Back in Chorzów, my uncle Kurt introduced me to his acquaintances who had been in Nazi camps. We shared our immediate past history, as we were all looking for remnants of our families. We followed any lead related to the fate of our loved ones. On one such encounter, I met a woman who was in Auschwitz-Birkenau at the time of our arrival. My hopes soared; possibly, she knew my mother and sister. However, she could not be sure what had happened to them, as they were not in the same barrack. On Yom Kippur 1943, while we were still there, the Nazis decided to select two thousand inmates from the women's camp and send them to the gas chamber. I remembered the event because we were confined to the barrack and we heard terrible screaming. As the men stood between the bunks and prayed, I climbed up onto the top bunk, looked through a slat between the wall and the roof and saw trucks loaded with naked women going past our barracks. The women were screaming because they knew where they were going. This was a scene that I never forgot and wished I had never seen. My uncle's friend thought that my mother and sister might have been on that selection because she did not remember seeing them after that. This information shocked me to my core, but I could not believe it.

All my thoughts were now preoccupied with the task of getting back to Bamberg. After spending time in Poland, I grew convinced there was no reason for us to stay. Our family and our community was gone. A few days after arriving back to Chorzów, I discussed our future plans with my father's family and we all agreed that Poland, with its Soviet presence, was not where we would want to live. I felt we should go to Canada, where my father's only surviving brother, Dave Leipciger, and his family lived. My memories of our family life before the war were sweet, but the intervening years brought terrible memories and every day I spent in my hometown I had to confront the reality of our losses. The pain was excruciating, and although I still hoped to find my mother and sister alive, there was the possibility that they would not come back.

Time was running out quickly and pressing on me to arrange my return trip to Germany. I was afraid that my father would leave Germany, as we had arranged, and that we would miss each other on the way and lose contact. In my last days in Chorzów I decided to walk through the city of my childhood, maybe for the last time. The memories of the tragedy were fresh in my mind but I wanted to assure myself that we had once lived there, and recall some of the better moments. In the city now devoid of Jews, I walked from my uncle's store past the smelter that was no longer active. I retraced the familiar paths from school to home. On the far side of a little park behind my grandparents' apartment building was Café Clubsz, where my grandfather Shimon would treat me to the best cup of hot chocolate I had ever tasted. I could still taste it, topped with a scoop of whipped cream and accompanied by a large piece of chocolate torte. The café was there as if nothing had changed. The surrounding park was overgrown and littered. I had loved to walk with my grandfather, my hand in his huge warm hand. He would take me with him to his glass shop and for walks through the busy streets of downtown. The memories brought tears to my eyes.

Walking past places I visited as a child with my mother reminded me of my happy, yet sometimes troubled, childhood. A small café where my mother would take me to meet her friends brought back some sweet and also hurtful recollections of my earliest preschool periods. I hurried on past the dark waters of the millpond. As children, we had been told it was full of poisonous minerals and chemicals and that if we fell in, we would dissolve instantly. Looking upon this pond, feelings of guilt and sadness returned to me. Our gang once put a kitten into an old potato sack, weighted it with a rock and tossed it into the pond. I never told my parents about it, but it caused me to have recurring nightmares. I was ashamed that I was an observer. Why did the kids do it? Maybe because kids can be cruel or maybe because there was no one to teach them differently. They exhibited a wanton lack of compassion and respect for life. For me this was the beginning of my terrible education that life was expendable at the whim of the ones with power. I wished I could forget that incident.

Just around the corner from my street, on Katowicka Street, was Hotel Graf Reden. This had been the place of Purim parties, weddings and celebrations of St. Sylvester, New Year's Eve. We loved when our parents went to the New Year's party and brought back confetti and paper streamers. The streamers were the most fun; we would blow through them and they would unfurl in a series of loops as they flew through the air.

One year at Purim, my sister and my cousin Roma were dressed up as pagegirl and pageboy, and they won a prize for their costumes. I don't remember the party, but I have a beautiful photo of that event, given to me by Roma. I don't know how it survived the war. The picture is the undeniable proof of a sweet life and of happy moments, even though sometimes life was hard. Now it was all gone. Yet, to remember only the tragedy, and not life's exciting and wonderful moments, would be a betrayal of that life.

Whenever I had walked these streets before, I had always seen a familiar face; now all faces looked strange and, in my mind, hostile. They seemed to ask, "What is this Jew doing here?" I could not have answered. Why was I there? Of the millions that perished, why was I spared? I was neither the smartest nor the strongest and yet fate caused me to survive. Survival meant pain and sorrow. In the camps, we had often questioned if we were the lucky ones or if those who had gone straight to the gas chamber were the lucky ones.

I came to the corner of Redena Street and Katowicka Street and painfully recollected how I had stood on this corner waving good-bye to my father on October 16, 1939, when he was crammed onto an open truck, being deported with other Jews from our city. The bakery shop was still there, but I had no desire to enter it. I suspected the owner was a *Volksdeutsche* like the majority of our city dwellers, and most likely left when the Germans withdrew.

The backyard of our former home on Redena 8 was empty. I was glad. I did not wish to encounter anyone. Most of our neighbours, too, were *Volksdeutsche* and most likely Nazi Party members who, fearing retribution from their Polish neighbours, had left with the retreating army. The yard looked the same; the garbage can stood in one corner near the gate and the pavement was still broken. I had never noticed the poor condition of our yard and our playground. I spent untold hours playing various games with laughter and, in tears, suffering disappointments and bullying from the older boys. Remembering my childhood games seemed so unimportant and yet I could not help but think back to those silly games. In the far end of the yard, the storage lockers, our clubhouse, was still there and looked much smaller than I remembered. It was padlocked; obviously, the kids no longer used it as a clubhouse.

I peeked into the window of our former ground-floor apartment and it seemed no one was there. I saw the little stove that we called *kaczka*. I noticed a woman at a window on the opposite side of the yard, watching me suspiciously from behind the curtains. I turned and left, not wanting any confrontations. I was anxious to leave this place, and I regretted that I had come. I was sure I would never return. I was wrong.

Lives in Suspension

I had no idea how to get out of Poland. Everyone I spoke to assumed it would take a long time and a lot of money to smuggle myself out. The route out of Poland went through Soviet-occupied Czechoslovakia. Since I had neither the time nor the money to pay a smuggler, I decided to get a visa and get out of Poland legally. When I told my family of my plans to obtain a legal exit visa, their response was laughter and skepticism.

On September 10, 1945, I went to the Provincial Office in Katowice and pleaded with the official. I explained that I had to go back to Bamberg to bring my father, who was sick and could not travel by himself, to Poland. After many questions, he believed my story but said I would need written permission from the Gmina Żydowska (Jewish Community Office) before he would issue me a *przepustka*, an exit permit. I immediately went to the Jewish community office a few blocks away. I was shocked as I walked through the front door – the hallway and the broad staircase was packed with people all the way up to the office doors on the second floor. I had arrived just before noon, and apparently, people started lining up at 6:00 a.m. I felt terribly sick and disappointed; it would take me days to obtain the document from the Jewish director.

I left the building not knowing what to do next. It occurred to me that the director and staff must have another entrance, as they would not attempt to get through the mob of people. I walked around the building, found it and decided to wait there between 1:00 and 3:00 p.m., the usual time that most European people ate their main meal. Shortly after one, a well-dressed gentleman emerged, and I approached him, ran beside him, and asked if he was the director. He nodded and kept on walking as I ran beside him crying and telling him the same story I told the Polish official, pleading with him to let me go to my father in Germany as fast as possible. At the entrance to a restaurant, he finally agreed to give me the required document. I waited for him outside the restaurant and walked with him to his office. He gave me a letter stamped with a seal. I was euphoric; I went back to the provincial office and thought that I was on my way to Bamberg. The provincial officer looked at the document and said it had the wrong seal and I must get the paper stamped with a round seal, not the square one. I immediately went back to the Jewish community office and tried to get through the people, showing them that I already had a document, but they just barred my way. I would have to come back the next day.

I went back to Chorzów dejected. The next day, I knew that the only way I would get the stamp was to repeat the process of the day before. When I saw the Jewish director at the restaurant and told him what the provincial officer said, he lifted his hand in disgust and told me to wait for him. I got the new stamp, returned to the provincial office and got my border-crossing permit to leave Poland. Then the officer told me that I needed a Czechoslovakian visa. It had been two and a half weeks since I left Bamberg, and I only had one-and-a-half weeks left to get back. It took me three long days to get through to the Czechoslovakian repatriation office to get the visa, which I finally received on September 14. My family was astonished at my persistence, and expressed doubt that the guards at the border would honour the exit paper because it was issued by a provincial office and not a national one.

The next morning, my family gave me some photos and I promised to keep in touch. My family's skepticism caused me to question the validity of both my exit permit and visa. As a precaution, I took a

train to an out-of-the-way border crossing. I was the only one crossing at that time and there was a single guard on duty. He examined
my papers and accepted them, then searched through my backpack,
with its meagre belongings, and found my prized possession, the
American Army blanket. He started to curse and called me names,
saying that the reason the Polish army was not getting anything from
the Americans was because the Jews get it all. He wanted the blanket.
I readily relinquished it, fearing he would otherwise use some excuse
to send me back to Chorzów. He let me through and I had no problem at the Czechoslovakian border. I arrived at a railway station at
dusk, happy to get on the train.

I arrived in Prague late that afternoon. Czechoslovakia was split
into two: the eastern part, including Prague, was occupied by the Soviet Union and the western part, including Plzeň, was occupied by
the Americans. At the train station all transients were directed to the
DP camp, where one could get a meal and accommodation. I got a
bed in one of the dorms and slept fitfully.

It was the middle of September but the sky was clear and the sun
was warm. As I was walking through the camp trying to orient myself and find out when the next transport would go to Plzeň, I could
not believe my eyes when I spotted my mother's cousin Elsa Percik.
Her father was Uncle Yehoshua, who was with us in Auschwitz and
had stood next to me in the lineup during the selection. She was the
youngest of his thirteen children. We had a very emotional reunion
and she told me she was there alone. She was my age and I was in
love with her in the early days in the ghetto. She was the one who had
looked like Shirley Temple, the model for the Polish chocolate company. Jokingly, I made a pass at her and she burst out laughing, saying
that I was just a child who had soft cheeks and did not even shave,
which was the truth, and a put-down. She looked like a young woman, well endowed, and I looked like a kid, especially in my knicker-
bocker pants and mauve stockings that my uncle Kurt had given me
because he could not sell them.

We spent the day together. She was also trying to get to the American Zone, where she had found out some of her siblings were. Two days later, I decided to try to get through to Plzeň in the American Zone on my own. I had the paper with the Czechoslovakian Repatriation stamp and thought that would get me through. It would be much easier to get from there to Bamberg, which was also in the American Zone. I bid my cousin goodbye, as she was waiting for the next transport from the International Red Cross, which would not come for another few weeks. The next time I would see her would be in Toronto some twenty-two years later.

At the Soviet checkpoint to Plzeň, we were told to leave the train and go through a passport check in the building. I showed them my document from Poland but they rejected it, detained me and put me on the next train back to Prague. When I arrived in Prague, I waited a few hours for the next train back to the border and to Plzeň. It was already evening by then, and I hoped to get to the border after dark. It was pitch black when we arrived at the border and, instead of going in for the passport check, I made a shortcut alongside the train to the front. My heart was bouncing in my chest for fear of being spotted, or even shot. I exerted the utmost control not to run. I walked slowly, with determination, as if I had just come from the checkpoint. It worked, and I re-boarded. I thought that there wouldn't be more checkpoints, but a few minutes after the train left the station, we arrived at the actual border point and a Soviet soldier came on board to check passports, which had to have a stamp from the checkpoint. I was beside myself. I thought I'd be arrested for illegally crossing the border and be sent to Siberia and no one would know what had happened to me. Next to me sat an enormous woman with a huge shawl around her body. I snuggled up to her. She did not wake up, so I draped the shawl over me as if I belonged with her. She stirred but did not say a thing. I pretended to be sleeping as well, and the soldiers didn't bother to check our passports. She must have been a regular passenger on this route. Adrenaline was pumping though me and I could not stop shaking for quite a while. A few hours later, we arrived in Plzeň.

I next had to find out how to get to the western zone of Germany. I saw a group of refugees at the station who looked Jewish and walked over, hoping to find out where they were going. I tried to strike up a conversation, but they looked at me suspiciously until I told them that I was Jewish and trying to get to the American occupation zone. They told me to take a train as far as possible toward the border, close to the town of Hof. I did not ask if I could join them, for fear of being refused, but I followed them onto the next train, and eventually latched on to them as they got off and met the guide they had hired to take them the rest of the way.

In Hof, I spent the night in a hostel and hitched a ride the next morning on an American army truck, arriving in Bamberg shortly after noon. I assumed that my father would be at dinner at our favourite restaurant around the corner from our place, and I went there directly. As soon as my father spotted me he jumped up and ran toward me with arms outstretched. The restaurant guests gave us a rousing applause – they thought we had only just found each other.

My trip to Poland had exposed me to various situations and decisions I had to make without my father's guidance. It was a good experience for me, and my father respected the fact that I had conducted myself well and did not get into any trouble. I spent hours with my father talking about my experiences in Poland. The most difficult part was telling him who had survived and who had not. He was devastated by the news of the possible loss of all his siblings. I could not bring myself to tell him what I had learned about my mother and sister. I continued to think that maybe the woman was wrong, and I did not want to quash his hopes.

We were determined to continue to look, and clung to each other as never before. Every few days we went to the DP camp in Bamberg to see if any new names had been registered. Bamberg was a lovely city – the part that we lived in had hardly been ruined by bombs, which was not so for the centre – but we had no joy in being there. Added to that, we were constantly on the lookout on the streets, in restaurants and everywhere Germans congregated, trying to see if we could recognize someone who was a guard in our camps. We didn't know what we would do in the moment if we recognized anyone, but we thought we could follow him, find out where he lived and report him to the authorities. We now lived in a lawful society and we could not take matters into our own hands. I was suspicious of all Germans and in my mind wondered: Where was he during the war? Was he involved somehow in the murder of our people?

Our lives were in suspension. I knew I needed an education, but I had no idea how to go about it in Germany. I wouldn't even consider entering a German school, sitting in the same classroom with German students. I had nothing in common with them, nor would I sit with children much younger than me. At that point, I wanted to have as little to do as possible with anything German.

We felt deeply depressed. We had decided not to go back to Poland, but where else could we to go? We ruled out staying in Germany. My father tried desperately to get some information to his only surviving brother in Canada. That would be our desired destination, but how to get there? My father remembered only part of his brother's address. Communication was extremely difficult except through people travelling. There was no Canadian consul in Bamberg to help us get information. My father was anxious to do something. Sitting and doing nothing was not his style, nor did he want to depend on the German welfare and UNRRA systems. He certainly wouldn't move into the Bamberg DP camp. To trade on the black market was dangerous and risky. My father tried to deal in currency, which was also illegal, and though on the first deal he made some money, he lost on the second and third deals and decided this was not for us.

By chance, my father met a Polish former prisoner and became friends with him. He worked in the American army tailor shop and he promised to try to get my father a job there. My father went for an interview and was accepted. Working for the army was fantastic – he was paid in American occupation dollars and also had access to the canteen. He also received an American uniform, which gave him status among the German population. My father befriended his US army boss, Ed, a Polish American from Detroit, and asked him if he would forward a letter to his brother through the military post. This was illegal, but Ed agreed to send my father's letter within a letter to his mother, who then mailed it to my uncle in Canada. Even though my father only remembered the city and street but not the number, the letter was delivered. A few weeks later, we received a letter from my uncle Dave through Ed's mother. We were overjoyed. We continued to correspond over the next few months. My uncle contacted his friend Anchel Weiss, who had good connections with the immigration office in Canada, and he promised to get us visas in a matter of months. In fact, it took years.

In 1946, few people received papers to emigrate anywhere. It appeared that we were stuck. No country was willing to admit us. Everyone we knew made applications to countries such as Australia, Canada, the United States and, of course, Palestine. We heard from Uncle Dave in Canada that his wife's sisters, who lived in the States, had also made applications to sponsor us to be admitted to the US. We were much more interested in joining Uncle Dave in Canada, but the US was our second choice. Time dragged on.

Our only consolation was my father's job with the US army and his access to the canteen, where he could purchase cigarettes, nylon stockings, coffee, chocolates and other staples that were scarce in occupied Germany. All of these items were in demand by German merchants and they were willing to trade rationed food such as meat, eggs, white bread, sugar and other produce. Trading for goods was not considered black marketeering.

Although we kept looking for relatives and friends, as time moved on it became less likely that we would find anyone. Our thoughts were always with our family – no matter what we did, we always reflected on what Mother or Linka might have felt or said. Nonetheless, my father felt that we had been granted a new lease on life and that we must not waste it. We could not remake the past and, as our future was unknown, the only thing to do was to live each day to its fullest and try to make a better tomorrow.

We had to be careful not to get into any trouble with the law, which could endanger our chances of going to Canada. We knew that in order to emigrate we would have to obtain a statement from the police that we did not have criminal records and that there were no outstanding charges against us. My father told me to be very careful, especially with women, not to get anyone pregnant or pick up anything. (Venereal diseases were so prevalent that special clinics were established and the American authorities provided penicillin to deal with the problem.) We were living in occupied Germany, but the Americans were very much in control and it was easy to be caught doing business on the black market. Some Jews ended up in prison – the American occupation police and courts did not make any allowances for our past experiences. But our cupboards were full of chocolate, coffee and other goods and we didn't need to buy anything on the black market. We also received parcels from the UNRRA with peanut butter, sardines, spam meat, tuna and other hard-to-get produce. No matter what we had, it did not matter. We knew it was temporary and we would eventually leave. Our greatest desire was to get out of Germany. Living among people who had so recently wanted to destroy us was complicated.

During the day while my father was at work, I had to fend for myself. Being alone all day, not having any Jewish friends, was boring and lonely. In the room next to ours lived a German radio technician whose door was always open. I saw him working on radios and it caught my interest, so I hung around his room and we started talking about radio and other things. His name was Paul Frohm and he was a former air force pilot. He was several years older than I was and attended the University of Fürth, a few miles from Bamberg. He introduced me to some of his fellow students and invited me to their parties. I liked this new experience, especially since many of his friends were women. Coincidentally, I always brought the vodka, and after a while I came to realize that may have been the reason for my invitation. When Paul saw the number on my arm, he started to ask questions. I was, at first, reluctant to tell him much.

In the meantime, I had befriended other Germans closer to my age, who were not directly involved in the war. They had been, however, part of the Hitlerjugend, a youth organization, and were indoctrinated to think that Jews were responsible for all the ills of the world and the cause of the war. It was a challenge for me to convince them otherwise. Whether I did or not, I will never know, but we discussed various topics, ranging from the right of the victor to judge the vanquished, the obligation to follow orders and the rights of the individual versus the state. I also had conversations with Paul as to what had happened to the Jews. Like most Germans, he held that he didn't know of the killings and gassing. He was very intent on letting me know that the Germans were not the only ones who did not like Jews; he pointed out that Henry Ford was an arch antisemite and wrote many articles that Hitler republished in Germany. It was the first time that I learned of this. Still, I asked him whether Ford actually advocated the genocide of the Jewish people, as Hitler did.

The term Holocaust was not used at the time; incidentally, I have always preferred to use the biblical Hebrew term, Shoah, which I feel encompasses the uniqueness of our catastrophe. But in Germany at the time, no one wanted to speak about what had happened to the Jews. Everyone blamed it on the SS and the Gestapo and claimed no personal knowledge, nor did they show remorse. No one was prepared to accept responsibility. "The Jews one day all just disappeared, no one asked any questions," was the typical comment. Some Germans wanted to know of my experiences, but the memories of our suffering and the loss of my family was too recent to talk about. It would bring on emotions hard to control; I told them only the barest of details.

Some of the Germans I met believed that their country was forced into the war by the Treaty of Versailles of 1919, and that all Hitler wanted was to get back the territories that were taken from Germany in that treaty. They didn't feel guilty about Germany starting the war. In their opinion, the only thing that Hitler did wrong was to lose the war, and they felt that Germany had invaded Poland only because it would not agree to give up part of Poland to unite Prussia with Germany. They said that Hitler never wanted to fight England and France and his true enemy was communism and the Soviet Union. Nevertheless, Hitler had entered into a "Non-Aggression Pact" with the Soviet Union before attacking Poland.

The Germans who ran from the invading Soviets told of rape and pillage and other atrocities. They cited the bombings of civilians and cities by the Allies and dismissed the fact that it was Germany who first bombed cities without strategic significance, resulting in massive civilian casualties. Although I did not excuse the acts of the Soviet soldiers, I would point out that it was the Germans who murdered millions of Soviet POWs and civilians. The Soviets were brutal, but it was in retaliation for the treatment they received at the hands of the Nazis.

By this time, most Germans who cared knew of the killing of Soviet prisoners and the murder of 1.5 million Jews by German killing squads in the East, as Germany invaded the Soviet Union. The Nuremberg trials were going on and the newspapers were full of the atrocities perpetrated. I followed the Nuremberg trials with interest and was disappointed that only a few of the top Nazis were caught and put on trial. To my friends' irritation, I contended that people had joined the Nazi Party voluntarily in order to improve their lives, and now they had to face the consequences and responsibilities of the acts perpetrated by the regime. The Allies attempted to subject German society to de-Nazification, a process that included removing former Nazi Party members from positions where they could influence the public.

Through Paul, I became very interested in learning radio mechan-

ics. He tried to teach me, but I soon realized that I lacked an understanding of algebra and trigonometry. I explained to him that although
I was eighteen, I had only had four years of public school education
because the Nazis, on occupying Poland, had closed schools for Jews.
He was impressed with my good knowledge of and proficiency in the
German language, given my lack of schooling, and suggested a fellow
university student could tutor me in algebra. His friend, also a pilot,
who was shot down in the early years of the war and was wounded in
the head, had restricted vision and was assigned to the German police force. For the rest of the war he was a gendarme, police officer,
in Paris. I had many questions about what happened to the Jews of
France and whether he was involved in any of the roundups. He told
me that by the time he got to Paris, there were no Jews to be seen. He
knew about the deportations to concentration camps but not about
the gassing and murder by mass shooting. I didn't believe him, but I
was satisfied that he was not directly involved in any criminal activity,
and I chose to concentrate on what I could learn from him. He was
an excellent teacher and he taught me algebra and some basic trigonometry. I paid him a handsome fee, but it was worth it and later on
saved me years of study.

By this time I had some Jewish acquaintances, mostly older, and
we discussed the issue of having sex with German women. We justified sex with Germans as a triumph over Hitler, who considered
any contact between a Jew and an "Aryan" as *Rassenschande*, racial shame. It became almost an obsession to have sex with as many
young German girls as possible. I was still a virgin and my desire to
experience sex was paramount; once started, the desire to have more
sex was insatiable.

The living conditions and values in Germany at the time were unusual and sex was as natural as any social intercourse. It was commonly accepted that if you took a woman out a couple of times it
would end up in a sexual relationship. My father befriended a beautiful woman, Martha, who lived with us for months. Her husband, a

former Nazi officer in the SS, was in a Soviet prisoner-of-war camp. On hearing our stories and learning about the atrocities that the SS committed, she sued him and got a divorce. Martha and her seven-year-old son slept with me and my father in the same bed. There was absolutely no privacy.

I began a relationship with a woman twice my age who had an insatiable sex drive. It was paradise. Once, she invited me to her home just before Christmas. I brought toys for her three kids, aged five to eight, but the most treasured gifts were the boxes of American chocolates. Her mother was not too friendly to me because of my age and the fact that I was Jewish. Most likely she was appalled with her daughter on both accounts. Our relationship ended when I saw her hand in hand with an American soldier. There was an acute shortage of men in the immediate post-war period in Germany, and American military personnel filled the vacuum. Sometimes, women who dated American soldiers were ostracized by the community, especially if they dated black soldiers. I had no problem getting a date with German women as most, at first, did not know that I was Jewish.

I then met Gertrude (Trudy) through Paul. She was an attractive eighteen-year-old and was anxious to make my acquaintance. I told her that I was Jewish and that I had lost almost all of my family. She listened attentively and then in disbelief to my experiences. I wasn't surprised, as she had lived a sheltered life up until the end of the war, when Bamberg came under severe bombardment. Even though the newspapers were now full of stories from war crimes trials, as I mentioned, she paid little attention to the papers. She told me that she was a debutante, and I had no idea what that meant. She was engaged to a wounded German veteran attending an out-of-town university. He was straitlaced, worshipped Trudy and did not make any sexual advances but I thought he probably wouldn't hesitate to murder innocent Jewish children and women. She didn't like him very much; her father had arranged the match because the veteran came from a wealthy, high-society family.

At first, we met only during the day and without her mother knowing. Eventually, Trudy convinced her mother that ours was a strictly platonic friendship. Trudy's mother didn't object to our friendship even though she knew that I was Jewish. Actually, she asked Trudy to see if she could get some nylon stockings and real American coffee beans from me, assuming that all Jews were dealing on the black market. I did not disappoint her, and provided her with whatever she wanted.

Trudy and I didn't have any opportunities for sex because she wouldn't come to my apartment. I asked her to go dancing with me to the Blue Elephant nightclub, which I frequented with my German friends, and reserved a table. She agreed to come, but when I picked her up, her mother came along as a chaperone. The nightclub had good schnapps, chocolate and, most importantly to Trudy's mother, real American coffee. I thought the evening would be a dead loss, but it turned out that her mother, although a stout woman, was very light on her feet and a better dancer than Trudy. After a few shots of schnapps, she became quite outgoing and I thought I would end up having sex with her instead of Trudy.

That evening, on the way home, we separated from her mother by taking a shortcut through a small park. We stopped to kiss, Trudy became quite passionate, and we had sex on the lawn behind some bushes. After that, unbeknownst to her mother, Trudy would meet me regularly during the day in my apartment. Trudy's sexual performance belied her prim and proper appearance. I was convinced I was not her first partner. We had an understanding that this was strictly physical, no emotional attachment, since she would soon marry and I would be leaving for Canada at some point. This relationship suited me very much. It added to my pleasure, knowing that I was having sex with a woman who would soon marry a former Nazi soldier.

There were few Jewish people of my age in Bamberg but within the first year, I befriended Ira (Izaak) Goetz and Barbara (Bronia) Goldfischer. I was a year older than Ira and about three years older than Barbara, but that was of no consequence. I also met Helen Ruff, who had recently arrived from Poland with her family. My relationship with Jewish girls was entirely different from that with German girls. I would not even think of making advances unless I was serious. All of us were in a holding pattern, awaiting emigration and unsure about our plans and futures. Helen, Barbara and I had strictly platonic friendships. Barbara was the sole survivor of a large family and was living by herself. Ira was also an orphan, having lost his entire large family except for an uncle, Aaron, who lived with him. Both Barbara and Ira were self-sufficient, strong-minded individuals.

Barbara, Ira and I spent hours boating and walking in the extensive parks along the river in an area known as little Venice. Our thoughts were mainly centred on getting out of Germany and starting a new life. We were impatient to do something constructive but didn't want to start anything that required a long commitment. We all wanted an education, and did not want to be burdened with a family. I also had misgivings about bringing Jewish children into this terrible world of hatred and murder.

Ira and I found a retired professor of German and we took lessons in German grammar and some Latin. Even though I had spoken German since I was a child, I could not read or write it. German was actually my first language because our housekeepers were German and we had lived in a predominantly German neighbourhood. My father and I also took English lessons from a former high school teacher. Our teacher was a vivacious young woman whom I adored and I liked to take lessons from her. I would have liked even more with her, but my advances went nowhere; she told me that I was much too young for her. She was from Berlin, spoke in a refined German known as *Hochdeutsch* and abhorred it when I spoke with the Bavarian dialect. I also learned to type and volunteered part-time in the office of the International Refugee Organization (IRO).

One would think that most people would lose faith given the tragedy that had befallen us. Yet, shortly after liberation, the Jews living in the city formed the Religious Committee of Jews in Bamberg and their first task was to establish a synagogue. They were granted the use of a facility for a synagogue and a social club. My father felt a need to say Kaddish for lost family members even though we didn't know the exact dates of their deaths or who was still alive. I myself felt no need to pray. I could hardly read Hebrew and my faith in God had waned.

Most survivors were left without any family members, and needed support and emotional security. Some were urgent to find mates, get married and start new lives and families and name their children after their parents. To me this showed that their Jewish roots were strong and they wanted to continue their families' Jewish tradition. Although it was not my priority, I respected and admired the young people who married and started families.

I had a lot of time on my hands. Bamberg is located about an hour's train ride from Nuremberg, and my father and I travelled there to attend operas. The opera house, although partially destroyed, improvised and gave wonderful performances. I had no knowledge and certainly no understanding of opera. My father, intent on educating me, took me every few weeks to see different operas and operettas. He knew the stories of most of the operas we attended and would give me a synopsis before the performance. He also knew most of the popular arias. Bamberg also had a symphony orchestra and my father encouraged me to develop a taste for classical music. Ira and I decided to attend a chamber music performance one afternoon and without thinking, we went to the performance in our short pants. The next day we were written up in the local paper's editorial, which read, "What has the German youth come to? How could German youth attend a concert in Lederhosen?" We were happy that the editor didn't know that we were Jewish, or he would have had a fit at our disrespect for the German tradition of getting dressed formally for chamber concerts.

On occasion, we travelled to Munich to see operas. Munich had been severely bombed and we revelled in the fact that the Allies had destroyed German cities; we actually felt that there was some justice in the destruction. We felt that the Western powers were now being too easy on Germany and the German people for what they had done, and that the only power that dealt appropriately with the Nazis were the Soviets.

Ira and I travelled to see the beautiful lakes and mountains of Bavaria, studded with magnificent villas and homes. We stayed in bed and breakfasts and enjoyed local cuisine, mostly various dishes of pork products and *Wurst*, sausages. We wondered how a people living in such a beautiful country and having developed such a rich culture could have so much hatred and commit such horrendous crimes. We were sure that some of those beautiful houses were once the homes or vacation places of Jews.

Ira and I even went to the devil's den in Berchtesgaden, Hitler's hideout in the mountains. The hideout, on the pinnacle of a mountain, overlooked the entire area of valleys and mountain ranges. Seeing the luxurious surroundings of the world's biggest antisemite brought our spirits down and our hearts ached. Life in the Bavarian mountains went on. In the guest houses, we heard stories of suffering and loss of fathers, husbands and sons and the mistreatment of the German people in the POW camps. I could not feel empathy for them; they may have been defeated militarily, but they remained unrepentant for starting the war and for the brutality of their forces. After the war, no one admitted to having belonged to the Nazi Party; they had enjoyed the benefits of being party members but did not want to take responsibility for that murderous organization.

Turning Points

In our unrelenting search for family, we found out that my cousin Roma Goldach (née Nadelberg) – who I had last seen in August 1945 in Chorzów – was with her family in Bavaria, in the Feldafing DP camp near Munich. West Germany was now overrun with refugees from the east, and especially from Poland. The Jews returning from the camps, the forests, coming out of hiding and from the Soviet Union had encountered a hostile Polish population. Many Jewish homes were occupied by Polish people and they were afraid that the Jews would want to reclaim their houses and even businesses. There was violence and pogroms against Jews, most notably in Kielce in July 1946, when a mob murdered forty-two people. This sent a shock wave throughout Jewish communities, and in the next few years more than a hundred thousand Jews smuggled themselves out of Poland, Roma's family among them.

We travelled to see them soon after they had arrived. They didn't know where they would go, which was a typical predicament, as most Western countries – as before and during the war – did not accept Jewish refugees in any great number, Israel was not yet a state and the British prevented refugees from entering Palestine. I agree with those who feel the British blockade contributed to the demise of hundreds of thousands of Jews during the Shoah by preventing their escape from Europe. Now they prevented the survivors from reaching

Palestine. Thousands of refugees were detained on the way there and forced into internment camps on Cyprus. When we visited them in the DP camp, Roma and her husband, Mietek, and their baby lived in a small room with no amenities. Roma felt they should not have to live in such conditions and became despondent; even though most Jews were leaving Poland, she convinced her husband to return.

In the summer of 1946, through the grapevine and through postings in the various DP camps, I found a number of Perciks, my mother's maiden name. We became very excited at the possibility that Mother could be with them. However, the names turned out to be those of my mother's cousins, the children of Uncle Yehoshua Percik. They were listed in the DP camp in Bad Salzschlirf near Fulda, about 150 kilometres northwest of Bamberg, and I decided to visit them. Of Yehoshua and Helen's thirteen children, some of whom had lived with us in the ghetto, six had survived, five of whom were in Bad Salzschlirf. As a family, their survivorship was out of proportion to most. The high rate could possibly be attributed to their being shipped to labour camps prior to the final deportation in 1943. The oldest daughter, Carola, was in Lwów in 1939, at the same time as my father. Carola and her family were among the people shipped to Siberia, and her husband was sent to a labour camp, where he died from hard labour and hunger. She and her two children returned to Poland and made their way to Germany. Elsa, whom I had met in Prague, was with them.

The DP camp at Salzschlirf was better than other camps I visited but still had few amenities. It was located in an old multi-storey building that had a number of rooms and each married couple was allocated a room. My cousins Adel and Fela both married in the camp. Carola and her children were given their own room. Everyone was anxious to go on with their lives, knew things were temporary and yet were uncertain as to their final destination. Carola's two boys went to a school organized by the Jewish Agency. One Zionist organization recruited people to go to Palestine, teaching them Hebrew and preparing them for eventual immigration to Israel. My cousins Carola, Fela and Zosia ended up in Israel in 1948; Elsa and Adel went to the US.

On hot days, refugees from the DP camp spent their idle days at the local river, and I went with my family members to the riverbank. I didn't know how to swim but was assured not to worry as the water was shallow. I was playing in the water, trying to learn how to swim, when the current swept me out. I realized that I was in trouble and started to shout *Hilfe*, help, in German. I continued bobbing up and down and at each breath I shouted *Hilfe*. I was told later that a man walking on the other shore saw me drowning, took off his shoes and jacket and swam to me. My family looked on in horror as I grabbed him by his neck; I pulled him down and when we came up, he told me to lie on my back and he towed me to shore by my chin. On shore, water poured out of my mouth and I started to cough. He waited to make sure I was breathing properly and then he swam back to the other shore. My cousins thought he must have been a German because none of the refugees were on the other bank. I never had the opportunity to thank him for saving my life.

After I recovered sufficiently, I went for a walk along the shore. I had become a celebrity; everybody knew that I had almost drowned. A couple of men told me, "When you yelled Hilfe we were not far from you in our boat but we thought you were German and turned away." At that point in time, many refugees did not empathize with the Germans and it wouldn't have bothered their conscience to see a German drown. I asked them what I should have called out – I was in Germany and so I called out in German. Well, they said, you should have called out in Yiddish. This irony stayed with me forever. The Germans had tried to kill me for years, and here some Jews almost let me drown, whereas a German did not stop to think that a Jewish refugee was drowning but jumped in and saved me. How could I hold all Germans in contempt? Millions of people did not join the Nazi Party. I felt that we could not generalize, although it was the easier way to handle our revulsion. This incident had a profound influence on my attitudes toward the average German.

~

Later that year, we received a letter from the Canadian immigration office in Germany saying that we should appear in regards to our application. We could not believe our good luck. We travelled to Regensburg, a beautiful, ancient city with castles and fortified walls. There were hundreds of refugees everywhere. We were directed to a building and lined up for fingerprinting and x-raying. We waited what seemed endless hours for our turn to be interviewed by the consul. He was a well-dressed young man in his mid-thirties, very polite. He opened what we surmised was our file, examined it and addressed my father, as if I was not there. "I am sorry to tell you that your son's x-ray has spots on it and we cannot approve your application at this time." We asked what that meant. He told us that I may be developing tuberculosis and we would have to wait for our next call-up in a year.

In Bamberg, I went to a doctor and told him what the Canadian official had found. The doctor ordered x-rays and confirmed the diagnosis, which, he said, was not unusual, as most people in Europe had been exposed to the tuberculosis bacillus and had calcification spots. He laughed and said that even a medical student could tell that there was no danger of developing tuberculosis from these spots – in fact, he said I was immune to tuberculosis. We were dejected and reluctantly accepted the fact that we would have to stay in Germany for at least another year.

In the summer of 1947, we again received a letter from the immigration office to report to Regensburg for an examination. This time, my father went for an x-ray at the front of the line and came back to where I was in the line; we changed places, and he went for another x-ray with my documents. Fortunately, these documents did not have photographs. Armed with two good x-rays, we thought that we wouldn't have any problems with the immigration officials, although we worried whether they could detect the identical x-rays. We were ushered into the office of the consul and again he did not speak to me. He told my father that my x-ray was okay but that my father's had spots on it and consequently we would not be able to go to Canada at this time. I spoke up, asking if I could go to Canada ahead of my father, as I wanted to go to school. I was anxious to get some education. Every year I missed would make it so much harder. He retorted that they do not separate families and I would have to wait. It was no great leap to conclude that Canada had a quota for Jews. Several of our Jewish acquaintances had the same experiences and were rejected for similar reasons.

That year, Ira and Barbara, as orphans, were able to receive immigration papers and they left Bamberg in November. Barbara went to Winnipeg in 1948, and Ira to New York. With Ira and Barbara gone from Bamberg, I spent more time with my German acquaintances, taking tennis lessons and riding my new bicycle, exploring Bamberg and the environs. My bicycle gave me a completely new sense of freedom. I also travelled by train to more distant places, sometimes with my father but mostly by myself. There was no lack of women to join me on these trips as long as I picked up the tab. A carton of cigarettes in my suitcase usually took care of all eventualities; a last-minute entry to the opera or a concert required one or two packs of cigarettes.

Without Ira my discipline and motivation to take lessons diminished, and I dropped German and Latin and decided to spend more time on English and algebra. I also spent more time with Helen, who was about two years younger than me. She, her mother and an older sister survived in Poland hidden by a Polish family. Her mother was very hospitable and had an open house. I was quite taken with Helen, but our friendship never went beyond being good friends. We liked the same things and took nature excursions, always chaperoned by her older sister or mother. This did not bother us, as we both knew that there was admiration but no romantic attraction. We shared an interest in music and ventured to afternoon concerts given by the

Bamberg symphony orchestra. We talked about our dreams but never about our wartime experiences. I imagined I would eventually find a girl like her. In the early summer of 1948, after the creation of the state of Israel, many of our acquaintances, including Helen Ruff, left for Israel.

My time in Bamberg dragged on and we anxiously awaited our next call up to the Canadian consul. The emigration situation generally seemed to improve as countries, especially the US and Australia, began to accept more Jews. It was not until years later that we found out the truth about Canada's terrible policy and dismal record regarding the admission of Jews. In the preface to their book *None Is Too Many*, scholars Irving Abella and Harold Troper wrote, "It is a story summed up best in the words of an anonymous senior Canadian official who, in the midst of a rambling 'off-the-record' discussion with journalists in early 1945, was asked how many Jews would be allowed into Canada after the war. His response, though spontaneous, seems to reflect the prevailing view of a substantial number of his fellow citizens: 'None,' he said, 'is too many.'"

It was not until mid-summer 1948 that we were summoned to appear before the consul again, but this time we had to travel to the DP Camp in Amberg. We decided not to play any games and we each took our own x-rays. We were again fingerprinted and photographed, and on June 24, 1948, we received our visas. Our departure time was set for September. The next few months were joyous and filled with anticipation of a new beginning, which was both overwhelming and terrifying. We tried not to feel too excited, so as not to be disappointed with what we would find in Canada. And our happiness at leaving could never be exuberant – the pain of losing our family was always just under the surface of our conscious minds. Leaving Europe meant leaving them behind, but we knew we would never forget them. Saying goodbye to some of our friends who still didn't know how long it would be before they could leave was hard. Our German friends were envious that we could leave the country. Life at that time in Germany was still very difficult, as the economic recovery was very slow. We promised to write and keep in touch, though we felt sure we would never again step on the soil of Europe.

My father and I travelled to Bremerhaven and on September 17 we embarked on the *Samaria*, a converted troop carrier used mainly to transport refugees and a few first-class passengers. We were assigned hammocks on the lowest deck of the ship. The motion of the hammock and the banging of the anchor against the hull kept me awake all night. As soon as the ship entered the English Channel, I became violently sick. The next morning I ran up to the infirmary to get some anti-seasickness pills. My seasickness did not subside until we docked in the port of Le Havre, France, where we took on some more refugees and passengers. The doctor who issued me the seasickness pills noticed that I spoke English reasonably well and asked me if I would translate for some of the passengers who spoke only German or Polish. This gave me something to do every morning and I was also given some privileges on the ship, including unlimited access to seasickness pills. I managed to sleep in one of the inside lounges on the upper decks and when the weather was good, I slept on wooden benches outside and suffered no more illness.

We arrived in Quebec City on Tuesday, September 28, 1948. One of my ship privileges allowed us to disembark and visit the city for the day. Our time constraint and lack of transportation allowed us to see only the lower part of the old city and we were very disappointed – the buildings were dilapidated and store windows were loaded with cheap merchandise in disarray. Even in destroyed Germany, the buildings and stores with little to sell looked better. My father assured me that Toronto would be different.

My father had not seen his oldest brother in thirty-six years. At the reunion at the railway station in Toronto, I felt overwhelmed at being with family but I maintained my composure. I was a stranger. The photographs our family members had sent to us from Canada were of poor quality and I would not have recognized anyone. I also felt that any show of emotion would result in a breakdown and create a scene. My father was the only one who showed emotion; for the first time in my life, I saw him cry, his tears flowing uncontrollably and his body shaking as he hugged his brother.

Even though it was the middle of the week and a workday, almost everyone came to greet us: my Uncle Dave, his wife, Helen, their son, Joe, and his wife, Rae, and Ralph Weingarten, who was married to my cousin Grace. Grace was the only one not there as she had given birth to their son, Paul, the day before. We travelled through the city to 224 Beatrice Street, in the heart of Toronto's Jewish neighbourhood. The house was a semi-detached, three-storey dwelling. We were shown to our room on the second floor. With our arrival and that of the newborn baby, the whole house had to be rearranged. My cousins Grace and Ralph vacated their room for my father and me; Joe and Rae, with their five-year-old son, Irving, moved to the third floor and gave up their room to Aunt Helen and Uncle Dave. They, in turn, vacated the front master bedroom for Grace and Ralph, who would now need space for a crib and dressing table. Both families lived with my uncle and aunt not out of choice but necessity, to save enough money to start a business and to buy a home. Our room was just big enough for a double bed and a chest of drawers at the foot of the bed. To access the drawers one had to sit on the bed. There was just enough space between the window and the bed for a small night table. The room was clean, and my dad and I were used to sleeping in one bed.

When I came downstairs, Cousin Joe led me toward a wall and explained that if I wanted to turn on the light I just pushed a button. He thought we came from a country that was backwards and had no electricity. I presumed this was what Uncle Dave told his kids when he described the conditions of Poland in 1912 when he left for Canada. I think he was a bit surprised and embarrassed when I told him that I was an electrician and had worked in an armament factory, and that I was very familiar with this type of switch.

When we first shared who of our family was lost, they listened attentively and asked a few questions as to how and where their family members were killed. They knew that the Nazis had killed thousands of people but no one knew for sure how many. The number of six million was not known until much later. They told us not to think back on those times any more, as we were now in a new country, and to devote ourselves to our new lives. There was no way they could have understood that it was impossible for us to turn off our memories of the past, even though we may have wanted to.

Social Studies

Toronto was, as my father predicted, a modern city. All of the buildings were intact; there was no sign of war. There were no lineups to get food and no ration cards. All the store windows were laden with a myriad of merchandise, beautifully displayed. One could buy anything, but we had no money and no need for anything. Being with our family was all that we needed.

Friday nights, after Shabbat dinner, we would go for a walk on College Street. The street was full of people. To me, they did not look Jewish, but my cousin assured me that most were. The most remarkable sight was young children and teenagers walking, running, playing tag, laughing and having fun. In Europe after the war, there was a noticeable absence of Jewish teenagers and children. The only children were the newly born. Almost my whole age group and generation had been murdered.

Uncle Dave was a senior designer in a women's coat factory on Spadina, and my father obtained a job as a tailor within two days of our arrival. My uncle made sure that my father was given more lucrative piecework. Consequently, he was earning a very good wage. He put his money in a drawer and I could take whatever I needed. We had had this arrangement in Germany: whatever we had we shared unconditionally. I would never take any money without letting him know. No one in Germany put savings into a bank and we did not do so for a long time in Canada.

We had arrived without any decent clothes and no winter coats. Aunt Helen's brother offered to take me to his jobber friend's places, and bought me a winter jacket with a fur collar that I loved. This was my first Canadian coat and when I wore it I felt less conspicuous, like I fitted more into my new environment. I was happy to discard my clothes from Germany, including my long overcoat and fedora. No one in Canada seemed to wear fedoras. In my new coat it was a pleasure to walk on College Street and window-shop. Anything that my heart could desire was available. This was a wonderful new experience and a realization of what could be possible.

Rosh Hashanah fell during the beginning of October, and Uncle Dave arranged seats for us in his synagogue. With no knowledge of Hebrew and hardly able to read it, I felt out of place. Yom Kippur was our most painful and emotional day. My father and I decided that we should consider the day of atonement the anniversary of my mother's and sister's deaths. Although it is customary to fast on this day, I refused to, as a protest against God. I thought the days of hunger during the war would last me a lifetime of fasting.

After the holidays, my cousin Joe agreed to take me to register as an apprentice electrician. On the way to the registration office, I asked if it would be possible for me to go to high school instead. He said, "I don't know, let's go and find out." He turned the car around and headed toward Harbord Collegiate. My heart pumped like mad with excitement and my knees were shaking. I had not been to school for nine years. After all my experiences in the ghetto, the camps and in Germany, living as an adult, this would be a totally new experience. Here I would find out if I had the intelligence and ability to study and get a higher education.

We entered the school and Joe asked to see the principal, who wanted to assess my knowledge of English. With my limited vocabulary, I tried to answer his questions as best I could. "Did I know any algebra?" he asked. I told him that I had studied some algebra and trigonometry. He called the head of the mathematics department,

Mr. Campbell, to interview me. "Can you solve (a+b) squared?" "Yes," I said, and gave him the answer without hesitation. The principal informed me I would not need to take Grade 11 algebra, and enrolled me in high school. Although I would not have to take algebra, I would have to take a variety of other Grade 11 subjects to complete my junior matriculation, which I could take while attending Grade 12. He made up my timetable consisting of a mixture of subjects at various grade levels.

Because going to the high school had been a spontaneous decision, I had not discussed it with my father. When I told him, he was very happy that I would at least have an opportunity for a high school education. He agreed to support me through whatever length of schooling I wanted. At that point, I had little hope of entering university. That was a dream far into the future and I did not even dare to think that far ahead.

The next morning, I dressed in a white shirt, tie and a blazer jacket, according to European customs. I was both fearful and excited. Before the war, I had finished only Grade 4. During the war, I had neither an opportunity for nor an interest in learning. As a child, I had had trouble learning to read and had often overheard my parents saying that I had a *farshtopten Kopf*, meaning a stuffed head. I had acquired an inferiority complex and was worried that I would be embarrassed in front of the students. I steeled myself as I entered the school building.

I reported to the office and was directed to a classroom. The teacher looked me up and down and said that English, Grade 12 A, would be my home classroom. He directed me to an empty seat at the back of the room. It was the middle of October and classes were well advanced in every subject and I had no idea what was going on. After nine years without formal schooling, it was incredible for me to sit in a classroom with sixteen-to-eighteen-year-old boys and girls with whom I had nothing in common. The student next to me leaned over and asked if I was a student teacher. At first, I did not understand what he meant. I could not understand how he would mistake me for a student teacher. He saw my puzzlement and explained that students normally did not wear jackets and ties to school. He suggested I wear a sweater instead.

That day after school, I told my cousin that I needed a sweater; he promptly took me to a jobber who suggested I look youthful and produced a white sweater with a huge green goose on the front and back. The next morning I proudly wore my sweater. None of my classmates made any comments but on changing classes the younger students snickered, laughed and sang a refrain from a then-popular song by Frankie Laine, "Cry of the Wild Goose." I asked one of my classmates what they were laughing at and he pointed to my sweater. This was the first and last time I wore the sweater. It appears, however, that I did not throw it away; years later, I found a photograph of my stepbrother, the actor Al Waxman, wearing it.

My mispronunciation of some English words provided much humour for my fellow students. In Grade 11 Ancient History class, the teacher asked the class to name the Roman general who crossed the Alps on elephants. Having studied that section of the text the night before, I put up my hand for the first time and said Hannibal, but to my fellow students it sounded like Honeyball. For days after, I was referred to as Honeyball.

The students tried to help me with my schoolwork; however, after school I felt very much alone. They were sympathetic, but they were not my friends. I had nothing in common with them. I could not express myself adequately in a general conversation and did not know how to behave in this environment. My self-confidence was very low. I was overwhelmed by the wide knowledge of academic subjects my fellow students possessed and this made me feel even more inadequate. Everything I read was new and required constant use of the dictionary. I doubted that I would be able to keep up and pass the upcoming tests and exams.

In Grade 12 English, we were studying *Macbeth* and I had to memorize some of the soliloquies. I had to look up word such as "clutch," as in "come let me clutch thee." I looked up the word, took it as a noun, and came up with "part of engine coupling." Other phrases, such as "draw the dagger," I came up with "tracing on paper." My frustration was increasing every day, and my insecurity carried over to my limited social life. I was asked by some of my classmates to join them after school but their world of baseball, football and hockey was totally unfamiliar and I was afraid to open my mouth for fear that I would ask a silly question.

In Germany I had lived the life of an adult and here I was masquerading as an eighteen-year-old boy. My stories about my life during the war, or after, would be totally beyond their experience and unbelievable. Once, I visited a classmate and met his mother. She would wring her hands and burst out crying every time she saw me, saying that I reminded her of the family that she lost. Not wishing to cause her grief and make my classmate uncomfortable, I stopped going over to his house.

My new life was very simple – I went to school, tried to take in as much as I could and then went home to study. I studied all the time except at meals. My only entertainment consisted of going by myself on Friday nights to a movie theatre for a double bill. I particularly liked westerns, which usually had little dialogue, and what was said was simple and within my knowledge. My cousin Joe had a floor tile setting business and he employed me on weekends. He paid me fifty cents an hour, and the two dollars I earned was enough for a double bill movie and some snacks.

The people with whom I had come over on the boat from Germany were years older than me and I had no friends among them. I was introduced to people who were closer to my age, but I had little in common with them. They all had jobs, and I was in school. This meant I had neither time nor money to spend the evenings with them. I had enormous amounts of homework to complete and new vocabulary to memorize.

The isolation was a blessing in disguise; it helped me concentrate on my studies. I immersed myself in schoolwork and studied every day, including weekends, late into the night. My cousins loved having me home every night to babysit. I didn't have a desk in my room, so I had to study at the dining room table, which was not always convenient or possible. My cousin Joe offered me a folding card table with wooden legs. I cut down two of the legs so they could rest on the bed with the others resting on the floor. This made an excellent desk and I could study long into the night. The only distraction was my father's snoring.

~

From a casual conversation one day, some students found out that I had been in Soviet-occupied Poland after the war and that I knew something about the Soviet Union. They invited me to a building on Christie Street to speak to some students at the United Jewish People's Order. It was not until sometime later that I found out that it was a communist organization. I was told that the daughter of the chairman of the Canadian Communist Party was present.

With my limited vocabulary and broken English, I related a short outline of my wartime experiences. The students were very interested in my experience after the war in communist Poland but were even more interested in my father's sojourn in the Soviet-occupied territory of Poland from October 1939 to early 1940. I told the story that my father had told us on his return, that he had considered bringing us to Lwów (Lemberg) but was discouraged by the overcrowding, lack of housing, impossibility of going into some businesses and the difficulty of obtaining a job. I relayed that the Soviet occupation was not very friendly to the Polish population and that I had repeatedly heard stories of rape and plunder. The Soviets issued a questionnaire to refugees and one innocuous question, according to my father, was would they like to return to Poland. Those who answered yes were considered a security risk and deported to Siberia. The Soviets would also deport people for the smallest infractions, such as not having a job or doing business as "black marketers." Everyone knew that deportation to Siberia was a potential death sentence, which is what happened to the husband of my mother's first cousin, Carola, whom I met after the war.

The members of the communist club were angered and thought I was exaggerating, and also did not believe the Soviets had behaved brutally, nor that they had committed atrocities and raped women. They argued that the deportation to Siberia saved thousands of Jewish lives. I told them that I didn't think that the Soviets sent the Poles to Siberia with the intention of saving their lives. Everyone at the meeting was very hostile to me, and I thought they would throw me down the stairs. My classmate, who was present at that meeting, avoided me for the rest of the year.

In December of that year, I wrote my first set of exams. My greatest challenge was Grade 12 English, which was divided into two subjects: authors and composition. The authors' exam was multiple choice. Since I had not read any of the books, I guessed the answers and I obtained a mark of 12 out of 100. On the composition exam I wrote an essay, " One Day in a German Concentration Camp." To my surprise, at the top of the paper "80" was marked in red ink but when I looked at the bottom of the page there were the notations "minus 20 for spelling, minus 20 for grammar, final grade 40." The teacher then left a comment about my "good imagination."

The weeks that followed the December exams, and especially the winter break and holidays, were filled with excitement. We met my aunt's extended family in Canada and from the United States. It was a fairy-tale existence. My aunt Helen was one of six children and they all had close-knit families. Although Aunt Helen's family was not related to us, they treated us as family. Our relationship grew and we had contact with some of them for years. During our stay in Germany, we had received parcels from the American family and I had corresponded with them in English. I wanted to tell them that I wished to reciprocate their kindness, but I had a hard time finding the right words; using my dictionary I found "to give back" or "pay back," which did not make sense, as I would not be in a position to do that. I wrote that I hoped there would be a time when I would be able to revenge their generosity. On our first meeting with the Americans, they wanted to know what they had done wrong and why I would like to "revenge" their generosity.

Few people were interested in our past. Most Canadians had heard about what happened to the Jews during the war but knew no details and were not interested in learning. On the rare occasion when we opened up just a bit, our stories were met with disbelief. As if to console us, some would tell us things like, "Yes, it was a bad time here too, so-and-so lost her son, we all suffered and were on rations, but now that the war is over there is no point in going over the past. It's over, let's forget it." However, for us, it was impossible to forget. And the better our conditions grew, the harder it was to forget – we missed our families and wished they could experience the good times with us. However, since no one listened, it was best to keep silent.

Some Canadian Jews thought that recent immigrants, who had lived through such terrible conditions and suffered the trauma of loss, could not possibly be normal and considered us somewhat strange or mentally unbalanced. This was untrue, and this kind of attitude was hard to accept and annoying. Like most immigrants, we were not well accepted by the established Jewish community and were derogatively called either "greeners" or "DPs." Some immigrants did have unrealistic expectations that their wealthy relatives would provide them with a lifestyle similar to what their Canadian families enjoyed. Some newcomers felt that because they suffered and lost everything, the world owed them a living. Family members in the ghetto had shared everything they had with each other. If a family member needed a place to live, we would take them in and share the little we had unconditionally. Some felt that their relatives in Canada should do the same. This entitled attitude of a few gave the newcomers a bad name. Some Canadian family members did take their newly arrived members into their businesses and eventually made them partners. Others lent their family members money or set them up in business. Most of us had no trades or skills to fit into the Canadian job market and going into some sort of business was one way to make a living. Many survivors struggled for years.

My father and I certainly did not have a sense of entitlement; we were grateful for what our family did for us. We wanted to make it on our own. Most of the friends who had come with us from Germany felt the same. There was help available from the Jewish Immigrant Aid Society, but we really didn't need anything. Uncle David and Aunt Helen provided us with a home and food. All we needed was to be with our family members, our cousins and their children.

At school, I still felt isolated from my fellow students by the lack of common experiences and differences in attitude toward life. They spoke incessantly about sports, of which I knew practically nothing. Their behaviour toward the opposite sex was understandably juvenile and innocent. They could not possibly understand my experience in Germany as a young man, especially my sexual experiences with German girls.

There were great gaps in my basic knowledge. Mundane information that students learned in the lower grades was absent from my experience. Although I had learned much about life and human beings, this was not what was being taught in school. I occasionally tried to make friends with the boys in my class by joining them after school, but they were not interested in anything that I had to say – either my English was too poor to make myself understood or the experiences I wanted to share were unbelievable to them. Most of the boys, I was told, did not want to become my friends due to their social insecurity and peer pressure. Comments that were not meant for my ears, such as, "Why do you want to hang around with the DP," were not uncommon. When I asked one student who belonged to a Zionist organization to introduce me to his group, he said I would make the boys and girls feel uncomfortable and I would not fit in.

I thought that it would be easier to make friends with girls, and what better place to try than at a school dance. I obtained some tips from a fellow student and my family as to what I should wear; unlike dances in Germany, where everyone wore a tie and jacket, here in Canada, I was advised that a shirt and sweater would be more acceptable. I thought I could impress the girls with my dancing skills. By this time, I was a good dancer but to my surprise, most girls did not know how to fox trot, tango or waltz. On the other hand, I did not know how to jive, so we just shuffled to the music, which was unfamiliar to me. Although I was not shy, I became tongue-tied. I tried to make small talk but was afraid I would use the wrong words or mispronounce a word, so I kept quiet, hoping that the girls would lead the conversation. I think they, in turn, were more interested in making contact with other Canadian students. I left the dance and went home alone.

As I mentioned, my family members did not wish to hear my stories either. They wanted me to assimilate into Canadian life as quickly as possible. They thought, with good intentions, that the best way to accomplish the transition was not to talk about my past, or my life in Europe, and to concentrate on becoming a "Canadian." My cousin Grace was home during the day and I practised my English with her. She corrected my essays and helped me with grammar. Usually, after school, she told me about the Canadian way of life and what was important for me to know about my new country. I tried very hard to become a Canadian by imitating my peers and studying the proper use and pronunciations of English words.

Grace's husband, Ralph, considered the weekend as family time and seldom worked then. Ralph was a war veteran and played trombone in the air force band. One weekend he took me with him on a band outing that involved a lot of music I liked, as well as my first

Canadian picnic. I ate too many hot dogs and hamburgers and drank lots of ginger ale. Having a newborn, the Weingartens were more homebound. Ralph drove a late model Pontiac that was his pride and joy, and he wouldn't let me drive it even months after I learned to drive. Most evenings and on the weekends, he did photography in his basement darkroom and taught me how to develop film, make enlargements and print photographs. Photography eventually became one of my hobbies.

My cousins Joe and Rae drove an old car and did not worry about appearances. He applied masking tape over the chrome of his Hudson for repainting and then got busy and did not remove the tape. After a few months, the tape was baked on and couldn't be removed. It bothered me that the car did not look nice, with all the chrome covered with tape. I attributed this to my upbringing, where appearances mattered in the clothes one wore and the condition they were in. Even during the worst times my parents always paid attention to their appearance in public. There was a saying, "It does not matter what is in your stomach, but people judge you by your appearance." I always took pride in my possessions and it bothered me that Joe's car did not look as nice as Ralph's. I tried to remove the tape but after an hour of scraping and not making any progress, I gave up. The car drove well, which is all that mattered to Joe. Joe and Rae lived their life to the fullest and material things weren't important to them. Although they had little money, they frequently went out to eat in restaurants and often invited me to join them.

In 1949, during my first summer in Canada, Joe and I became more like brothers. He hired me again to help with his tile laying and paid me more than the going rate for my time. When we worked in the city, we would go to a corner coffee shop and for a dime I would be served a fried egg with a bagel and coffee. He helped me feel more independent. Joe tried to get jobs out of town and make it into a short working vacation. Usually it was somewhere up north in Muskoka and we would take a day off after the job was finished and go fishing.

On those occasions, he allowed me to drive even though I had no learner's licence yet. It was scary but exciting.

That first summer, I got a taste of Canadian life and was happy. My life assumed a new direction and I loved every minute of it. Uncle David spent one week of his summer vacation fishing with his three friends, and invited me and Joe to join them. He rented a separate cabin for us on a small lake in Muskoka. For the rest of summer vacation, Uncle David and Aunt Helen went to Detroit to visit Helen's two sisters and their families. They took me with them across the border illegally. Aunt Helen's nephews and nieces were a few years younger than I was, but I enjoyed their company. I really did not need to make friends. I was busy all the time.

~

My father was a handsome man, well dressed and a good conversationalist – mainly in Yiddish, but he also spoke Polish and German perfectly. He was a very eligible bachelor and several people introduced him to women. One day, he met a woman whom he told me very little about, but his behaviour changed – he was happy and full of new energy. My father had always been immaculately groomed and elegantly dressed, but now he purchased some new clothes and looked even more dapper. I knew that this was serious. I asked to meet her and he said, "In time." The only thing he volunteered was that she was from Poland, had been in Canada a long time and had two teenage sons. Her name was Toby Waxman and she had been widowed three years earlier. He spoke of her in superlatives and I knew he was in love. I was apprehensive, for I was depending on his support in order to get through school, but he assured me that he would continue to support me.

When I met Toby and her two sons, it was a short, formal get-acquainted visit. Toby was well dressed, good-looking and stately, but also warm and interested in pleasing my father. Her two sons and I felt awkward and impatient for the visit to end. Toby gave me a Parker pen and pencil set as a gift. I was overjoyed but Albert, the younger of her two sons, appeared upset. Many years later, when Al Waxman, of "King of Kensington" fame, wrote his memoirs, *That's What I Am,* I found out Toby had taken one of Al's bar mitzvah gifts without asking him and given it to me. He had several sets and she felt he would not mind parting with one. A few days later, my father and Toby were married in a private ceremony at city hall. I was not invited to witness the ceremony and was deeply hurt, but I later found out that her sons were not invited either. My father moved out of my uncle's home and I now had the room and the double bed all to myself.

The separation, although painful at first, was good for me. I was too busy to pay attention to anything, and I saw my father once a week. The school year continued uneventfully; I wrote my exams and passed all subjects, except English. Although I had passed the final exam, my average resulted in a failing grade. Before I left school, I was told I would have to repeat Grade 12 English next year. I was extremely disappointed.

Toby soon sold her house and bought a new, beautiful four-bedroom house on Glen Cedar Road, in the northern part of Toronto. The area was new and not very developed. Eglinton Avenue, a few blocks north of the house, was the northern boundary of development. The house was finished in the summer and we moved in. It was an exciting time for me. One of the four bedrooms, with new furniture, was mine. The room was large and I had a desk, dresser and closet. I now had privacy and my very own space.

It felt strange to sit with my father's wife and her two sons at a Shabbat table. It was my new family and yet, I did not feel that it was. The background of these people was entirely different, but I very much wanted to be a part of this family. I could not come to terms with calling Toby "Mother." The memory of my mother was still fresh in my mind. Would I betray her memory by calling another woman Mother? Al and Benny also felt awkward calling my father "Dad." The three of us discussed this and next tried uncle and aunt, but eventually concluded it would be best to use their first names.

Through one of her good friends, Toby managed to get me a summer job in a junkyard. The work consisted of sorting different metals into separate piles, and it was so boring that I could not stay awake. After a week, I requested a different task. I was assigned as a helper on a truck picking up scrap metal. Working on the truck was much harder but I liked it. We travelled all over the city, which was fun. Our main job was to pick up entire cars from other junkyards and bring them back to the hydraulic press. It was amazing to see three or four cars compressed into a small cube.

That summer, I met Irv Solnik, who lived a few houses north of me. Irv convinced me to leave my job and he managed to get us both hired at a hotel, he as a waiter and I as a busboy. The job did not last long. Irv was caught eating while waiting on tables and was fired. Without asking me, he told the owner I would quit in solidarity with him. So we both lost our jobs. I soon realized that Irv had said this because he needed a companion. Irv and I were next hired by his father's soda company to go from house to house selling seltzer water on commission. I found out he was a much better salesman than I and a good storyteller; I still had a language disadvantage, and I made few sales. Fortunately, I had made some money in my previous job, and having a part-time job gave us time for adventures. Irv had the use of his father's car and we would visit summer camps trying to make contact with some of Irv's counsellor friends. It was a good summer and I appreciated having Irv as my friend.

In the fall, the principal suggested that I take Grade 13 in two years, which would give me an opportunity to get better marks for university entrance. I was not prepared to lose another year – I was in a hurry to get on with life. I also did not want to be a financial burden to my father any longer than necessary. I didn't panic though, because I had already decided to take Grade 13 English at night school. To my surprise, the principal refused to enrol me because they did not allow students to take Grade 13 and Grade 12 English in the same school year. Unbeknownst to me, there was a competition among Toronto high schools to graduate the largest number of students with the highest marks, and the principal didn't want my low grades to pull down his record. After the initial shock, I went back the next day and the vice-principal, who was in charge and did not know me, allowed me to enrol.

Repeating Grade 12 English in day school, I once again studied *Macbeth*. At night school, I could choose *Hamlet* or *Macbeth*, and I of course chose *Macbeth*, for the third time. By the end of the year, I knew most of the soliloquies by heart. I wrote the Grade 13 English provincial exam in the University Armoury and I passed.

Meanwhile, I lived in the opulent surroundings of Toby's home with my father, my stepmother and my stepbrothers, and yet our interactions were not extensive. Partly this was because of my poor English. We could all speak some Yiddish, but were not comfortable enough to have a long conversation in it and, in reality, there was little to talk about. How could I impose my experiences – my sorrow and my nightmares – on these people?

Benny was only a year younger than me, but we had very little in common. He was a dedicated Zionist and member of Hashomer Hatzair, a socialist organization. His plan was to go to Israel and live on a kibbutz, where everything would be shared. He told me that his group practised free love, which I was interested in because I was unattached. He invited me to come to a meeting with him to find out more about their ideas and way of life. I was intrigued and I went a few times. I soon found out that the idea of free love was a myth – everyone in the group was paired up. The more I learned, the more disillusioned I became. Benny believed communism was the ideal way of life and government. I found his idea of a communist utopia naive and nothing like the communism I knew. The paradox was that he enjoyed the fruits of capitalism: he loved to drive his mother's luxurious Studebaker, to live in a big house and to frequent expensive restaurants. His life was far removed from the socialist existence of a kibbutz. My talks with him in my broken English soon deteriorated into strong disagreements and I retreated from those discussions.

Albert was several years younger, but I could relate to him more easily. He had a zest for life and I envied his innocence. Through Al, I lived vicariously; I tried to understand what it would feel like to be a teenager again, to live at home during peacetime and to have everything I wanted and needed. But it was impossible to imagine. I had been thrust from being a child to having to be a man, and I found it difficult to talk about, even with Al. I didn't want to burden him with my past, to spoil his innocence. Our common ground was parental loss – it is terrible to lose a parent at any age, but it was catastrophic for him at age twelve. I could identify with his feelings of grief for his father, who had died suddenly from a heart attack.

My father tried to be a father figure to Ben and Al and at the same time tried to fit me into that category, but my relationship with my father had long since taken an entirely different form. Having lived together for two years in camps and three years after the war in close quarters, we were more like brothers, almost equals. I resented that my father wanted to assert himself as a parent again. I loved him dearly but I could not accept his new and assumed parental attitudes. Although he was entitled to these, I wanted to retain our previous rapport. Once, we had an altercation where, after a few strong words, he tried to discipline me by striking me. I grabbed his arm and looked at him in anger, and he understood that I was not a child. He never again told me what to do. One day, I asked him to lend me the car for a date and he refused because he would never have dared ask his father to borrow a car. I asked if I should refuse my future child bread because I did not have any at his age. He soon realized the absurdity of this situation and we laughed.

My father was the only link to my past and I was afraid that I was losing his attention and affection. Although he tried to treat Benny and me in the same manner, in reality he did not. It bothered me that he gave in to Benny's wishes so easily; I was convinced it was to gain his acceptance. At the same time, I resented sharing his attention. I could feel that Al and Benny also resented his approaches, but for different reasons. I thought it was because their mother was the authority figure and they didn't want another. Toby was strong and definitive but also very sensitive; she tried not to come between me and my father or take sides, for which I was grateful, and she also did not tell me what to do.

I continued to struggle with my identity. Who was I in this new world? How should I behave? I wanted to be accepted but I did not have a role model. I knew that I had to leave the past behind to make a new life. I was grateful that fate had put me together with this family and to have an opportunity to see the life of a normal family, surrounded by people with love and understanding. However, the horrible past still intruded. I wondered whether I was having a dream or if my experience was real. After a number of years, when I began to question whether the past was a nightmare or reality, I would inevitably think back to the images of occupied Poland and my memories of our hometown of Chorzów. I could never truly leave my past behind.

Moving Forward

My English was improving and I concentrated on pronunciation. I stood in front of the mirror and watched my mouth as I spoke, paying special attention to the pronunciation of the "th" sound and trying not to interchange the "w" sound with "v." The W and V plagued me for years, but eventually, people couldn't tell if my accent was German or western European. This was an improvement, as I did not want to be known as a DP or refugee. Irv introduced me to girls and as I was getting more secure in my English, I even asked a few for dates. However, I experienced many disappointments, with one girl in particular. She had agreed to go out with me but then broke the date. I was surprised and tried to make another date with her but she refused and wouldn't give me a reason why. Through her cousin, who was my neighbour, it came out that her mother found out that I was a DP and would not allow her daughter to go out with me. The mother considered all DPs, because of our traumatic experiences, to be mentally unbalanced. I found the students were generally more accepting than their parents. Eventually, I gained enough self-confidence to grow a goatee at a time when facial hair was bizarre, if not eccentric. My outward appearance as a person at ease with himself belied an inward feeling of insecurity and inferiority. My DP status lingered.

Irv was not too popular with the boys in my class but he fascinated the girls. He was good-looking and always had amazing stories to tell. Most, if not all, were fabrications, and he would ask me to back him up. I thought it harmless and amusing and I went along, although others accused him of being a habitual liar. After a while, I realized he believed that the stories he fabricated had actually happened. He had a fantastic memory and he never faltered in retelling the same story days later. He opened a new phase in my life. I tried very hard to imitate him, become a Canadian and lose my DP status. When he introduced me to new friends he would introduce me as Chicago Nate. The name was a moniker given to me in Grade 12 by a non-Jewish student who found my accent funny. To new acquaintances, I was known simply as Chicago Nate.

On Sunday nights, Holy Blossom Temple, located not far from our home, held teenage dances. The price of admission was attending a lecture given by the temple educators, different members of the Youth Leadership or Rabbi Fackenheim. Most of the time we would arrive after the lecture and have some of our friends open the back door for us. One time, I decided to attend and, by chance, Rabbi Fackenheim was giving the lecture. Rabbi Emil Fackenheim was from Germany and managed to escape in 1939. During the discussion period, I volunteered my opinion that I would not want to bring children into a world that persecuted Jews for centuries and murdered us during the Nazi regime. Why should my children possibly be subjected to such a fate? The rabbi became agitated and asked me to come forward. "Young man, this is exactly what Hitler intended. Don't you see you are giving Hitler a posthumous victory?" His words jolted me into the realization that the Nazi indoctrination and propaganda had worked on me: I was its victim. Little did I know, at the time, that this proclamation would one day become Rabbi Fackenheim's thesis and be the basis of his proposal for a 614th commandment.

This incident stayed with me and I realized that the Nazis had destroyed not only my family but also my belief in God. Years later, Rabbi Fackenheim's words prompted me to study the various religions of the world to see if I could find faith. I disagreed with the concept of God as presented in the basic teaching in the bible. In reading about other religions, I found I could not accept other interpretations and beliefs either. I could not come to terms with the concept of an omnipotent, all-seeing and all-knowing entity who had control of everything that happened in the world. How could an omnipotent and loving God allow the murder of "His Chosen People," especially the children? My return to faith came years later, from a suggestion by Elie Wiesel: "Don't ask where was God; ask, where was man?"

In 1950, the summer after Grade 13, Irv convinced me to apply for a job in a summer camp. I thought that it was unlikely I would even be considered, without experience, but there was no harm in trying. Irv, whose interview was before mine, convinced the camp director of my qualifications as a tennis and dance instructor. When the director asked me if I had any camp experience, not wanting to lie, I responded with, "Do I have camp experience?" I didn't volunteer that I had a different camp in mind. She did not pursue the issue and I got the job as a counsellor, tennis, photography and dance instructor.

The camp, Balfour Manor, was located just south of Gravenhurst in Muskoka, on a lake surrounded by lush forests. The view was breathtaking and serene. The summer camp environment was so different from anything that I had experienced. I doubt many Holocaust survivors had this opportunity, and I felt very fortunate. I immersed myself in camp life. Although the images of the past still tormented my dreams, I was intent on leaving the past behind. I pretended to be a young person like anyone else. I identified with the kids and the adults at different times of the day. The camp had a well-equipped photographic dark room and I loved developing films, experimenting with different exposures and enlargements. Nobody questioned my time or what I did. I took and developed photos of various camp activities, campers and counsellors, pictures that I still have. I cannot believe how lucky I was. I was in charge of twelve-year-old boys and I encouraged their mischievous nature and observed them with interest. I wished I had experienced this type of pleasure at their age.

I also enjoyed the easygoing camaraderie of the counsellors as we sat around the campfire singing songs in both English and Hebrew. They were amazed that I did not know even the most common songs. Morley Markson, my co-counsellor, introduced me to sailing. Every time I went out with him, I was terrified. I still couldn't swim well, and we were always on the brink of going over, although Morley tried his best to assure me that the boat wouldn't tip. From all my experiences at summer camp, I developed a sense that it was not too late for me to catch up on my lost youth and that I could be a "normal" person; my horrible experiences did not need to dictate my future.

Irv and I visited the Gateway Hotel in Gravenhurst, where Murray Adler's new and upcoming dance band was playing. This in itself was an attraction, but we also knew Renee Drevnik would be there, whom I had tutored in algebra during the year. Renee introduced me to Bernice Collis and we spent the evening together. I was very attracted to Bernice, although she appeared to be much younger than me. Irv kidded me about this but it did not discourage me from dating her the following year. Our relationship developed slowly. Unlike other girls, she was interested in my past, and asked me questions. Years later, I found out she was intrigued by my stories but did not believe them to be true, or thought that I exaggerated grossly. Although she was seventeen, she looked much younger and, later, my older friends complained that I was bringing a fifteen-year-old to frat parties, telling me that their dates were embarrassed to be intimate in front of a child.

That summer, I agonized about what I should do next. I wanted to apply to university for engineering, but my family and friends told me this was not for Jews because there was a lot of antisemitism and it would be almost impossible for me to get a job. They gave me examples of graduate engineers with honour degrees and cum-laude designations having to go into the insurance or travel industries. I had already encountered discrimination in obtaining entry into Canada. On the other hand, camp experience gave me a lesson in motivation. One day, I was sitting in the shade under a tree; it was an oppressively hot day and I was observing a group of campers playing baseball. I could hardly move without exhausting myself, and yet these young people were running and playing, ignoring the heat. I concluded that if you like what you are doing, the temperature and conditions under which you are doing it do not matter. I hoped that I would like university life and the hardship that I was sure to encounter.

In the end, I applied to the University of Toronto dental school. I had As in algebra, trigonometry, geometry and chemistry; Bs in German and physics; and credits in English and music. Everyone assured me that my application would be accepted. Members of the dental fraternity were interested in me becoming a member and asked me to pledge. I was convinced that dentistry should be my profession and was hoping to be admitted. Eventually, I received a letter requesting me to attend an interview with the dean of dentistry. The interview was short and direct; he asked my reasons for wanting to go into dentistry and I thought I satisfied him with my answers. He then told me that there was a problem: I was in competition for the space with a student from a rural area. He explained that I had just arrived in the country, whereas the other applicant's family had lived in Canada for generations and paid taxes for umpteen years. And, he would most likely practise dentistry in his home area, where there was a need for dentists, while I would most likely practise in Toronto, where there was an oversupply. He closed the interview by saying that he would not admit me. I protested and told him about the hardships I had overcome, that I was mature and interested in dentistry. I asked what he suggest I do and he advised me to enrol in a four-year course of Honour Science, which would lead me to a physiology or biochemistry degree, and on graduation from either of these I would be admitted directly into dentistry and not have to take the pre-dentistry year.

I faced a dilemma. I had no idea what the course was like. On inquiry, I was told that Honour Science was tough and not many students could handle it. It seemed I had no choice but to enrol. I thought this would determine if I had the intellect and the ability to master a university education. I had a terrible inferiority complex, thinking that Grade 13 was not a real test of my intelligence, as it had required merely the regurgitation of the information given to me during the year. I was sure that *Coles Notes* got me through high school. Honour Science would determine my ability to learn and think critically. I applied and was accepted.

~

My high school graduation was a milestone that I had never thought I could reach. I think my father was also pleased with my first visible academic achievement. I was looking forward to the ceremony and managed to get tickets for my dad, Toby, my uncle Dave and Aunt Helen. As I lined up with my fellow graduates, I suddenly heard my name being called on the PA system. "Mr. Leipciger to the office, please." I was told that I could not graduate from Harbord Collegiate, as I did not have Grade 13 English. I was beside myself. How could they do that to me? I told them I had written Grade 13 English exams at the Armoury and been admitted to Honour Science at the University of Toronto. I pleaded it would be an embarrassment to me and to my family in attendance. They did not care – in order to graduate, I was required to take and pass all subjects at Harbord Collegiate. Eventually, they compromised by letting me attend the graduation ceremony, but they told me not to open up the certificate, as it would be a blank piece of paper.

~

Honour Science was not as hard as I had imagined. As it happened, Irv Solnik also enrolled in the course, as did many of my classmates from Grade 13. On the first day, the professor of the chemistry class said, "Look to the right and look to the left; only one of the three of you will pass this course." I did well on the midterms and even better on the final, with second-class honours. I stood seventh in the class, which had started with eighty students, but only twenty of us passed into second year. Through this experience, I gained confidence in my ability to handle any course and my self-esteem went up. My social life was also much more active and the problems of being labelled a DP fell to the wayside. After this year, I saw Irving much less; he had transferred into a different stream and our paths diverged. The influence of other friends began to play a greater role in my life.

Eventually, after discussions with my family, I decided to drop out of Honour Science because I would have another seven years of university ahead of me if I pursued dentistry. I was twenty-three years old and would be thirty before I graduated, and only if everything went well. I was impatient to get on with my life; that much study and economic hardship did not appeal to me. I decided to enrol in an electronics technician course at Ryerson community college. I went to the college, filled out an application and put my documents from high school and university on the registrar's desk. He looked at my papers for a few minutes, scooped up the documents and disappeared.

When he returned, he told me that the principal wanted to see me. I thought, what now? The principal asked me why I wanted to enrol in Ryerson, which required only completion of Grade 12 for admission. He had reviewed my documents and seen that I had good marks from Grade 13 and second-class honours from the Honour Science course. He appeared to be a decent fellow and I thought I should be up front with him. I told him about my European experiences and the antisemitism that I encountered on entry into Canada, and that my family had advised me that I would not be able to get a job as an engineer. I also told him about my experience with the dental college. In view of all that, my plan was to become a licensed technician and after a few years go into business repairing and selling radios and TVs, which were just coming on the market. He asked me if I could afford to go through university and I said I lived at home, I worked during the summer and my father had agreed to help me financially. He advised me to go to the university and apply to Electrical Engineering; he felt that with an engineering degree, I could still work as a technician, but it would be much harder to get a degree in engineering later. He agreed there was a lot of prejudice and anti-semitism but he felt that, at this time, there were a lot of war veterans graduating from engineering, which would saturate the market. He said that by the time I graduated, the demand for engineers would be greater than the supply and discrimination would diminish. He gave me a letter of introduction to the dean of Electrical Engineering at the University of Toronto.

I made an appointment to see the dean, who received me courte-ously. He read the letter and pondered for a while. I repeated my rea-sons for wanting to apply to Ryerson College. He agreed that there was antisemitism and an oversupply of engineers but said he was glad that I had taken the Ryerson principal's advice. We sat together for four hours telling each other stories; during the war, his son had been shot down over Italy and was in a German prison camp for four years. At the end, we both cried and he asked me to keep in touch with him and keep him informed of my progress.

After enrolling in first year at the engineering faculty, I was asked to join the BSR Fraternity. Entering engineering had put me back on track to my chosen profession; joining BSR changed my social life and, together, these changed the direction of my life. I was very fortu-nate to get to know two superb individuals who were instrumental in furthering my growth and development. Two of the fraternity broth-ers, Herb Green and David Merkur, became lifelong friends. Herb and I "pledged" together to enter the fraternity. Herb was in civil engineer-ing. Dave was a year ahead of us and became our fraternity mentor.

In the summer following my first year, I got a job with Ontario Hydro. I would finish my daily assignment by noon and had a hard time staying awake in the afternoon. I had already obtained the books prescribed for second-year engineering and I decided to try to study calculus in the afternoons. I concealed my book in a half-open roll of drawings and after a four-week period, had solved every problem in the book. I was then transferred to a Hydro office in Tecumseh, near

Windsor, Ontario. On the weekend, being alone in the town, I decided to go to Detroit, where my Aunt Helen's two sisters and families resided. I didn't have a passport or visa to enter the US, so I decided to try to get through on foot and took the Detroit-Windsor tunnel. I approached an immigration officer with a story that I had a girlfriend in Detroit and that my papers were in Toronto. He bought the story, or maybe he felt sorry for me, and he let me through on a couple of weekends.

During my trips to Detroit, my family made me feel welcome and I experienced a taste of Detroit and some of its problems. From the tunnel to their home I had to travel through a mainly black neighbourhood and was warned by my family to watch out, as this could be dangerous. I could not understand how in a country as rich as America there could be so many destitute people who resorted to crime. I was quite happy that we had managed to get to Canada instead of the US. For one thing, had we gone to the US, I would have had to serve in the army, as did my friend Ira, who immigrated there a year before my departure to Canada.

I found the second year of engineering not very challenging. I attended only the first two classes of calculus; I knew the work and the class was boring. I stopped going to class and to my surprise, I got 100 per cent on my calculus exam. This was my first and last perfect paper. In the following summer of 1953, Bernice was back working at the Gateway Hotel. I suggested to Herb and his girlfriend, Joyce, that we go there for the August long weekend. We travelled in Herb's truck up north. It was that weekend of August 1953 that I offered Bernice my fraternity pin as a commitment to "go steady." I was elated that she accepted. Our official courtship began.

The third year of engineering took second place in my life. Now, my life revolved around Bernice. The following year, I became engaged to my beautiful young bride and my love. My feelings for her were different from any others and I knew shortly after meeting Bernice that she would be my partner for life. Bernice and I spent a lot of time together and my marks suffered. Still, it was a marvellous year, with many dinners and parties put on by Bernice's parents and my parents. Toby and my father really liked Bernice. They could see what I could, that she was not only beautiful but also sensitive, not something one sees often in such a young person. When I confided to my father about a fight I had with Bernice, he attributed the fault to me. He always took her side. In his eyes, she could do no wrong.

On September 7, 1954, our parents made a big wedding with more than two hundred guests. Bernice had just turned nineteen and I was twenty-six. The traditional wedding started at my house with a festive celebration. I waited nervously and impatiently for Bernice's father, Saul, to come and pick me up. Joyce and Herb had married in June of that year and I had filmed their wedding. Herb reciprocated and filmed every aspect of ours. The bridal party was picked up and taken to the bride's house for the *bedeken*, the viewing of the bride. This tradition, of the groom lifting and then replacing the bride's veil, goes back to the biblical story of Jacob, who was married to Leah instead of Rebecca. From there we went to the marriage ceremony at Beth Shalom synagogue and then to the wedding dinner. I was very happy to have Ira at our wedding, who had to obtain special permission from the US army to be with us. Both Bernice and Toby had large families, and most were invited. My family, consisting of Uncle Dave's family members, was very small, a sad reality of the Holocaust. The loss of our families echoed in my mind. My father did not say anything, but I could see it in his eyes. I missed my mother and my sister and thought of the pleasure and satisfaction they would have had to see me get married. The sadness of these thoughts made me indulge in alcohol a bit more than I should have and my slurred and emotional little speech reflected this. I found the wedding overwhelming; it all seemed like a dream, and I could not believe my good fortune. It was the beginning of a wonderful life, not without challenges, but wonderful. Bernice's extended family accepted me unconditionally and they became my family.

After our honeymoon in the Catskills, which ended too soon, we had to return to reality and go home to finish our education. Bernice entered what was then called "Normal School" for teachers and I had to complete my fourth year of Electrical Engineering. The fourth year, I was told, was not tough, but being married, living with my wife's parents and studying at night in the bedroom was stressful. I just did not have enough hours in the week to attend lectures, write my thesis, keep my part-time job and spend hours going to interviews with prospective employers. In retrospect, getting married seemed a mistake and our relationship suffered, but we both managed to pass all the exams and graduate.

We had hoped antisemitism would disappear by the time I graduated in 1955. It had not. My fears of unemployment became real. Some companies quite openly indicated that they could not hire me, not because their company was discriminatory but because their customers would not like to deal with me. Everyone in my year had at least two or three job offers. I was getting desperate. The situation was not totally hopeless, as we lived with Bernice's parents, but we wanted to move out on our own as soon as possible.

After my last exam, I noticed a new company, H.H. Angus, listed on the bulletin board. I ripped off one of the slips, called the company and got an appointment for an interview. It was a consulting engineering firm and I prepared myself for a disappointment – from the name I assumed this would be a "WASP" company and I was sure that they would not hire me. I went to the interview with a chip on my shoulder. After being introduced to Don Angus, the son of the boss, I told him, "Look, sir, I am a new immigrant from Poland and I am Jewish and if you have any hiring restrictions... let's not waste time." He got very annoyed and said something to the effect of "I will decide if you are a candidate for the job or not, no matter where you come from and whatever your religion may be."

He hired me. I was the first Jew to work in the firm, but not the last. Don was of the new generation – more open-minded. After I joined the firm, I met Tom Saar, an Estonian immigrant who worked there, and a Lithuanian immigrant, Eugene Cuplinskas. The firm hired immigrants and Jews and never discriminated based on religion or race. I enjoyed working at H.H. Angus and gaining experience. I worked on a new project known as "Mid-Canada Line," a series of Air Force installations at the 55th parallel. The job gave me an opportunity to travel from Dawson Creek, BC, right across Canada to Weenusk and Knob Lake on James Bay.

~

Being married changed my attitude to life. With the possibility of bringing children into the world, my thoughts turned to the search for meaning. My quest started with what other religions and societies thought of God and the place of man in the universe. I had time to read on the bus and streetcar going to work and returning home. I started with Hinduism and proceeded to read about Shinto, Sikhism, Buddhism, Baha'i and the beliefs of Aboriginal people on various continents, and I came to the conclusion that all societies were looking for a deity or some supreme being to regulate their social behaviour, to pray and to give thanks to. The next phase was to read about atheism, existentialism and Mordecai Kaplan's Reconstructionism, which resonated with me the most. I even dabbled in Gershom Scholem's books of Jewish mysticism and Kabbalah, all of which were interesting. I engaged Bernice's curiosity and she read a number of these books, too. In the end, I didn't find answers to my questions. I started to read books about Judaism, including some by the philosopher Martin Buber, and became more confused than ever.

My search for the meaning of life became a theoretical exercise when we were confronted with a new, real life. On March 26, 1958, our daughter Lisa was born. Bernice had a difficult delivery that I unfortunately missed. In those days, the father was kept far away from his wife during delivery. I went home, got a good night of sleep and at 7:00 a.m. the doctor called me to say, "Mazel tov, you have a beautiful daughter." I drove down to the hospital as fast as I could. Bernice, just then, was wheeled out of the delivery room. She was high, and said, "I am sorry it is a girl." She thought I would be disappointed, but I was overjoyed and I did want a girl. I had to wait some time to see Bernice and the baby, but when I did, it was a moment of jubilation. Bernice looked happy, tired but radiant, and the baby looked beautiful. To me it was a miracle, a miracle of life. At that moment, I thought of my mother and was sure she was with me; her soul hovered above me and I knew we had made the right choice to name our firstborn in her memory. I was happy that her spirit would live on. We named her Lisa, after my mother, Leah, and after the first Jewish woman, Sarah. For me she was the beginning of a new world after the Shoah. This was a new generation and a triumph over Hitler and the Nazis, as my encounter with Rabbi Fackenheim had taught me some years earlier. The birth of a child to a survivor was not only a triumph of survival, but also of continuity of Judaism and our traditions. The birth of my daughter was a turning point in my life. Now I had new responsibilities and new fears – would I be a suitable father, after what I had experienced? A flash of my past crept into my consciousness and I blocked it out. I cradled my daughter in my arms in disbelief that this new baby was ours. The reality of having a daughter suddenly frightened me. I was awkward in handling her; she seemed so fragile. I was happy to return her to Bernice's arms.

That same year, Herb suggested that I meet with his brother-in-law, who was enlarging his electrical contracting firm, Plan Electric, and was looking for an engineer. I met Sid Cohen and his partner, Saul Ellis. We had a couple of positive meetings and they offered me a job at a much higher salary than I was making at H.H. Angus. I told my boss about the offer and asked him what I should do and what my prospect of advancement in his firm was. He said that the chief electrical engineer was a young man and that it would take years for me to get a position that would pay the amount offered. He advised me to take it, and he also told me to keep in touch.

Plan Electric consisted of the two partners, an expeditor and me. Saul and I were the estimators. My assignment was to review engineering drawings, to prepare lists of materials and labour needed and to make out a bid on the work. After a while, it became tedious. I started to examine the drawings to try to find shortcuts and acceptable alternatives to meet the specifications of the project. That was more interesting and matched my engineering skills against those of the project engineers. I also found I had good negotiating skills. We expanded the business and I negotiated a better salary but the more money I made, the more insecure I became. I thought that my only security would be in becoming a partner, but Sid and Saul had had a bad experience with a third partner and did not want to do that again.

Working for Plan Electric allowed us to purchase a house. Most of our acquaintances lived in the Bathurst area known as Downsview. Our current apartment was on Bathurst Street just north of Eglinton, which was a predominantly Jewish area. I considered it like a ghetto, which brought back negative memories, and I refused to consider buying a house there. At the time, the Winfield farm of Don Mills was being developed with designated residential, commercial and industrial areas. Young couples moved to the area, only a few of whom were Jewish. This suited our goal of living in an integrated community. In Poland, I had also lived in a mostly non-Jewish neighbourhood, and I felt that isolation would breed misunderstanding, intolerance and antisemitism. We thought it would be better for us to live in a mixed community so our children would be exposed to other religions and cultures. In keeping with our idea of living in a multiethnic community, when our children entered the public school system we joined in the campaign to stop religious education in public schools. The paradox was that we sought out our few Jewish neighbours and became close friends with them, as we felt more comfortable in their company. But we also had a group of non-Jewish friends in the area, including my former co-worker Tom Saar, a group that grew when, a couple of years later, I joined the local Civitan Club, where I was elected president, eventually becoming its district director. There were not many, if any, Jewish members in Civitan clubs, and this experience helped me attain more self-confidence in dealing with non-Jewish clients in my future role as a consulting engineer.

On October 25, 1959, our second daughter was born. We named her Ronda Beth, after my father's mother, Rudla, and after my sister, Linka, whose Yiddish name was Blima, meaning flower. Two years later, Bernice delivered our third daughter, Arla, on October 30, 1961. Our third daughter was named in memory of Bernice's paternal grandmother, Adel. Her second name became Naddene, in memory of Bernice's uncle Nathan. He had died that year, and Bernice was very fond of him. Our family was complete; I had three beautiful daughters and a beautiful wife. Out of the ashes of Auschwitz and the hell of the Holocaust arose our new family. My father was overjoyed to have three granddaughters of his own.

~

In 1962, after four years at Plan Electric, I decided I would rather be on my own. Although I had graduated as an engineer, my job didn't require engineering skills, and I was getting bored. I liked being a consultant and having to work out new problems on each project. After reviewing a few opportunities that came my way and after meeting with prospective partners, I decided to approach a couple of engineers at H.H. Angus. When I had left the firm, two engineers asked me to stay in touch and told me that if I ever wanted to open a consulting engineering firm, I should call them. I talked to Ed Okins, who was immediately interested, but we needed a third person to round out our expertise and be able to offer a full mechanical and electrical consulting service. Eugene Cuplinskas, who had worked at the firm for years, heard that we were looking for another partner with his particular discipline and we quickly came to an agreement for a partnership.

We opened for business on April 2, 1962, as Okins, Leipciger, Cuplinskas and Associates Ltd. The fact that Ed was a Polish Catholic and Eugene was a Lithuanian Catholic did not matter – what did matter was their mechanical engineering expertise. I knew them well enough to know they were decent and honest. I never experienced any antisemitic sentiments from them, but Ed uttered some stereotypical phrases and referred to the cash register as a "Jewish piano." On one occasion, when we had to lower our fees to get a certain project, he considered that we were "Jewed down" even though the architect was not Jewish. When I pointed out to him that those terms were derogatory, I realized he was completely unaware of their connotations. In a similar way, people use "Gypped" without realizing it is an ethnic slur.

The initial few weeks were fun; we were busy finding a place for an office, buying furniture, setting up a drafting room and office and hiring staff. We still had no work. Ed had been promised projects before we went into business, but they turned out to be just that, promises. I suspected the reason we did not get any work from his old drinking buddies was because of his Jewish partner, but I never voiced it and Ed never suggested that was the reason. After two months without work, we were getting nervous. Then I found out that my friend Joe Godfrey was in the process of hiring an architect to design a luxury apartment building and needed engineers. This became our first project. Ed also managed to get a large industrial plant project through a friend and this connection helped us obtain other work. Slowly, our office grew busy.

A few months after we went into business, my father's wife, Toby, had an operation. Her condition was not life-threatening, but on her return from hospital, she had a massive heart attack and died almost instantly. This premature death changed my father's life and greatly affected us. Two years after Toby died, my father met a woman named Rose through some friends. Rose decided to divorce her husband and marry my father. My father felt flattered by her; she was twenty-five years younger than he was. He did not ask me what he should do, and Rose became his third wife.

About a year after opening our doors for business, we took in David Kaminker as a partner and the firm's name became Okins Leipciger Cuplinskas Kaminker. An unwieldy name, but we became known simply as Okins. Through the firm, I was able to fulfill my professional ambitions and social responsibility. It became a feature of our firm that we did not discriminate against anyone's religion or ethnicity. Our office was a reflection of the immigrant population in Toronto – with each influx of refugees and every world crisis that produced refugees, we were in the forefront, accepting them. We had a working relationship with the Jewish Vocational Services and they brought us excellent people, many of whom became managers and partners. The Vietnamese boat people had a large impact on our firm. We hired people with unrelated experience and trained them to become excellent designers; some went on to get their engineering degrees, while others became partners. When the Soviet Union opened its gates and allowed Jews to leave we took in refugees who became important members of our company and some were with us until retirement. The firm, in time, merged with Mitelman Engineering and expanded, and through this merger, we became one of the first consulting engineering firms to use computer-assisted drafting. The firm assumed the name Leipciger Kaminker Mitelman. The company expanded to a staff of 110, in Toronto and Sudbury. After forty-five years of successful operation, the firm was sold to snc Lavalin in 2007, and continues to function as a division of snc Lavalin with our daughter Lisa at the helm.

The Last Connection

I had kept in contact with my aunts Zosia and Ruzia since 1945, but we hadn't seen each other for two decades. After the war, my aunts had remained in Poland. My father had offered to bring them over after we arrived in Canada, but Zosia wouldn't consider it because she was engaged to the man who had hidden her and saved her life during the war. My father confided in me that he would have married Zosia had she come to Canada. Ruzia and her husband, Antek, also would not leave Poland and Antek's large family. They now lived in Poland as non-Jewish Poles. They had careers and didn't want to start new lives in a new country, and there was no pressure or incentive for them to leave Poland. In the summer of 1965, Bernice and I had planned a trip to Poland but just before departure, I was informed by the Polish consul that I was a *persona non grata* (undesirable), and I was refused an entry visa. In my application I had revealed that I'd been in Poland in 1945 and left soon after, and I suspect this did not sit well with the Polish government of the day. The communist government considered anyone who left Poland after the war a traitor and reactionary.

Instead, we went to Greece for one week, and then to Israel. I am sure my anticipation of Israel was different from Bernice's. To me Israel represented all that other countries could not fully provide – freedom from antisemitism, freedom from persecution, freedom from fear for my life. In 1965, my mental bags were still packed. I still felt very insecure, even in Canada – I did not feel the security I would feel in later years. I was of the opinion that our safety depended on the well-being of the Canadian economy. I felt that antisemitism was everywhere, just below the surface. When we arrived in Israel, I had the unexplained urge to get down on my knees and kiss the ground, which I resisted, but I saw others do it. Even though the state of Israel had existed for seventeen years, I had not absorbed its full meaning and I was surprised and overwhelmed as we stepped down on the tarmac. This was a Jewish state, where you could be free and not worry what the gentiles would think. Here, I felt I was at home, although I had never set foot on the soil before.

That evening, we went for a walk in the neighbourhood. We had chosen the hotel in Tel Aviv based on its price, because after the inexpensive accommodations in Greece, we felt spending four times as much per night was decadent. When we saw prostitutes working the street, we soon realized that our hotel was located in the red light district. We discovered the true nature of a Jewish state – even the hookers were Jewish. I was not surprised; even in the ghetto a Jewish sex trade had existed.

The next day, we met my cousin Cesia Leipciger Freiman, whom I had last seen in Poland in the fall of 1945, on my return to my hometown. She was now married to Salek, whom she had known from Chorzów, and they had a daughter, Hedva. The reunion was emotional. They were not impressed with our choice of hotel and tried to convince us Israel had better ones, but our stay in Tel Aviv was only five days and we didn't intend on spending much time in the hotel. Salek and Cesia were working, so we spent the days on our own. During the day, the streets were full of life. We realized that the garbagemen, the mail carriers and the bus drivers were all Jewish. We felt very comfortable as everyone on the street looked like they could be related to us. We enjoyed walking on the beach and strolling through streets lined with shops of all descriptions. We spent the day wandering through the ruins and excavations of ancient Jaffa and ended up having supper in a small fish restaurant on the waterfront.

In Jerusalem, we stayed in a modest but much more expensive hotel. We could only visit New Jerusalem; the Jordanians occupied the Old City. Wire fences divided streets; armed guards were stationed on the old citadel walls looking down on us with their guns aimed at no one in particular. Even though it had been twenty years since my liberation, the view of the guards, the barbed wire and the guns pointing at us evoked painful memories. This time, though, I was not behind the barbed wires, and I was free. The Jewish Quarter, the western wall of the Temple, the university and hospital were inaccessible to us. Although we could visit only parts of the old city, walking through the narrow streets worn down through the centuries was exhilarating. The new city built in sand-coloured Jerusalem stones looked magnificent, especially at sunset when the city was enhanced by a golden glow. It felt good to be in Jerusalem. We walked for hours and enjoyed every bit of what we saw.

~

As Expo '67 neared, we decided to bring Zosia and Ruzia from Poland for a visit and take them to Montreal. Since we couldn't go to Poland, we thought bringing them to Canada would be even better. I envisioned it as a fantastic reunion, though it was hard to anticipate how I would feel when we met. It would be twenty-two years since I had last seen them, when I had been a young man of seventeen. We made the arrangements for them to come to Canada. They could get travel papers only for themselves, provided their husbands stayed behind in Poland.

The time came and we picked them up at the airport and brought them home. On opening the door our three daughters greeted my aunts in unison with the refrain, "Polske Ogórki." My aunts were perplexed as to why they were being greeted as Polish Pickles. I had to explain that the girls wanted to say something in Polish to make them feel at home and the only thing they knew was what they read on a jar of Polish pickles.

The next day, my father and Rose came and we had a family reunion. We spoke for hours in Polish; my Polish was that of a teenager's, unsophisticated, but Rose knew even less and her pronunciation was with a heavy accent since she came from a small town and spoke mainly Yiddish. We reminisced about our life before and during the war, painful memories that revived our suffering. It seemed that time had not healed the deep wounds of loss. For the previous twenty years, no one had been interested in hearing about the war, and no one was prepared to talk about it. In 1961, the trial of Eichmann in Jerusalem had made headlines and spurred some interest, but many survivors still did not speak about the Holocaust.

I knew that Ruzia had married Antek after my grandmother's death just before the war, in a civil ceremony. I did not suspect that she and Zosia had converted until Ruzia's purse fell to the ground and her rosary fell out. They explained that they both became Catholic to make life easier for their husbands' families. They did, however, go to their mother's grave on Rosh Hashanah and fasted on Yom Kippur. Their mother's grave was all they had left of their entire family; they didn't know where their father was buried. They didn't know how we would feel about the conversion and perhaps hadn't thought it was important to tell us. We assured them that it didn't matter, as long as it made sense to them. They were relieved.

⁓

My involvement in Jewish religious life happened almost by accident. Before having children, we had little interest in attending synagogue other than on high holidays. However, when Lisa was in kindergarten, we thought that she should be going to religious school, and it was natural for us to join the nearest synagogue, which was Beth El, a conservative synagogue with a liberal outlook. Coincidentally, it was the same synagogue that our friend Joe Godfrey, who had sold us our first house, kept asking us to join. No sooner had I joined than I was asked to participate in synagogue activities, the most interesting of which was the Education Committee. My Hebrew school experience had been unpleasant, and I wanted to make sure the same type of experience was not forced on my children. I wanted the education offered in our synagogue to give students a good grounding in Hebrew language and religious education. I agreed to go on the education committee and after one year, I was elected as the chair. The next few years saw me advance from education chair to vice-president.

In 1968, our synagogue underwent a crisis as our religious layleader and congregation debated changing affiliation from conservative to reform. This resulted in the departure of the conservative members, and our merger with the congregation of Temple Emanu-El, which had been struggling with a small membership. Three years after the merger, I became president of Temple Emanu-El. The two years I served as president changed my outlook and my role in the community. I became more self-assured and less afraid to take on responsibilities. Bernice and my family aided my personal development. Many long and involved discussions with Rabbi Bielfeld and his teachings broadened my understanding of what it was to be a modern Jew. All this helped me to overcome the *galut* (exile) mentality that I carried with me from Europe. I stopped packing my mental bags; my fear of a recurrence of the Shoah receded. Our children were now teenagers and I had started to look at their lives in comparison to my experiences at their age. There was no comparison. I learned to move on from the images of the past and to look to the future with even more optimism.

~

During the fall of 1972, Ronda was preparing for her bat mitzvah. Two weeks before the occasion, Rose called me to tell me that my father was in the hospital. My father had had a massive stroke that left him in a coma. My world suddenly changed. The prognosis was not good. My stepbrother Benny Waxman, who by that time was a physician, spoke to the doctor in charge, who held out no hope of total recovery. At best, he would be severely handicapped, without speech, and most likely confined to a wheelchair.

After one week, my father seemed to come out of it. He was responding to my words and he squeezed my hand as a sign of recognition. I was there when the nurse came by with some water; he took a sip, coughed and instantly fell back into a coma, from which he did not recover. He died two days later during the night, when Rose was with him. When my Uncle Dave had had a stroke, during his prolonged rehabilitation my father had said he hoped for a quick death if that should happen to him. My father had his wish.

The sudden death of my father was the most traumatic experience for me since the Shoah. Part of my life ended as well. He was the last connection to what I still considered "home." I owed my survival to him. He was not only my father, but also my friend, and although we had grown somewhat apart, the bond was always there. We were brothers in suffering and had experiences not commonly shared by father and son. Our relationship after the war was also unusual, and many events and experiences were sealed in our memories. I loved him dearly; although we never declared our love for each other in words, we knew how we felt about each other and indirectly confirmed our feelings. We communicated our feelings by touch, a squeeze of the hand. Whenever I was sick and he visited me, he would just squeeze my hand and that was enough for me.

Until his death, my father was the spokesperson for the past; he talked about our experiences from his point of view. I never corrected his narrative. He spoke mostly in Yiddish, was a good speaker and generally told the stories accurately as we both remembered them. He respected my "secrets" as they were, and we never reminisced about events that only concerned me. He never mentioned that he was a police officer in the ghetto and I never asked him about it. Nor did he speak of the time that I provided him with food, and although that bothered me, I never spoke of it either.

A couple of years before his death, I spoke to the confirmation class at Beth El synagogue and one student wanted to know if I believed in God while I was in the concentration camps. I told them that I did, but that my belief in God was very simple and I did not question it at that time. I was curious to know if my father had believed. I asked and he responded in Yiddish, "Silly boy, how do you think we survived? I prayed every day, and that's why we managed to survive." As a boy, my father had studied in a yeshiva until he was sixteen years old. He knew most of the daily prayers by heart. After the war, when we were in Bamberg, he was one of the people instrumental in establishing a small synagogue. His faith was never shaken, which surprised me greatly. On his death, I re-examined my relationship with him before the war. I loved him dearly, but it had not always been like that.

After the death of my father, and thirty years after the war, the experiences of Auschwitz-Birkenau started to feel like nightmares and not real experiences. I considered trying once more to go back to Poland, also because my aunts were getting older and I wanted to see them again. It was also very important to me that Bernice see a bit of Poland, at least the part in which I grew up. I applied for a Polish visa, only this time I did not volunteer the information that I had been back in Poland after the war. We received our visas, and in the summer of 1975, we were on our way to Germany and Poland.

We landed in Frankfurt am Main and rented a car. I was apprehensive that when we arrived at the Polish border there might be some information about my first refused visa that I failed to mention in my second application. For this reason, I scheduled the arrival at the Czechoslovakian-Polish border on a Sunday, hoping that the Warsaw immigration office would be closed and they would not be able to check my previous records.

We drove to Prague, set to enjoy a few days in this beautiful city crowded with historic castles, ancient buildings and old synagogues and cemeteries. Prague, once a vibrant city with over a thousand-year Jewish history, was a skeleton of its former Jewish life. A number of synagogues were filled with ritual objects that Hitler had confiscated from various synagogues of Europe and planned to display in a museum of the "vanished people." The Old-New synagogue, dating back centuries, which had been the spiritual home for untold thousands of families, now served a few old men. We were told it was a constant struggle to get a minyan of ten men to say the evening prayers. They depended on visiting Jews to fill the synagogue for holidays and daily prayers. I only vaguely remembered the city that I once went through as a young man on my way back to Germany in 1945. At that time, I was not interested in its beauty – I had only wanted to leave it as soon as possible to be reunited with my father. Now the city lay before us in its diminished splendour, deteriorating for the last thirty years under the communist regime. Our guide, an electrical engineering graduate, told us in hushed tones of the hardship of his life, that he was guiding to make ends meet and to share his love of the city's past glory with tourists for a few dollars in tips. We met some elderly Jews who had once had a good life there but were now dependent on the communal kitchen for their daily meal, a kitchen that was supported by foreign visitors. We left most of the Kronen we had with them.

On Sunday morning, we left Prague and arrived at the Polish border midday. All the cars in front of us were waved through. An officer took our papers, examined them for a minute and asked us to park our car. We were ushered into a separate room and left by ourselves. I was nervous that they had found out about my refusal ten years prior. After an hour, I became concerned and criticized myself for risking the life we had established in Canada. I told Bernice that if I was detained or arrested, she should get in touch with an influential Member of Parliament and a member of our synagogue, and ask for help. After two hours, I was beside myself and in a panic. Finally, after three hours, the officer returned with our papers and we were allowed to go on. Our schedule was off; it was late in the afternoon and we still had at least four hours to get to Katowice, where Ruzia and her husband, Antek, lived and where Zosia would join us.

We arrived at my aunt's apartment late in the evening and after a quick and emotional greeting, they took us to a nearby hotel. It was a hotel for railway employees and had no amenities. The beds were cots and the towels were threadbare, and the shower, toilet and sink were communal, and down the hall from our room. The cost per night was equivalent to five dollars. Bernice was horrified and depressed by the surroundings, especially since it was her fortieth birthday, but I didn't want to insult my aunts by complaining. We stayed the night and didn't get much sleep; every few minutes a train would come rattling through, sounding as if it went right through our bedroom. That was it; I agreed with Bernice that this was unacceptable even in Poland. I asked my aunts if there was another hotel with more amenities. They told us that a better hotel would cost twenty-five or thirty dollars per night, which was enough money for them to live on for a month. We decided to move to another hotel, but felt guilty for giving in to our selfish comforts to which we had become accustomed. We asked them to take us to their bank, opened special US accounts in their names and deposited a sum of American dollars, on which they could live for many months, that could also be used in specific government stores to obtain goods not available for their local currency. Now we could enjoy our stay in an international hotel, which was still third class, but at least was clean and had a private bathroom.

Ruzia and Antek's apartment consisted of one room with a small kitchen across a common corridor, which they shared with another couple. Their neighbours didn't know my aunts' Jewish background, and anytime we spoke of our family, they closed the windows and doors, in spite of the oppressive heat of the summer. Their room, although large, appeared small, as it was crowded with oversized furniture bearing Antek's family crest. Antek was a member of a Polish aristocratic family, which, in communist Poland, was a mark against him. In addition, he had been a member of the élite military Polish Legion before the war, which was outlawed by the Communist government. Those two facts were considered reactionary and consequently, although he'd had a professorship designation before the war in the Katowice Polytechnic, afterward he was given the position of lab demonstrator and lecturer. Before the war, Ruzia had a good position in the state fertilizer monopoly. As she was not politically active, she was rehired in a similar position, which had given her access to a very good retirement program with benefits not available to most governmental positions. At the time of our visit, they were both retired.

My aunts actually thought that communism was good for the country – no one had much, but everyone shared what little there was. They took pride in the accomplishments of the communist regime, a view I did not share. The Polish communist government was very antisemitic, and we could not celebrate their accomplishments. The Poland of my youth was gone. My family was destroyed, all our possessions gone. It was still painful to speak of the family we lost.

Our aunts wanted to take us to Warsaw because they were proud that although it was destroyed in 1939 and again in 1943 and 1944, it was totally rebuilt according to the original design and styles. I couldn't participate in their enthusiasm – we had come to be with my aunts and not to visit Poland as tourists. How could I go to Warsaw and see a new city built on the ruins of the destroyed ghetto? I didn't want to hurt them so I made the excuse that it was too far, and we agreed to go with them to Krakow instead. Krakow is a medieval city that was never destroyed. I knew of the Jewish district of Kazimierz and I wanted to visit it even though I was told the old synagogues were partially destroyed and abandoned. To please my aunts, we visited the Wawel castle, but they wouldn't take us to the former Jewish district. They were afraid to be seen there by the communist agents who monitored the area, worried their Jewish roots would be discovered. In view of the 1968 anti-Jewish political propaganda campaign that had resulted in thousands of Jews emigrating from Poland, this was a justified fear. We wanted them to accompany us to Auschwitz-Birkenau but they refused; they were afraid it would be too emotional for them.

We also visited my former residence in Chorzów, where nothing seemed to have changed. We took pictures and I noticed that although our old accommodations were far from luxurious, this had been a place of happiness and joy. We travelled up the hill to the park where my family had spent May Day celebrations and outings. For the first time I became aware how large that park really was and that as a child, I had explored only a very small section of it. After four days with my aunts and uncle Antek, we left, knowing this reunion could be the last time we would be together.

Before our trip to Auschwitz-Birkenau began, I was terrified, not knowing what to expect. I was afraid of reliving the painful moment of separation from my sister and mother and disturbing the old wounds. We started out at the Stammlager (main camp) of Auschwitz, which had been turned into a museum. One room was filled to the ceiling with hair. I had to do my utmost to control my emotions; I imagined that somewhere in the mountain of human hair was the hair of my sister and my mother. Each lock of hair had belonged to an individual, an individual with hopes and aspirations for a full life that had been brutally cut down. The next room had a mountain of shoes: men's shoes, women's shoes, children's shoes and baby shoes. Each pair represented a human being who had walked in innocently, trusting humankind, only to be murdered in cold blood. Other rooms were filled with different objects, such as cooking utensils, shaving brushes, eyeglasses, prostheses and Jewish prayer shawls. My chest felt as if it would burst from pain and anger. Over the last thirty years I had read many books about the Shoah and seen many of the iconic photographs of the objects displayed in front of us, but to see them in actuality evoked a new and painful emotion.

One of the buildings displayed hundreds of photographs of former prisoners; very few of them had Jewish faces or names, and this disturbed me terribly. How could it be? Why were there no pictures of the hundreds of thousands of Jews who were brought here? It was obvious to me that the Communist regime considered Auschwitz-Birkenau to be a Polish memorial of resistance and heroism, considering the victims as fighters against fascism and capitalism. The situation was incongruous – the articles I had just seen exhibited belied the presentation of hundreds of photographs of Polish males as being the main prisoners of Auschwitz. Years later, I found out that until 1942 the majority of prisoners in Auschwitz were there for being politically active in the underground movement and were mainly Polish-Christian, although there were a few Jews among them. After 1942, the situation changed and by 1944, most prisoners were Jewish. These facts were totally hidden, as it did not fit into the Polish Communist narrative.

We left Auschwitz, I dejected and sorrowful. We drove the three kilometres to Auschwitz II-Birkenau. The view of the gates, the railway tracks and the memories of this place paralyzed my mind and tears welled up in my eyes. I was seeing it all from a very different perspective. We climbed the stairs into the gatehouse tower to the observation room, where we could see the entire camp. This view was not one we could see as prisoners. I never knew the enormity of the camp. This, without a doubt, was a huge murder factory. No one could dispute it. It was overwhelming.

The women's camp, with dozens of brick barracks, stretched out to the left. Through the centre of the camp ran a rail-line, which I did not remember seeing. I remembered disembarking on a railway siding in the middle of nowhere. Could my memory be that mistaken? On the right side of us stood a row of barracks. I remembered our barrack was toward the centre of the camp but closer to the latrines. Beyond these barracks were dozens of chimneys as far as we could see. These were the remnants of the housing barracks and kitchens.

We listened to the audio guide tape in English and in Polish. The English tape explained that the railway line into the camp was built in 1944 to receive Hungarian Jews and other nationals. The Polish tape enumerated the nations from which the victims came but did not mention that they were Jewish. It described the murder of four million people of various nationalities from all over Europe (which was wrong, later research put the number at 1.5 million), but there was no mention that 90 per cent of the victims were Jewish. It appeared as if the Jews of Europe who were murdered here never existed. The Nazis robbed us of our lives; the Polish communist regime robbed us of our identities.

We walked the one-kilometre road from the gate to the memorial and ruins of gas chambers ii and iii. Nineteen plaques in different languages announced that the Nazis murdered four million people here. The monument, although massive, did not mention the murder of children, just men and women, as if this massive crime had not occurred. Children had been brought here with no chance for survival and were taken directly to the gas chambers. The plaque on the main memorial extolled the heroism of the people against Hitler's fascists and was decorated with the Grunwald Cross, the highest Polish military honour. This was hardly a fitting monument to the innocent civilian men, women and children. I left Birkenau for the second time in thirty-two years, only this time as a free man. I swore that I would never return. I was completely emotionally exhausted.

We next travelled through the Carpathian Mountains to Zakopane, a once famous resort area frequented by Jews. The trip to Auschwitz and the memories had depressed me; I was unable to function and had to go to bed. Bernice became concerned and called for a doctor who examined me and could not find anything wrong. It took me two days to regain my will to carry on. We spent two more days in the beautiful Carpathian Mountains and drove over the mountain pass into Czechoslovakia. We arrived in a small village at dusk and we stopped at the only hotel and tried to obtain a room; the hotel was obviously empty, but we were told that all the rooms were reserved and that nothing was available for "you" meaning "you Jews." It was the only hotel for miles. We finally did get a room in a small guest-house. The next morning we travelled through Bratislava and crossed over the border into Austria. After leaving the communist area, it felt as though I was liberated again.

As I Remembered

I had thought that the death of my father would separate the past from the future, but it did not. The past, and my memories of the Shoah, drove me to do many things and continued to govern my decisions and actions in various areas of my life. I had been given another chance for life and believed I should live it as fully as possible. It was in 1973 that I took up sailing, and for twenty years it took up a major amount of my spare time. I was lucky that Bernice went along with my newfound passion, even though she did not particularly like sailing. It was a concession on her part, which I did not always recognize, and was somewhat selfish of me.

By 1975, I was quite involved in the Jewish community and in synagogue life. Four years later, our good friend Joy Cohen, a member of Holy Blossom Temple and of the Toronto Jewish Congress's Yom HaShoah (Holocaust Remembrance Day) Committee, suggested that I be on this committee and gave my name to Rabbi Mark Shapiro, the chair. I was asked to meet the committee and see if I would consider serving on it, and I soon became a member. I didn't know any of the people, including the survivors. Through all my years in Canada, I hadn't had much contact with other survivors. I moved in other circles socially and professionally, and felt I had little in common with survivors. I considered them a part of my father's generation, even though some of them were only a few years older than me. I identified with the second generation, children of Holocaust survivors who, although much younger than me, had a similar education and interests and were more assimilated into Canadian culture.

In 1982, Rabbi Mark Shapiro asked me to join him at a meeting to discuss the construction of the future Toronto Jewish Congress building. Eventually, this also led him to ask me to create and chair a committee for a Holocaust Memorial Centre, which would be included in the building. A week later, I met with architect Jerome Markson to review his proposal for the space. It was obvious it was much too small for a walk-through type of exhibit used in other museums, such as Yad Vashem. One way to solve the issue was to project pictures on a wall, which I believed would be appropriate for our exhibit. In the centre of the proposed space was a round room that Jerome envisioned as a commemorative area. The project intrigued me and I was excited by its possibilities. I had never undertaken such a venture and spent a few sleepless nights thinking about what to do with this enormous task that lay before me.

At the next building committee meeting, with butterflies in my stomach, I proposed that we hire Morley Markson – whom I knew from my youth, and who had designed a well-received exhibit at Expo '67 – to prepare an outline for the centre, and my suggestion was accepted. I was informed, however, that my committee would be responsible for fundraising. Two months later, armed with a proposal and budget, I went to a meeting with the president of the Toronto Jewish Congress (TJC) and the executive director. They approved the project and told me to go ahead and raise the funds – the president suggested I raise one million dollars. Overseeing the construction of the project was in my line of professional expertise but I had never been comfortable raising funds because I considered refusals as personal rejections.

The executive director expressed doubts the project would ever get off the ground and forbid his staff to provide any assistance; I was also told I could not involve the TJC staff in the fundraising or construction of the project. Nevertheless, Ruth Resnick, the director of the Remembrance Day committee, offered to help on her own time and she gave me suggestions of people who could form a fundraising committee. I met with some prominent community members and we had a pleasant evening, but no one was prepared to chair the fundraising committee.

Only a few weeks after Rabbi Shapiro's request that I chair the committee for the newly formed Holocaust Memorial Centre, he was appointed to a pulpit in the United States. I received a call from Wilfred Posluns, president of the Toronto Jewish Congress, who asked me to assume the chairmanship of the Holocaust Remembrance Committee. I protested that I had just assumed this great responsibility to create the Holocaust Memorial Centre and that I could not manage both. I don't know what Rabbi Shapiro told Wilfred about me, but he expressed his confidence in my ability do both. He overcame all my objections and doubts and I agreed to consider accepting the position. By this time, I had a good grasp of the workings of the committee and all of its sub-committees. I had another meeting with Ruth Resnick, a very accomplished professional whose opinion I respected very much. She convinced me to accept the position. She was my major advisor and morale booster.

In 1983, Ruth Resnick and I went to the Gathering of American Holocaust Survivors in Washington, D.C., and for the first time I felt like a member of the survivors' community. There were survivors of my generation involved, and the event was an eye-opener; my previous perception of not belonging to the survivor community had been just that, a perception. The meeting attracted thousands of survivors from all over the States, Canada and other countries. Elie Wiesel was among the prominent speakers. The Gathering included government officials, Members of Congress, the vice-president of the United States and the Canadian Ambassador to the United States, Allan Gotlieb. At this meeting, I met many of the Toronto Holocaust survivors who later became members on my committees.

At the gathering in Washington, the idea of a Canadian Gathering occurred to me. In 1985, I introduced the idea to the national chair of the Holocaust Remembrance Committee of the Canadian Jewish Congress (CJC). He accepted the idea, but months went by and he did not do anything. Sharon Weintraub, a member of the second generation and a member of my committee, asked me to assume the chairmanship of the gathering and I eventually agreed to assume the co-chairmanship with Mendel Good of Ottawa. My first step was to convince some Holocaust survivors to support the project financially. I approached some of the survivors who were at the gathering in Washington and easily obtained ten preliminary pledges. Armed with these pledges, I went to see Milton Harris, president of CJC, and presented him with my proposal. At first, he hesitated, but soon he recognized the viability of the project and offered the help of his professional staff to make it a national event.

Mendel Good and I met with survivors and second-generation groups in Ottawa, Toronto and Montreal and committees were formed to deal with the various aspects of the Gathering. I asked Gerda Frieberg to become the entertainment chairperson and she convinced professional entertainers to volunteer their services. We hired Srul Irving Glick to compose and arrange special music for the event. In the end, we had a fantastic gathering, including a public meeting in front of the Parliament Building with speeches from the deputy prime minister, both leaders of the opposition and other prominent officials. The event attracted more than two thousand attendees for the opening ceremony and even more registered for the entire three-day program. From a portion of the surplus funds, I was able to establish the videotaping of Holocaust Survivors' Stories. I hired historian and educator Paula Draper to educate interviewers and prepare the interview questionnaire. Over the next few years, we recorded more than three hundred survivors' stories.

Meanwhile, after a number of unsuccessful attempts to find a fundraising chair for the Holocaust Memorial Centre, Ruth Resnick suggested that I approach Gerda Frieberg. Gerda agreed to do the fund-raising provided she could take over the Holocaust Memorial Centre committee. I agreed and Gerda threw herself into the project. We worked closely together; we had gained mutual respect and confidence in each other from planning and creating the 1985 Gathering. Morley Markson accumulated some 3,500 black-and-white images of old photographic slides from various sources. Gerda and I insisted we review each slide to be included in the final program. We agonized over each one – many brought back memories for both of us. Out of the thousands of images, we chose ones that created a stream of memories that would be enshrined and thus become icons of the presentation.

The funds for the centre were slow in coming. Together we organized parlour meetings in people's houses and involved personalities such as Stephen Lewis, my stepbrother Al Waxman and others. We prepared lists of items needed in the centre and allowed people to sponsor various items. We established a policy that no living people's names were to be displayed in the centre except for on a donors' plaque at the exit door.

The circular room in the middle of the centre was designed by Jerome Markson as a shrine with a Star of David on the ceiling, surrounded by clerestory windows showing only the sky and introducing daylight into the space. The centre of the star was designed for a hanging light, a *Ner Tamid*, eternal light, that would be "on" all the time. We thought this circular room would be well suited to display plaques with the names of lost family members. Most families had erected monuments in cemeteries, and as the centre was not yet established, it was not a place of prestige that attracted donations. In the end, we were able to reduce the required donation to a nominal amount due to Gerda's successful appeals to the Ontario government and the German government to make substantial donations. In 1986, the centre opened its doors to the public and has since attracted nearly 20,000 students and other visitors yearly. In the year 2000, the governor general of Canada awarded both Gerda and myself a Meritorious Service Medal for the creation of the centre.

In 1988, I was able to convince a member of our committee, Robbie Engel, to take over the chair of the Holocaust Remembrance Committee. Coincidentally, I was appointed by the CJC president, Les Scheininger, to the executive of the CJC as chairperson of the National Holocaust Remembrance Committee (NHRC). Becoming a member of the executive introduced me to the greater organized Jewish community. The Canadian Jewish Congress was a national organization, involved in advocacy and representing Jewish community interests. My role was to bring a Holocaust survivor's point of view to the executive and to engage in furthering Holocaust education in Canada. The NHRC staff person was Josh Rotblatt, a prince of a fellow. The NHRC received a grant from the federal government to produce and distribute eight videos of Holocaust survivors' stories to various secondary school boards. Each video was accompanied by a written lesson plan for high school students. The material was well received and the videos reached a wide audience across Canada.

⁓

In the fall of 1990, I received a call from CJC president Les Scheininger and vice-president Moshe Ronen. They had been meeting with the Polish government on some other matter when they found out about the establishment of an International Council of the Auschwitz-Birkenau State Museum. I was asked if I would be interested in participating and if I would be prepared to go to Poland in three days. The last time I had been in Poland was in 1975 and at that time, I swore I would never return. Of course, things had changed since that time – the Communist government was no longer in power and there seemed to be a change in attitude of the new Polish government toward Israel in particular and the Jews in general. After the fall of the Communist government in 1989, the Jewish community became very interested in commemorating the site of Auschwitz-

Birkenau, and rightly so. Now Poland was having its first free election and Solidarność, the trade union movement and party, was vying for power. I wanted to challenge my impression from 1975, so I accepted without hesitation. To my surprise and relief, my son-in-law Cary Green offered to join me.

On arrival in Warsaw, we saw walls covered with antisemitic graffiti, some of which accused one of the leading candidates of having Jewish roots. Casting these aspersions was enough to disadvantage the candidate and there was suspicion one of the other candidates had fabricated the information. This showed that even though there were few Jews in Poland, there was still latent antisemitism. President Walesa's support group was accused but he denied any responsibility and, after the elections, he was the first Polish president to appear before the Knesset, the Israeli parliament. He assured Israelis he was not an antisemite and apologized for any wrongs the Polish people had committed during the war.

My membership on the International Auschwitz Council was reaffirmed by the prime minister of the Republic of Poland. Twenty-eight representatives from around the world attended a conference in the former administration building of the SS camp establishment. On entering the building, I noticed a wall with photographs displaying various dignitaries and political leaders who had visited the Auschwitz museum in the last few years. All of the people in the display were identified by their name, title of office and the country they represented. Out of the dozens of pictures, only one person was identified as prime minister, but it did not show what country he represented. That person was the prime minister of Israel. This indicated that the state of Israel had not been recognized by the Communist government and that the museum still adhered to this policy. I brought this to the attention of the museum director, who apologized profusely and claimed that it was a simple oversight. But the next day, rather than adding the identification, the picture was removed.

The first time I had come back to Auschwitz-Birkenau, in 1975, there was nothing I could do to change the problems I saw, and I had left with utter disgust, certain I would never return. This time, I looked at the area with great care to see all the problems the council would have to deal with. As a former prisoner of Auschwitz II, or Birkenau, and having obtained a wide array of information in the intervening years through extensive reading and study on Auschwitz and the Shoah, I was now able to identify which statements were misleading. This was especially challenging at a time when Holocaust deniers like Ernst Zündel and James Keegstra in Canada, and David Irving in Britain, were on a campaign claiming that the murder of six million was a Jewish fabrication. For forty-five years, the Polish government had denied the victims of the Holocaust their identity. To the Communist government, people brought to Auschwitz from France were Frenchmen, regardless of their religion. They purposely ignored the truth – that the only reason these people were brought to Auschwitz to be murdered was that they were Jewish – to suit their ideology. Only one photographic billboard showing the arrival of Hungarians in Birkenau was identified as "Hungarian Jews."

At the conference, Sigmund Sobolewski, one of the earliest former prisoners, who had the number 88 on his arm, tabled a whole list of inconsistencies: the exhibits were not identified; there was no indication that the items were brought from Birkenau and were taken from Jewish victims before or after being murdered in the gas chamber. Barrack 27 was turned into a Jewish museum and memorial showing the crucial events of the history of the Shoah with iconic images. It told the story adequately, given the limited space, however, it included some unfortunate generalizations; this was later corrected. A memorial at the exit was a replica of a Warsaw ghetto bunker, invoking the struggle and sacrifice of the ghetto fighters. There, some visitors chanted the mournful tune of Kaddish.

There was still the large monument I had seen last time, bearing the Grunwald medal and dedicated to men and women (with no mention of the children) as heroes who opposed fascism. In front were the same inscriptions on nineteen brass tablets that announced the murder of four million people. Research by many scholars, including Mr. Piper, a member of the Auschwitz research team, concluded that 1.5 million people were murdered and not the four million the plaques indicated – this gave the revisionists and Holocaust deniers more fuel for their arguments. These tablets were inscribed in nineteen different languages, including Hebrew and Yiddish, indicating that the Jews were one group among all the other nations whose citizens were murdered here. The explanation for this, from the museum administration, was that since the Communist regime did not recognize any religion, only the nationality of the victims was displayed.

At the end of the camp at Birkenau, a large area was identified as the Field of Ashes. This field contains the buried ashes from the crematoria and it was also the place where bodies of the victims were burned on pyres when the crematoria were unable to burn the massive numbers. The first victims of mass murder by gassing were buried in mass graves; these remains were eventually exhumed and burned. Polish Boy Scouts had erected crosses in this field, without any control by the museum directorate. The Jewish community objected, as most of the victims were Jewish. The scouts then tried to solve the problem by hanging large Stars of David on the crosses.

The martyrdom of Christian individuals was prominently displayed but there were no memorials specifically for Jewish victims. Even the heroic uprising of the *Sonderkommando* men on October 7, 1944, was not noted, and although Sigmund Sobolewski had witnessed the revolt and ensuing massacre of the *Sonderkommando*, the International Council did not appoint him to the council. When Sobolewski presented a painting and a plaque commemorating the uprising, the museum refused to display them and put them in storage.

The ruins in Birkenau were crumbling and, if left unsupported, would soon dissolve into dust. Signs were misleading, referring to ruins by the Nazi designation "crematorium" instead of "gas chamber and crematorium," disguising the true nature of the building. The fields of ashes and the pond of ashes, "Kanada" and other camp areas were not identified and their significance was not explained. Most signs were in Polish only; some had very poor English translations. Only in two instances was Hebrew or Yiddish used.

~

After the conference, Cary hired a car and driver and we went to Sosnowiec and the Środula ghetto. I was amazed that I could remember almost every detail. In Sosnowiec, I took Cary to the apartment house where we had lived in 1939 and to the building that we had lived in 1942 in the open ghetto. I walked the streets as if it was a few days ago, rather than fifty-one years. Little had changed in the interval, except that the buildings were in terrible disrepair. We tried to find the factory where I had worked but the area had been converted into a pedestrian mall.

We travelled to the ghetto in Środula, taking the same route I had walked daily from the factory in Sosnowiec. Środula lay in ruins, most of the houses falling apart due to neglect; Polish peasants occupied a few of the buildings still standing. The ghetto office building was also in ruins; only some structural elements remained. We climbed up the perilous structure and found remains of nails on the gateposts of rooms where *mezuzahs* were once affixed. A man approached us and wanted to know if we were interested in purchasing the site.

We left with a mixture of bitterness and sadness. From there we drove for hours through Galicia to find Józefów, the hometown of Cary's grandfather Lipa Green (formerly Gruenwald) and some other family members. In the village of Józefów, we found a woman who remembered the Gruenwald family and directed us to a local teacher who took us around to the cemetery and synagogue. The cemetery still had a fence but was overgrown and headstones had been removed. Apparently, the Nazis and local people used the headstones as paving stones, foundations and other things. Next, he took us to a forest where, in 1942, the Einsatzgruppen assembled almost the entire

Jewish population of men, women and children and marched them into the forest and shot them. This provided a tragic and painful closure to Cary's family's existence in eastern Poland.

~

Over my next fifteen years on the International Auschwitz Council, most meetings took two days, requiring us to stay overnight. On one occasion the meeting took place on Friday, and I had to stay over Shabbat in Auschwitz. I was billeted in the German youth hostel, a very spartan facility but clean and bright. The thought of spending a Friday evening in Auschwitz in a German youth hostel made me shudder and I felt anger and regret that I had decided to stay. However, it turned out quite differently from how I'd envisioned.

With me were Sigmund Sobolewski and Jonathan Webber. Sigmund, as I mentioned, was a survivor of the first transport to Auschwitz. In 1940, when he was seventeen years old, the Nazis had come to arrest his father, who was an officer in the Polish army. Since his father was not home, they arrested Sigmund instead. He, along with more than one hundred men from the Tarnów region, was the first to be brought to Auschwitz. Among the group were some Jews, but they were not singled out as such, since they had been arrested for political activities. He told me the harrowing story of his treatment and conditions at the camp on arrival. He eventually became a firefighter, which gave him a privileged status.

Jonathan Webber was a professor of social anthropology at Oxford. Together we lit candles, made Kiddush over the wine and a blessing over the bread. Of all the Jewish members on the council, I identified with Jonathan the most and our views coincided on most aspects regarding the museum policy and work. The other members were of my father's generation and we had little in common, except that we were survivors of Auschwitz. On Saturday, we visited the old town of Oświęcim and discovered remnants of Jewish life in the town; before the war the town had been about 30 per cent Jewish.

Whenever I visited Birkenau alone, the events of years past came to me as if they had occurred yesterday. The silence that surrounded me on those occasions was shattered by the sounds in my head, as I slowly walked toward the gas chambers. I relived our family's arrival and selection on a similar ramp located halfway between Auschwitz I and Birkenau. I relived the painful separation on the ramp. I relived the selection and the courageous act by my father. I relived the horrendous and devastating news of what was happening to our people. I relived my miraculous rescue. I relived the days in the transition camp, the weekly selections and the fearful hiding. I relived the terrible screams and the sight of the women on trucks driven past our camp to their deaths in the gas chamber.

Any place I walked I could be walking on the ashes of our people. The pain in my chest mounted, and I often sat down on the steps of the memorial and cried. I would sit there for a while, unable to move. Voices of people passing me would bring me back to the present, my family and our life in Canada, and my spirits would rise. At the memorial, people lit candles. One day I was there at sunset, the red sun setting behind the memorial; the red sky reminded me of the clouds illuminated crimson by the flames of the crematoria.

It took time to change the memorial tablets with the wrong information on them and add new ones. It took several meetings before we all agreed on a suitable inscription and years before the tablets were cast and mounted. Over time, in meeting with the staff of the museum, I noticed a marked difference from the early days: the overt antisemitism was gone. The new political reality in Poland manifested itself in the way the museum and government employees were more cooperative and accommodating. However, the government was in financial straits – any proposed changes that cost money would take years to implement. I appealed to the council to make a timetable. I felt that without a timetable, no one could judge the progress of the required changes.

One of the continued problems we had to deal with was the Carmelite Convent. In 1984, before the fall of the Communist government, the Carmelite nuns, at the request of the Sisters of Our Lady of Sion, were granted a long lease to use the former theatre as a convent. According to some wartime reports, the former theatre was allegedly used by the Nazis to store the canisters of Zyklon B gas. The Jewish community had previously raised objections to the convent being there and asked the communist government to rescind the perpetual lease granted to the nuns. The government refused. Knowing they would have little or no influence on that government, they next appealed to several church leaders to intervene and relocate the convent.

According to the museum administration, there was a lot of misunderstanding about the convent. The theatre, located in a separate building, was not part of the camp itself, being located outside the high brick prison walls. The building could not be accessed from within the camp, nor was it visible unless one knew exactly where it was. Some people claimed the convent was located next to the gas chambers and crematoria; however, it was located outside the camp itself and on the opposite end. The controversy arose when the sisters expressed their desire to be close to the camp's grounds to pray for the salvation of the souls of the non-Jewish and Jewish victims. This was, understandably, an outrage to the Jewish community, for any Christian group to pray for the salvation of Jewish souls.

Over the years, there were various protests by Jewish leaders regarding the location of the convent and a large papal cross that the convent had erected. There were some altercations and the Polish press claimed that a rabbi and his group tried to invade the convent and attack the nuns, whereas, in my opinion, the group was trying to engage in debate. A war of words ensued and tempers flared on both sides. The convent was eventually relocated in 1993; however, the land was subleased to an arch antisemite who, along with a radical group, erected 152 crosses for the 152 Poles executed in the gravel yard located next to the theatre building and held weekly prayer meetings there. These crosses were eventually removed by order of the state; now, only the one papal cross remains.

In the following years, problems arose when a report was published that the antisemite who rented the theatre was attempting to build a shopping centre, restaurant and hotel across from the main gate to Auschwitz I. Images of a huge, American-type shopping centre and boisterous parties in the hotel and restaurant were imagined. Some thought a nightclub and dance hall would be included. People claimed that the sanctity of the area just outside the camp would be permanently destroyed. Heated discussions in the Western media took place and things were blown out of proportion. On my next visits I went to the sites and found that the "shopping centre" was a small food store that had replaced a rundown market, and the restaurant was a coffee shop frequented by the bus drivers who sat for hours in the front parking lot of the museum waiting for their passengers. The museum administration welcomed the additions and changes. I did not visit the new hotel but could not imagine it being worse than the only other hotel at the railway station.

The following years saw a lot of changes and improvements. By the time I left the Council in 2006, after serving for fifteen years, most of our original ideas had been implemented, as were other innovations. My knowledge of Auschwitz had increased and I attained a level of expertise that was very helpful in my later work with the March of the Living.

My Past and My Future

In 1991, I thought it would be fitting for survivors, their children and Canadian Jews to go to Poland in 1993 for the commemoration of the fiftieth anniversary of the Warsaw Ghetto Uprising. I proposed the idea at a board meeting of the Canadian Jewish Congress, and the board agreed to organize it. The trip became known as the "Presidents' Mission to Poland and Israel." The original aim was to have 120 participants but in the end, 163 people went on the trip. Most of the participants were survivors and their children.

In the spring of 1992, in preparation for the trip, I went with a group of ten people – composed of elected officials of the CJC and staff members – to arrange the logistics with Polish tour operators. By coincidence, I met my friends Joyce and Herb Green in Birkenau. I was unaware that they were on a trip to Poland at that time. Our reunion caused a cathartic outburst and I had an uncontrollable breakdown. I think I had been holding it back for many years. Meeting friends in a place where my mother, my sister and other members of my extended family had been murdered was painful and joyous at the same time. It was an unforgettable experience for the three of us. I thanked God that I had the good fortune to start a new life in Canada and to make such good friends as Joyce and Herb, both of whom I loved and respected.

In 1993, the fiftieth anniversary of the Ghetto Uprising took place in Warsaw. It was held in the former ghetto area and was organized and carried out by the Polish government. The commemorative service started in total darkness, with candles then lit in every window of the apartments surrounding the huge square, followed by the piercing sound of locomotive wheels grinding to a stop. The light and sound production that followed was sensitive, moving and appropriate. Heads of state, including the president of Israel, vice-president of the US, Elie Wiesel and the president of Poland, made passionate speeches and extolled the survivors for their tenacity and determination to make new lives for themselves and to start new families. It was interesting that many countries were ready to honour the memory of the six million murdered but none of them had been prepared to lift a finger to help us when it was desperately needed. The speeches were eloquent, promising never to forget and pledging "Never Again." Yet, almost fifty years after the Shoah, the world had not changed; genocide and murder were being perpetrated with impunity. The United Nations, the hope of the world in the 1950s, proved to be powerless to intervene. The ceremony moved most of us but it did not promise a changed world, one where hatred would be relegated to the back pages of history.

~

How does one measure the loss of thousands upon thousands of prominent scientists, philosophers, scholars, musicians, doctors, engineers and inventors? How can one estimate the loss to our people and the world? How can anyone understand what it feels like to be a lone survivor of a generation? How does one impart these feelings to family, never mind the world?

In 1995, as the fiftieth anniversary of my liberation neared, I felt an urgency to take my family to Poland and let them experience a bit of my pre-war world, to see the place where I came from, where I had a life before the war. The fiftieth anniversary of my rebirth was a significant event in my life and Bernice and I decided to mark that occasion by taking our children and their husbands – Lisa and Steve Pinkus, Ronda and Cary Green and Arla and Zvi Litwin – to Poland. The time seemed right. It was six years after the fall of the Communist government and things were stabilizing in Poland.

Visiting my birth city of Chorzów with my grown family was like nothing I had experienced before. We entered the courtyard of my apartment building and it was as if I never left. There in the corner was our old storage shed where we had our gang clubhouse; the ground of the yard was broken up a bit more than twenty years earlier when Bernice and I had visited with my aunts. We went up to the ground floor window where I had lived and I peeked in. A man came out and asked if we wanted something; when I explained that I had lived there, he asked if we wanted to see the place. We jumped at the opportunity, and he led us into the apartment. The two rooms, consisting of a kitchen and bedroom, looked as I remembered; the most surprising thing was that in the corner of the bedroom, next to the window, stood the huge wardrobe/commode that we had had to leave behind when we were expelled from our home. From this backyard, we proceeded to my grandparents' yard, where again all things looked as I remembered. Opposite my grandparents' apartment building, in the place where our big and beautiful synagogue had once stood, was now a supermarket. The school building situated behind the synagogue was still there but was now a city government office. I could feel that our children understood my childhood and were now part of it.

Our trip followed our resettlement route to Sosnowiec and to the apartment on 12 Prosta Street. We walked up to the third floor and found nail holes in our apartment doorpost where our *mezuzah* was affixed. Next we went to Towarowa Street, where we lived in the open ghetto before the first deportation of the elderly from Sosnowiec to the east. This time we went into the courtyard and I told of the thousands of people who were detained here under horrible conditions.

They could not believe that five thousand people could be held in this space for over a week.

Next we visited old Sosnowiec, where I worked in the shoe factory, but things had changed beyond recognition. We drove from that area along the same route that I walked every day to and from the ghetto. We arrived in the village of Środula, which lay in ruins. Five years earlier with Cary, we had found the ruins of the Judenrat buildings but did not venture any further. This time we located the ruins of my last home as a family before we were taken to Auschwitz-Birkenau. My vegetable garden was overgrown, the huge pear tree stood in the yard, the basement area and the adjoining building where we hid had collapsed – painful memories of fifty-two years earlier were brought back as if it was a few days ago. My stories took on a more profound meaning to our children.

The next day we travelled to Auschwitz; it rained all day and created the appropriate mood. Auschwitz in the sun, with green grass and tall birch trees, does not fit into my memory. A gloomy rainy day does. Bernice stayed with the driver because by this time she was emotionally drained. It felt unreal to walk the one-kilometre ramp in Birkenau with my three daughters and their husbands. At the ruins of Gas Chamber III we tried in vain to light memorial candles in the rain. I said Kaddish and we all cried. It was the right moment to introduce my family to my sister and mother. In a way it provided closure to that period. Lisa is named after my mother, Faigel Leah, and Ronda Beth after my sister, Linka (Blima).

The following day the tone of our trip changed – we were in Krakow and we went to a first-class restaurant, famous for generations, and had a typical Polish/Jewish meal consisting of frozen vodka and herring, followed by boiled carp. The window of an antique shop in the hallway to the restaurant was laden with incongruous items for sale: Nazi emblems, bayonets and other paraphernalia. In the next window were Jewish candelabras, Kiddush cups and other Jewish ritual objects. We wondered how these objects came into the store.

Were they traded for a piece of bread or stolen from their Jewish owners' homes?

Our moods changed drastically after Auschwitz. Although I had some feelings of guilt, we had a good time together as a family and we were relaxed, joking about some of the inconsistencies of our trip. The trip created a coherent timeline for my family and sequenced my stories that had been told in bits and pieces over the years. I felt we reached a closer bond and that my references to past events were better understood. We drank the Polish vodka and celebrated life and our good fortune as a family. The past can never be forgotten, but it assumed a proper space in my family life. This trip to Poland was and still is my most important. It cemented my past and future into a continuum.

~

Early in 1998, Norman Godfrey, the son of my friends Joe and Rose, approached me and asked me to go on the March of the Living as a survivor. A survivor and a member of the Israeli Knesset had conceived the March of the Living as an educational experience that involves taking Grade 11 students on a two-week voyage, spending the first week in Poland and the second week in Israel. Canada participated in its first March in 1988. Approximately four months prior to the trip, the students come together to learn about the Holocaust and to study the history of pre-war European Jewry and of Zionism. The students learn about the struggles and sacrifices Israelis had to make in order for the beleaguered country to become a reality and to maintain its security, surrounded by and attacked at various stages of its existence by five Arab nations determined and avowed to destroy it.

In Poland, the March visits some towns in which Jews had constituted between 30 and 50 per cent of the population, and others where they had been as much as 75 to 80 per cent of the population. Once the students understand who the victims were, they are taken to the places where they were murdered in a systematic and brutal manner: the death factories of Auschwitz-Birkenau, Treblinka, Belzec and Majdanek, and forests where mass executions took place. Emphasis is placed on not traumatizing the students, although some trauma will, of course, be experienced. The second week is spent in Israel. The students visit historic sites and cities including Jerusalem, Tzfat and Tel Aviv. They participate in the observance of Yom Hazikaron, the day of remembrance of fallen soldiers and victims of terrorism, and the celebration of Yom Ha'atzmaut, the day of declaration of independence.

The March focuses on Poland because the Nazis committed most of the murders against Jews who were concentrated in various ghettos and camps in occupied Poland. I have often heard people ask the question: Why did the Nazis choose to locate the six death camps in Poland? Those same individuals are quick to answer their own question with the misguided response that they were located in Poland because the Nazis knew that most Poles were antisemitic. I think this allegation is terribly wrong. It is only logical to construct the death camps where the victims are located. Poland had three million Jews in 1939, the most in the world. There have been many papers written on the reasons for locating the murder factories in Poland. This is not the place to provide a detailed discussion, but the Polish people had no say as to what was happening in their occupied territory.

I was hesitant to join the March because I was familiar with the Israeli attitude toward the Diaspora – that Jews were not living as a free people, and that to live freely, their place and future was only in Israel. I thought that I would never want to be part of this type of program, which made the students feel guilty if they did not make aliyah to Israel. However, I was assured that the attitude of the Israeli leaders vis-a-vis the Diaspora was changing and that we were being considered as partners rather than outsiders.

My own attitude toward Poland had changed during the fifteen years I spent on the Auschwitz International Council, and I was concerned that the Jewish student participants were very anti-Polish and that little was done to dispel their prejudice. The prejudice was usually acquired from their grandparents' experiences. Although based on actual, but limited, occurrences, it was a generalization and, like all generalizations, was derogatory. I had no intention of minimizing or whitewashing the crimes of the Shoah, but I felt that Poland should not be blamed for crimes it had not committed. There were enough proven crimes, and Poland had to live with its past. Crimes perpetrated by no matter how many Poles could not be transferred to the whole nation, and certainly not to the subsequent generations. I believe we must break the cycle of hatred based on past injustices. We must stay dedicated to educating the public and especially our children to be not only tolerant of other cultures but to accept them. It is easy to say that others should change and become like me and then I will accept them. Acceptance is not easy, but that is what must be done – only then will we destroy intolerance, achieve harmony between nations and individuals, and keep hatred in check. The Shoah is the strongest and most poignant example of group hatred and intolerance. Nevertheless, I do hold the state responsible for the crimes of their citizens, especially if the state has benefitted materially from crimes of the previous regimes.

I also felt that the emphasis on the March was on the way the victims were murdered and not on the way they had lived for a thousand years and what they had contributed to the Jewish community, Polish society and the world. I felt that the victims should be honoured and the participants should learn who they were and how they lived – not only in Poland but also in Europe generally. I was promised that I would have some input into the programming. I decided to go. Little did I know that this decision would change my life.

I was completely unprepared for the emotions that I experienced going for the first time on the March of the Living with 155 bright, articulate, dedicated teenagers. During the Shabbaton held prior to our trip, we quickly developed a mutual respect and understanding with the students and the chaperones. This event set the interaction and chemistry between the students, chaperones, two other survivors and me. The terrible realization came upon me as I looked into those beautiful faces and bright eyes that in 1943, these young students would have been doomed. The teenagers' faces reminded me of my sister and her friends. These high-spirited people singing and dancing at the Shabbaton made my heart grow with pride and hope. This experience charged me with new energy, kindled my dedication and hope in the future and gave me strength I did not know I possessed. I felt that Jewish continuity would be assured through these young people. I felt that this voyage must not be a voyage of despair and defeat but one of remembrance, triumph, victory over our enemies and hope. Above all, it must be a voyage of discovery and education, to learn that our religion and traditions go back thousands of years and that the people who were murdered were educated, creative, religious and secular, with different ideological persuasions. They lived full and productive lives, not always untroubled, but flourishing in spite of untold obstacles.

A few weeks later, after spending thirteen sleepless hours on a transatlantic flight, we arrived in Poland. Our first stop and lunch was in the rain at a local gas station parking lot on our way to the death camp of Treblinka; the cold air saturated with moisture penetrated our clothing and added to our discomfort. We gathered in a circle and sang Hebrew and English songs of remembrance and of hope. We linked hands and swayed slowly to the rhythm of the songs. Tears appeared in our eyes. We hugged each other and we started the trip with a kindred spirit of mutual support.

On the bus to Treblinka, I told the Israeli *madricha*, guide, that my father's family of twenty-four was deported from Częstochowa on Yom Kippur day 1942 but that I did not know where they had been sent. From her resource material she told me that the Częstochowa transport of that date was sent to Treblinka. I was devastated by the information that twenty-four members of my father's family were murdered on this site. At the monument I read the names of all those who came here and were murdered in cold blood. My composure gave way and I recited each name in tears. The students accompanied me with their own tears, and together we intoned the sorrowful words of the Kaddish, the mourner's prayer. This was a moment I will cherish forever.

On Yom HaShoah, Holocaust Memorial Day, we assembled in Auschwitz I for the three-kilometre march to Birkenau. Eight thousand young Jews from around the world marched together. My thoughts went back to August 2, 1943, when I marched with my father, when we did not know that this was the last road with our family, to an unknown destination and fate. The day before, I had spoken of my experience in one of the barracks in Birkenau to two hundred students from Toronto. With their faces wet with tears, they sat on the mud floor and listened in silence as I recounted my arrival with my family on that fateful day. Retelling the story in this environment brought tears to my eyes, and my heart was filled with grief and anger. I choked up and thought I could not go on, but the students gave me strength to go on, for I could see that they shared my pain as we cried together.

The next day we visited the cemetery of Kielce, the town of the 1946 pogrom. One of our participants angrily asked me, "Don't you hate the Poles?" "No," I responded, "I do not hate all Poles, but I think that those responsible for this and any other crime must be brought to justice." I explained that I felt that hatred only begets more hatred. Hatred is like a double-edged sword – it cuts both ways. Hatred is blind and it stops us from acting rationally. Besides, hatred consumes one with bitterness and despair, and it does nothing to those you hate. The student was amazed and asked, "Don't you hate the Nazis who murdered your family?" Of course, I hate what they did, and I am angry, but I would not take the law into my own hands and take revenge, which does not serve any purpose. Bringing them into a court of justice would establish that murder does not have a time limit and that criminals must be pursued as long as they live. The videographer on our trip recoded part of this episode and it became my hallmark.

That evening, we welcomed Shabbat in Warsaw in the Nozik synagogue, filled to overflowing with people from around the globe, including some from the small but growing Jewish-Polish community; we all sang in unison, in our ancient, common language of prayer. This in itself was remarkable, and it was bittersweet to feel that the Nazis had not succeeded. I reminded the students about the uprising led by Jews no older than most of our participants. At the ghetto fighters' memorial I spoke of the young heroes who fought with courage and fierce pride, not to survive but to die with dignity and honour. In Krakow we visited old synagogues that were in terrible states of disrepair, but we danced with the spirit and joy and energy of the people who once lived there and were no more. Some of the synagogues retained the smallest fraction of their original splendour.

We also visited the death camps of Belzec and Majdanek, where various survivors spoke of their families who were murdered there. Each of the students had different reactions; some broke down and cried on the shoulders of their friends, the chaperones or the survivors, and others were stoic. When we met in the evening to review what we felt, each had the opportunity to express their feelings. We assured the students that there was no right or wrong reaction. The trip was a rollercoaster of emotion. We emerged from the depth of sadness in Poland to the joy of life in Israel.

We arrived in Israel on a Friday and went directly to the Kotel, the Western Wall, for prayers. On Yom Hazikaron, we spent a solemn day remembering the brave soldiers in all Israel's wars, and stood still with all Israelis as sirens wailed for two minutes at 11:00 a.m. That evening, we participated in a national ceremony at Latrun, where participants recited poems of bravery and sacrifice. A student choir sang national hymns and the anthem, which ended the solemn observance of Yom Hazikaron. Next a band struck up folk and dance music to start the joyous celebration of Yom Ha'atzmaut on the fiftieth anniversary of the declaration of independence. We danced with unbridled energy and exuberance. The next day we marched from the City Hall to the Kotel in joy and high spirits.

The participants' exemplary behaviour raised my hopes for a better future. These young men and women, focused, intelligent and articulate, gave me assurance for Jewish survival. They are the future leaders in our communities and the world, and their dedication and commitment gives meaning to the slogan "Never Again." The March of the Living has proved to be a life-changing event and an unequalled, unique educational experience. Many of our community leaders come from the alumni of the March. I have dedicated years to the study and teaching of the Holocaust and I feel that the March of the Living is the most effective method of teaching the lessons of the Holocaust in a rather short time. I have decided to dedicate much of my time to the March of the Living and I intend to continue as long as my health and strength will allow me.

~

While the March of the Living involves only Jewish students, the March of Remembrance and Hope is open to non-Jews mainly. In 2003, this trip comprised university students and their professors from all over Canada and the US. The students were mature but had a limited knowledge of the history of the Nazi regime and very little knowledge of what happened to the Jews. On the trip, students from the University of Saskatchewan who were Aboriginal Canadians identified with many aspects of my story because their people were terribly treated by white settlers. Some of their parents suffered greatly through forceful resettlement and some were removed from their families and sent to residential schools. One of the students was inconsolable because one of her brothers committed suicide shortly before the trip. She blamed the governments and their policies for the unbearable conditions that existed in their communities. Most young people in her community had little hope of finding a job.

On the trip were two sisters and their brother who were Muslims from Pakistan. The two women wore traditional Muslim attire. I was careful in my encounters with them, especially in relation to Israel. We talked about the history of the Jews in Israel, of which they had almost no knowledge, and they were convinced that the Jews had no rights to the land. They came with preconceived ideas that Israel had come into existence because of the Shoah, and weren't aware of the continuity of Jewish presence in the Land of Israel throughout the centuries. I explained that Zionism started long before the war and was more a response to antisemitism. Our discussions were non-confrontational and we sat late into the night talking and exchanging opinions and facts. In the end, I think they came away with a different impression of Israel and the Jewish people. One of the sisters, a PhD student, spoke at the conclusion of the March about the need for all people to be tolerant and accepting.

～

Between 2006 and 2013, each of my grandchildren accompanied me on the March of the Living. The trips do not get easier as I age; the emotional toll is heavier and more difficult to control. I took the first trip with my grandchildren Mira and Jennifer. I did not know how I would react to being with them in places such as Birkenau and Belzec. I was afraid they would resent my presence and decided to give them as much space as they needed. My fears were unfounded, as both were very responsive and sensitive.

In 2007, I triumphantly marched with three generations of the Leipcigers, something that the Nazis would have thought could not occur. We were here to remember my mother and sister, to honour the memories of those who were murdered and to march the road to life instead of death. We marched in silence and with pride, with arms linked, my grandson Josh on one arm and my daughter Arla on the other. This was the first time that I publicly revealed that my father was in the Jewish police in the ghetto. In 2007, my grandchildren were older and I felt I could explain the circumstances under which he had to accept the position. It was a choice-less choice. I never heard from anyone who was with us in the ghetto that he did anything wrong, such as beating people or using his position to gain any advantage. My father's participation in the Jewish police had bothered me for years, but I had never had the courage to ask him what he did or did not do. Maybe I was afraid of the answer, and of judging him. In all the years that I heard him tell the various bits and pieces of our experience to his wife and their friends, he had never mentioned that he was in the police.

Arla knew about my father being a policeman. During her second year at Hebrew University in Jerusalem, she shared my family's story in her Holocaust history course. Her professor was of the opinion that the only way our family could stay together in the ghetto until the final deportation was if my father was in the police. On her return home, she confronted me with the question and I did not hesitate to confirm it was true. She understood that some choices were not choices. She remembered my father as a kind and thoughtful man and did not hold that against him.

In 2008, I travelled on the March of the Living with my grandson Jason. Jason was the most demonstrative of our grandchildren and he clung to me, which I appreciated. He freely showed his emotions and cried and that in turn caused me to be more emotional than usual. I cherished his closeness.

In 2009, my oldest grandsons, Daniel and Jonathan, accompanied me as young adults. This trip was very different as the participants were over twenty-one, most in university or working in a profession, and the group was small. They were mature adults, knowledgeable and articulate, and their questions were penetrating and deep in scope. They challenged me and I enjoyed being with them. In Birkenau, the small group allowed us to have an intimate conversation about my experiences. I talked about the helplessness we felt at the time and how the situation for the Jews changed with the existence of Israel. It was months after this trip that, to my surprise, my grandson

Daniel told me that it was in Auschwitz, in the barracks, that he had made the decision to volunteer in the Israel Defense Forces (IDF).

One year later in 2010, my daughters Lisa and Ronda and my grandchildren Adam and Jordana came with me on March of the Living. This was unquestionably the most emotional and painful trip and yet it was a triumphant one. As in past years, we were there to pay homage to my mother, Leah, and sister, Blima. Although this was not my daughters' first trip to Birkenau, it was special in that they were there with their children. This was very significant, representing two new generations and the renewal of our nation.

This was my tenth trip. As I told my story of entry into Birkenau and my exit to Fünfteichen, somehow, unplanned, I also told the story of my sexual abuse, without going into any details. The sexual abuse was something that bothered me all my life. At first, I was ashamed to admit it to anyone, except my wife, and thought it was my fault. I certainly would not tell my father about it, but I suspected that he knew what was happening at the time. Sexual abuse was the most difficult narrative for me to tell, and it took me years to get up the courage to talk about it. It is one thing to talk about it to strangers and another to tell the story when members of your family are present. I was afraid it would evoke shame in me, and I didn't know how it would affect them. How much detail should I go into, or does it matter how and when it occurred? This was the last secret. What gave me the courage to reveal it was the climate of understanding of the difficulties encountered by young boys in compromising situations. Today, many abused individuals have come forward and shared their suffering at the hands of people in power over them.

The special characteristic of my next trip, in 2011, was that my grandson Daniel was now in the paratroopers' division of the Israel Defense Forces special detachment of Lone Soldiers, and he travelled four hours to spend Shabbat with our group. The young men and women were interested in hearing his motivations in becoming a lone soldier, one who joins the IDF from another country, without having immediate family in Israel. I think his presence added much to the group's understanding of the importance of Israel to our life in the Diaspora.

On March of the Living 2013, our youngest grandchild, Gary, accompanied me. Gary was the last of our children and grandchildren to participate in the March. My family assumed this would be my last time going on the March, but it was not. The March of the Living is such an important educational event, and I feel if I can add some measure of value to it, I should continue to go. The March has not only changed the lives of thousands of young people, but it has also changed and enriched my life. This was my thirteenth March of the Living, a significant number in Jewish religious life. Thirteen is the coming of age for our young adolescents, a moment of accomplishment for them and their parents. It was, likewise, for me. I resolved long ago that I would dedicate my senior years to the March as long as I am able to make a difference and the organization wants me to participate.

Epilogue

In the year 2000, as chairperson of the CJC, I had the privilege to attend the First International Forum on the Holocaust conference in Stockholm. I was excited that the twenty-first century was starting with an optimistic event. Forty-six nations gathered to commemorate the Holocaust and to promote Holocaust education. At the same time, I was angry, because during the Shoah, no nation came to our rescue or even offered help to escape.

During his opening speech, French prime minister Lionel Jospin said, "It is significant that the first conference in the new millennium is not on economics but on morality." I heard speaker after speaker emphasize that the Holocaust is unique and is a warning of man's ability to commit the most heinous crimes. I, too, believe the Shoah was unique. Jews have experienced pogroms and random killings through the ages, but there was no precedent of a state-planned, organized and executed genocide involving arrays of individuals, professionals, organizations and modern technology for the sole purpose of destroying a whole nation.

All heads of state at the conference time and time again reiterated the importance of examining their nation's history honestly to teach the next generation not to repeat the mistakes of the past, and to sensitize them to the dangers of demagogues and their undemocratic quick-fix solutions. Holocaust studies can and must give us a clear and unmistakable early warning signal of impending dangers when human rights are unceremoniously abrogated and minority groups are used as scapegoats. The Holocaust provides examples of the choices people had in being a bystander – complicit through silence, a rescuer or a perpetrator.

I hoped the International Forum would have as profound an impact on most participants as it did on me. I sat and listened to the various prime ministers speak and heard their admission of their nation's complicity, collaboration, inaction and silence at the darkest time of the civilized European world. The speeches were inspiring and uplifting and I hoped they would be heard by the world but years later, as other genocides were perpetrated, I realized they were empty words.

In an essay in *Time* magazine on April 12, 1999, Roger Rosenblatt wrote, "The Shoah lies not only beyond compensation, it also lies beyond explanation, reconciliation, sentiment, forgiveness, redemption or any of the mechanisms by which people attempt to set wrong things right." That must apply to those who have committed crimes and those who participated in their execution. Even bystanders are not free of blame, especially those nations that by refusing refuge and safe havens contributed to the ability of the Nazis to carry out their heinous scheme of the "Final Solution."

Students often ask, "Why are you still trying to go after the old men who were involved?" I believe that the answer is simple: The world cannot establish a precedent where time will render the guilty innocent; there cannot be a time limit on the prosecution of murderers. It is also important to remember that accusing someone of a crime is not sufficient in a civilized community; we must prove guilt beyond a shadow of doubt. We cannot consider it revenge but, rather, justice. Once the guilt is established, the court has the option to take into consideration how the individual conducted his or her life. Are they remorseful and do they regret their actions, or are they defiant to the last day of their lives? For sure, no one suggests that an octogenarian should be executed. However, they should not be able to flaunt their crimes and live out their lives in the comfort of respect and freedom.

Another question that comes up is "why the Jews." It is difficult for me, as a Jew, to confront this historic fact. I could suggest that they ask their teacher, or refer them to a book such as *Constantine's Sword* by James Carroll. That would be a copout. I say that, historically, the Catholic Church created a climate of hatred and discrimination against the Jews. The Gospels accuse the Jews of betrayal and then of murdering Jesus. For centuries, we have been marked with yellow patches and segregated from the population in ghettos. There is practically no country in Europe where the Jews, at one time or another, were not expelled or murdered.

We must also think of the pre-war times when, in 1938, President Roosevelt convened a conference in Evian, France, to which he invited thirty-two nations to resolve the crisis of 600,000 refugees, created by the Nazis after the *Anschluss* of Austria, which deprived Jews of their citizenship. In the end, no nation decided they had room for the refugees; only the Dominican Republic agreed to take some.

In 1939, the ship SS *St. Louis* arrived on the shores of Cuba, the US and Canada, but there was no room for the 937 desperate Jews. Although Cuba admitted several, the rest were sent back and eventually accepted into four nations in Western Europe. Of those, approximately 250 were ultimately murdered when Germany occupied those nations in 1940. In addition to closing its own borders, the British established a naval blockade of Palestine, thus closing off that escape route. The world, in my opinion, gave Hitler a free hand to do with the Jews as he pleased.

There have been times when students ask me questions that make me feel like I have failed to convey the enormity of what happened during the Shoah. Obviously, the number six million cannot be grasped. After one such question, I thought the students might understand it better if I personalized my history. This has become my starting point in my talks to high schools:

"I would like to ask you to do a mental exercise. I ask you to take into your mind all your brothers and sisters, your parents, your grandparents, your uncles and aunts, your cousins and your best friends. I would guess you have about forty or fifty of your dearest people in your head. Now, think how you would feel if in a short period, say two years or less, all of them would be gone. Gone, by death due to starvation, disease, shooting or gassing. How would you feel? How would you feel if you were left alone, possibly with a brother, or a father, as in my case? In addition, out of the 110 of you in this room, only 15 would survive. How would you feel? You would be a survivor."

After a few seconds of silence, I proceed. "I do not want you to leave this room with these terrible thoughts in your minds. I would like to ask you to do something for me when you get home. I want you to go to your siblings, your parents and your friends and tell them 'I love you.' If they ask you if you are out of your mind, or what has come over you, I want you to tell them this: If by accident of birth, you were Jewish and lived anywhere in Europe during World War II, you would have lost them. Tell them my story and tell them how much you appreciate having them as your family and friends."

There is one question I ask myself: Why me? Why did I have to suffer and lose everyone? Why did I survive, while others who were better educated, stronger and bigger in body, smarter and better looking, did not? My friends tell me, "You survived to tell the story, to bear witness, to inspire others to reduce the hatred in the world and to do *tikkun olam*, heal the world." I hope they are right.

Glossary

Akiba (Agudat Hano'ar Ha'ivri Akiba; Association of Hebrew Youth – Akiba) A youth movement founded in 1924 in Krakow, Poland. Named after an important first-century rabbi, it advocated adherence to traditional Jewish values and return to the Jewish homeland of Palestine. *See also* Zionism; Zionist and Jewish movements in interwar Poland.

Allied Zones of Germany The four zones that Germany was divided into after its defeat in World War II, each administered by one of the four major Allied powers – the United States, Britain, France and the Soviet Union. The American Zone included parts of Austria, Czechoslovakia and southern Germany. These administrative zones existed in Germany between 1945 and 1949.

Allies The coalition of countries that fought against Germany, Italy and Japan (the Axis nations). At the beginning of World War II in September 1939, the coalition included France, Poland and Britain. Once Germany invaded the USSR in June 1941 and the United States entered the war following the bombing of Pearl Harbor by Japan on December 7, 1941, the main leaders of the Allied powers became Britain, the USSR and the United States. Other Allies included Canada, Australia, Czechoslovakia, Greece, Mexico, Brazil, South Africa and China.

antisemitism Prejudice, discrimination, persecution and/or hatred against Jewish people, institutions, culture and symbols.

Appellplatz (German; the place for roll call) The area in Nazi camps where inmates had to assemble to be counted. Roll calls were part of a series of daily humiliations for prisoners, who were often made to stand completely still for hours, regardless of the weather conditions.

Auschwitz (German; in Polish, Oświęcim) A town in southern Poland approximately forty kilometres from Krakow, it is also the name of the largest complex of Nazi concentration camps that were built nearby. The Auschwitz complex contained three main camps: Auschwitz I, a slave labour camp built in May 1940; Auschwitz II-Birkenau, a death camp built in early 1942; and Auschwitz-Monowitz, a slave labour camp built in October 1942. In 1941, Auschwitz I was a testing site for usage of the lethal gas Zyklon B as a method of mass killing, which then went into wide usage. Between 1942 and 1944, transports arrived at Auschwitz-Birkenau from almost every country in Europe – hundreds of thousands from both Poland and Hungary, and thousands from France, the Netherlands, Greece, Slovakia, Bohemia and Moravia, Yugoslavia, Belgium, Italy and Norway. As well, more than 30,000 people were deported there from other concentration camps. It is estimated that 1.1 million people were murdered in Auschwitz; approximately 950,000 were Jewish; 74,000 Polish; 21,000 Roma; 15,000 Soviet prisoners of war; and 10,000–15,000 other nationalities. The Auschwitz complex was liberated by the Soviet army in January 1945.

bar mitzvah/bat mitzvah (Hebrew; literally, son/daughter of the commandment) The time when, in Jewish tradition, children become religiously and morally responsible for their actions and are considered adults for the purpose of synagogue and other rituals. Traditionally this occurs at age thirteen for boys and twelve for girls. Historically, girls were not included in this ritual until the latter half of the twentieth century, when liberal Jews instituted an equivalent ceremony and celebration for girls called a bat mitzvah. A bar/bat mitzvah marks the attainment of adulthood by a ceremony during which the boy/girl is called upon to read a portion of the Torah and recite the prescribed prayers in a public prayer service.

Betar A Zionist youth movement founded in 1923 that encouraged the development of a new generation of Zionist activists based on the ideals of courage, self-respect, military training, defence of Jewish life and property, and settlement in Israel to establish a Jewish state in British Mandate Palestine. *See also* Zionism; Zionist and Jewish movements in interwar Poland.

British Mandate Palestine The area of the Middle East under British rule from 1923 to 1948, as established by the League of Nations after World War I. During that time, the United Kingdom severely restricted Jewish immigration. The Mandate area encompassed present-day Israel, Jordan, the West Bank and the Gaza Strip.

Canadian Jewish Congress (CJC) An advocacy organization and lobbying group for the Canadian Jewish community that existed from 1919 to 2011. Between 1947 and 1949, it helped to bring 1,123 young Jewish refugees to Canada. The CJC was restructured in 2007 and its functions subsumed under the Centre for Israel and Jewish Affairs (CIJA) in 2011.

Carmelite Nuns Members of the Order of the Brothers of the Blessed Virgin Mary of Mount Carmel, a Roman Catholic religious order founded on the mountain range in northern Israel. The nuns separate themselves from the outside world to focus on prayer.

Chanukah (also Hanukah; Hebrew; dedication) An eight-day festival celebrated in December to mark the victory of the Jews against foreign conquerors who desecrated the Temple in Jerusalem in the second century BCE. Traditionally, each night of the festival is marked by lighting an eight-branch candelabrum called a menorah to commemorate the rededication of the Temple and the miracle of its lamp burning for eight days with one day's worth of oil.

chametz (Hebrew) Food that is produced by, or associated with, leavening and fermentation, and therefore must be removed from Jewish households during the festival of Passover; a product that is made from wheat, barley, spelt, rye or oats and that has undergone fermentation as the result of contact with liquid. *See also* Passover.

cheder (Hebrew; literally, room) An Orthodox Jewish elementary school that teaches the fundamentals of Jewish religious observance and textual study, as well as the Hebrew language.

cholent (Yiddish) A traditional Jewish slow-cooked pot stew usually eaten as the main course at the festive Shabbat lunch on Saturdays after the synagogue service and on other Jewish holidays. For Jews of Eastern-European descent, the basic ingredients of *cholent* are meat, potatoes, beans and barley.

Civitan Club An international association of groups committed to volunteer services, founded in 1917. The organization particularly focuses on providing services to children and adults with developmental disabilities.

De-Nazification The effort by the Allied countries to eliminate the influence of Nazi ideology from post-war Germany by removing members of the National Socialist Party from public office and positions of influence.

displaced persons (DPs) People who find themselves homeless and stateless at the end of a war. Following World War II, millions of people, especially European Jews, found that they had no homes to return to or that it was unsafe to do so. To resolve the staggering refugee crisis that resulted in October 1945, Allied authorities and the United Nations Relief and Rehabilitation Administration (UNRRA) established Displaced Persons (DP) camps to provide temporary shelter and assistance to refugees, and help them transition towards resettlement. *See also* United Nations Relief and Rehabilitation Administration (UNRRA).

Eichmann, Adolf (1906–1962) The head of the Gestapo department responsible for the implementation of the Nazis' policy of murder of Jews (the so-called Final Solution), Eichmann was in charge of transporting Jews to death camps in Poland. In 1942, Eichmann coordinated deportations of Jewish populations from Slovakia, the Netherlands, France and Belgium. After the war, Eichmann escaped from US custody and fled to Argentina, where he was captured in 1960 by Israeli intelligence operatives; his ensuing 1961 trial in Israel was widely and internationally televised. Eichmann was sentenced to death and hanged in May 1962. *See also* Gestapo.

Fackenheim, Emil (1916–2003) A Jewish philosopher who served as a rabbi at Reform temples in Hamilton and Toronto and was a professor at the University of Toronto. Fackenheim was born in Germany, arrested on Kristallnacht in 1938, and held for three months at Sachsenhausen concentration camp before being released and fleeing to Scotland. British authorities sent him to Canada as an enemy alien in 1940. In 1984 he immigrated to Israel, where he taught at the Hebrew University.

Flossenbürg The fourth concentration camp built in Germany, established in 1938. Flossenbürg was comprised of a main camp and approximately one hundred subcamps. By the time the camp system was liberated by the US army on April 23, 1945, more than 30,000 people had perished.

Fünfteichen A forced labour camp that was part of the Gross-Rosen concentration camp system. Fünfteichen was established in 1943 near what is now Miłoszyce, Poland. At the height of its operation, as many as 30,000 prisoners were incarcerated there, working mainly in munitions plants. Two days before the camp was liberated by the Red Army on January 23, 1945, 6,000 prisoners were sent on a death march to Gross-Rosen, during which about 2,000 were killed by SS guards. *See also* Gross-Rosen.

Generalgouvernement The territory in central Poland that was conquered by the Germans in September 1939 but not annexed to the Third Reich. Made up of the districts of Warsaw, Krakow, Radom and Lublin, it was deemed a special administrative area and was used by the Nazis to carry out their murderous plans. From 1939 onward, Jews from all over German-occupied territories were transferred to this region, as were Poles who had been expelled from their homes in the annexed Polish territories further west.

Gestapo (German; abbreviation of Geheime Staatspolizei, the Secret State Police of Nazi Germany) The Gestapo were the brutal force that dealt with the perceived enemies of the Nazi regime and were responsible for rounding up European Jews for deportation to the death camps. A number of Gestapo members also joined the Einsatzgruppen, the mobile killing squads responsible for the round-up and murder of Jews in eastern Poland and the USSR through mass shooting operations.

ghetto A confined residential area for Jews. The term originated in Venice, Italy, in 1516 with a law requiring all Jews to live on a segregated, gated island known as Ghetto Nuovo. Throughout the Middle Ages in Europe, Jews were often forcibly confined to gated Jewish neighbourhoods. During the Holocaust, the Nazis forced Jews to live in crowded and unsanitary conditions in run-down districts of cities and towns. Most ghettos in Poland were enclosed by brick walls or wooden fences with barbed wire.

Gross-Rosen A village in western Poland, now named Rogoźnica, where a labour camp was established in 1940. As the camp was expanded to include armaments production, Gross-Rosen became classified as a concentration camp and was the centre of a complex of at least ninety-seven subcamps, including Fünfteichen. As of January 1945, 76,728 prisoners were held there, of whom about one-third were women, mostly Jews. Liquidation of the subcamps began in January 1945 and Gross-Rosen was evacuated in early February 1945, with 40,000 prisoners, including 20,000 Jews, being forced on death marches. The camp was liberated by the Soviet Red Army on February 13, 1945. It is estimated that 120,000 prisoners passed through the Gross-Rosen camp complex; 40,000 died either in Gross-Rosen or during its evacuation. *See also* Fünfteichen.

Hitlerjugend (German; in English, the Hitler Youth) The Nazi Party's youth organization, founded in 1926, that focused on creating soldiers for the Third Reich who were properly indoctrinated in Nazi ideology. By 1935, 60 per cent of the German youth – boys and girls – were members of the HJ and on December 1, 1936, all other youth groups were banned. In 1939, HJ membership was made compulsory for youths over seventeen, after which membership comprised 90 per cent of German youth. Boys over the age of ten were eligible for membership, but in 1941 membership became compulsory for them as well. The girls' branch of the HJ was the Bund Deutscher Mädel (BDM).

Hochdeutsch (German; high German) A term referring to a standardized form of the German language. It also applies to the High German languages, dialects spoken in certain parts of Austria, Germany, Liechtenstein, and Switzerland.

International Refugee Organization (IRO) A United Nations agency that existed between 1946 and 1952 to assist those displaced by war in Europe. It replaced its predecessor, the United Nations Relief and Rehabilitation Administration (UNRRA), in maintaining refugee camps, providing vocational training and assisting in resettlement and in tracing of lost family members. *See also* United Nations Relief and Rehabilitation Administration.

Jewish ghetto police The force established by the Jewish Councils, under Nazi order, that was armed with clubs and carried out various tasks in the ghettos, such as traffic control and guarding the ghetto gates. Eventually, some policemen also participated in rounding up Jews for forced labour and transportation to the death camps and carried out the orders of the Nazis. There has been much debate and controversy surrounding the role of both the Jewish Councils and the Jewish police. Even though the Jewish police exercised considerable power within the ghetto, to the Nazis these policemen were still Jews and subject to the same fate as other Jews. *See also* Judenrat.

Judenrat (German; pl. *Judenräte*) Jewish Council. A group of Jewish leaders appointed by the Germans to administer and provide services to the local Jewish population under occupation and carry out Nazi orders. The *Judenräte*, which appeared to be self-governing entities but were actually under complete Nazi control, faced difficult and complex moral decisions under brutal conditions and remain a contentious subject. The chairmen had to decide whether to comply or refuse to comply with Nazi demands. Some were killed by the Nazis for refusing, while others committed suicide. Jewish officials who advocated compliance thought that cooperation might save at least some of the population. Some who denounced resistance efforts did so because they believed that armed resistance would bring death to the entire community.

Kaddish (Aramaic; holy) Also known as the Mourner's Prayer, Kaddish is said as part of mourning rituals in Jewish prayer services as well as at funerals and memorials. Sons are required to say Kaddish daily for eleven months after the death of a parent and also each year, on the anniversary of the death. The word Kaddish comes from a Hebrew root word meaning "holy."

kapo (German) A concentration camp prisoner appointed by the SS to oversee other prisoners as slave labourers. A *Hauptkapo* was a head kapo who worked under direct Nazi supervision.

Kanada The name prisoners in Birkenau gave to the warehouses that stored enormous amounts of goods seized by the camp authorities; the name came from the widely held belief that Canada was a land of wealth.

Kiddush (Hebrew; literally, sanctification) The blessing over wine that is recited on Shabbat and other Jewish holidays. *See also* Shabbat.

Kielce pogrom The July 1946 riots in a city in Poland where about 250 Jews lived after the war (the pre-war Jewish population had been more than 20,000). After the false report of a young Polish boy being kidnapped by Jews, police arrested and beat Jewish residents in the city, inciting a mob of hundreds of Polish civilians to violently attack and kill forty Jews while police stood by. Combined with other post-war antisemitic incidents throughout Poland – other pogroms occurred in Rzeszów, Krakow, Tarnów and Sosnowiec, and robberies and blackmail were common – this event was the catalyst for a mass exodus; between July 1945 and September 1946, more than 80,000 Jews left Poland.

Lagerälteste (German; literally, camp elder) A camp inmate in charge of the prisoner population.

Leonberg A town in southwest Germany that served as the location for a subcamp of the Natzweiler-Struthof concentration camp in northeastern France. More than 3,000 prisoners were held in Leonberg, most working in twelve-hour shifts at a Messerschmitt aircraft factory established in the Engelberg Tunnel, a nearby motorway. While 389 prisoners are confirmed to have died there, the number of deaths due to starvation and illness is believed to be much higher. A few days before liberation in April 1945, the prisoners were sent on a death march to Bavaria.

March of the Living An annual event that was established in 1988 and takes place in April on Holocaust Memorial Day (Yom HaShoah) in Poland. The March of the Living program aims to educate primarily Jewish students and young adults from around the world about the Holocaust and Jewish life before and during World War II. Along with Holocaust survivors, participants march the three kilometres from Auschwitz to Birkenau to commemorate all who perished in the Holocaust. The concept of the event comes from the Nazi death marches that Jews were forced to go on when they were being evacuated from the forced labour and concentration camps at the very end of the war. Many Jews died during these marches and the March of the Living was thus created both to remember this history and to serve as a contrast to it by celebrating Jewish life and strength. After spending time in Poland, participants travel to Israel and join in celebrations there for Israel's remembrance and independence days.

Merin, Moniek (Moshe) (1905–1943) The leader of the Judenrat in

Sosnowiec and chairman of the Council of Jewish Elders in the region of eastern Upper Silesia. Merin believed that being economically useful to the Germans offered the best chance of survival and oversaw the selection of Jews for forced labour under brutal conditions. Merin was arrested in June 1943 and deported to Auschwitz-Birkenau, where he was murdered. *See also* Sosnowiec.

mezuzah (Hebrew; literally, doorpost) The small piece of parchment inscribed with specific Hebrew texts from the Torah – usually enclosed in a decorative casing – that is placed on the door frames of the homes of observant Jews.

mikvah (Hebrew; literally, a pool or gathering of water) A ritual purification bath taken by Jews on occasions that denote a change in time, such as before the Sabbath (signifying the shift from a regular weekday to a holy day of rest) or in personal status, such as before a person's wedding or, for a married woman, after menstruation.

Molotov-Ribbentrop pact Also known as the Treaty of Non-Aggression between Germany and the USSR. The treaty that was signed on August 24, 1939, after signatories Soviet foreign minister Vyacheslav Molotov and German foreign minister Joachim von Ribbentrop. The main provisions of the pact stipulated that the two countries would not go to war with each other and that they would both remain neutral if either one was attacked by a third party. One of the key components of the treaty was the division of various independent countries – including Poland – into Nazi and Soviet spheres of influence and areas of occupation. The Nazis breached the pact by launching a major offensive against the Soviet Union on June 22, 1941.

Mühldorf A complex of four subcamps, one of which was Waldlager, established in Bavaria by the SS in the middle of 1944. Under the supervision of Organisation Todt, the more than 8,000 prisoners who were held there constructed subterranean factories for the production of aircraft and weapons. An estimated 2,200 to 3,900 people were killed in the Mühldorf camps – from abuse, over-work and disease. SS guards sent about 3,600 prisoners on death marches from the camp in April 1945 in an attempt to evade the approaching US army. How many survived is unknown. *See also* Waldlager.

Nuremberg Trials A series of war crimes trials held in the city of Nuremberg between November 1945 and October 1946 that tried twenty-four key leaders of the Holocaust. A subsequent twelve trials, the Trials of War Criminals before the Nuremberg Military Tribunals, was held for lesser war criminals between December 1946 and April 1949.

Orthodox Judaism The set of beliefs and practices of Jews for whom the observance of Jewish law is closely connected to faith; it is characterized by strict religious observance of Jewish dietary laws, restrictions on work on the Sabbath and holidays, and a code of modesty in dress.

Passover (in Hebrew, Pesach) One of the major festivals of the Jewish calendar, Passover takes place over eight days in the spring. It commemorates the liberation and exodus of the Israelite slaves from Egypt during the reign of the Pharaoh Ramses II. The festival begins with a lavish ritual meal called a seder, during which the story of Exodus is retold through the reading of a Jewish religious text called the Haggadah. With its special foods, songs and customs, the seder is the focal point of the Passover celebration and is traditionally a time of family gathering. During Passover, Jews refrain from eating *chametz* – that is, anything containing barley, wheat, rye, oats, and spelt that has undergone fermentation as a result of contact with liquid. *See also* chametz.

Piłsudski, Józef (1867–1935) Leader of the Second Polish Republic from 1926 to 1935. Piłsudski was largely responsible for achieving Poland's independence in 1918 after more than a century of being partitioned by Russia, Austria and Prussia. Piłsudski's regime was notable for improving the lot of ethnic minorities, including

Poland's large Jewish population. He followed a policy of "state-assimilation" whereby citizens were judged not by their ethnicity but by their loyalty to the state. Many Polish Jews felt that his regime was key to keeping the antisemitic currents in Poland in check. When he died in 1935, the quality of life of Poland's Jews deteriorated once again.

pipel A slang term used by concentration camp prisoners to refer to a young male forced to perform chores or provide sexual favours to another prisoner in a position of authority. In exchange, the *pipel* was usually given special privileges.

pogrom (Russian; to wreak havoc, to demolish) A violent attack on a distinct ethnic group. The term most commonly refers to nineteenth- and twentieth-century attacks on Jews in the Russian Empire.

Polish Legion (in Polish, *Legiony Polskie*) The armed forces established in 1914 by Józef Piłsudski while he was head of the Polish Socialist Party. During World War I, the Legion formed a unit within the Austro-Hungarian Army. Comprised initially of eastern and western branches, the Eastern legion was disbanded in September 1914, while the Western one fought against Russia until 1916, when it was reorganized as the Polish Auxiliary Corps and was transferred to German command. Its members refused to swear loyalty to Germany and were either drafted into the Austro-Hungarian army or interned in prisoner-of-war camps. After the war ended, Legion officers became part of the Polish Army.

Purim (Hebrew; literally, lots) The celebration of the Jews' escape from annihilation in Persia. The Purim story recounts how Haman, advisor to the King of Persia, planned to rid Persia of Jews, and how Queen Esther and her cousin Mordecai foiled Haman's plot by convincing the king to save the Jews. During the Purim festivities, people dress up as one of the figures in the Purim story, hold parades and retell the story of Haman, Esther and Mordecai.

Shabbat (Hebrew; in Yiddish, Shabbes, Shabbos) The weekly day of rest beginning Friday at sunset and ending Saturday at nightfall, ushered in by the lighting of candles on Friday evening and the recitation of blessings over wine and challah (egg bread); a day of celebration as well as prayer, it is customary to eat three festive meals, attend synagogue services and refrain from doing any work or travelling.

sheitel (Yiddish; wig) A head covering worn by Orthodox Jewish women to abide by religious codes of modesty. *See also* Orthodox Judaism.

shtiebel (Yiddish; little house or little room) A small, unadorned prayer room or prayer house furnished more modestly than a synagogue. Most observant Jews in Eastern Europe prayed in *shtiebels* on a daily basis; they attended services in a synagogue on holidays or sometimes on Shabbat. *See also* Shabbat.

Sosnowiec A town in southern Poland that was part of an enclosed police boundary known as the *Oststreifen*, or Eastern Strip, during the war. Over time, numbers of Jews living there were sent to forced labour and concentration camps; between May and August 1942, more than 11,000 Jews were deported to Auschwitz-Birkenau. In October 1942, the remaining Sosnowiec Jews were relocated to a ghetto in the nearby village of Środula.

SS (abbreviation of Schutzstaffel; Defence Corps). The SS was established in 1925 as Adolf Hitler's elite corps of personal bodyguards. Under the direction of Heinrich Himmler, its membership grew from 280 in 1929 to 50,000 when the Nazis came to power in 1933, and to nearly a quarter of a million on the eve of World War II. The SS was comprised of the Allgemeine-SS (General SS) and the Waffen-SS (Armed, or Combat SS). The General SS dealt with policing and the enforcement of Nazi racial policies in Germany and the Nazi-occupied countries. The SS ran the concentration and death camps, with all their associated economic enterprises. *See also* Gestapo.

SS *St. Louis* An ocean liner that sailed from Hamburg, Germany, on May 13, 1939, with 937 passengers on board, most of them German

Jewish refugees fleeing the Nazis. Their destination was Cuba, where they sought temporary refuge before being admitted into the United States. Both countries, however, refused entry to the passengers – as did Canada – and the ship was forced to return to Europe, eventually docking in Belgium. Passengers were given refuge in Britain, France, Belgium and Holland, but after the May 1940 Nazi invasion of France and the Low Countries, the passengers were once again targets of Nazi persecution. It is estimated that approximately 250 perished in the Holocaust.

Star of David (in Hebrew, *Magen David*) The six-pointed star that is the ancient and most recognizable symbol of Judaism. During World War II, Jews in Nazi-occupied areas were frequently forced to wear a badge or armband with the Star of David on it as an identifying mark of their lesser status and to single them out as targets for persecution.

Stubenälteste (German; room elder) A prisoner who served as the overseer of a room, ensuring order, cleanliness and the distribution of rations.

Stubendienst (German; room orderly) A prisoner in charge of maintaining the cleanliness of the block, next in command to the *Stubenälteste* (room elder or head). *See also* Stubenälteste.

Stubenschreibe (German; room scribe) A prisoner who served as a secretary, engaged in record-keeping and similar tasks.

tallit (Hebrew; prayer shawl) A four-cornered ritual garment traditionally worn by adult Jewish men during morning prayers and on the Day of Atonement (Yom Kippur). One usually wears the *tallit* over one's shoulders but some choose to place it over their heads to express awe in the presence of God.

Toronto Jewish Congress Formed in 1976 as a local organization providing the educational and social services then offered by the Canadian Jewish Congress. The organization has been restructured several times and is now known as the UJA Federation of Greater

Toronto. It raises funds for welfare, education and community-building activities. *See also* Canadian Jewish Congress.

Treaty of Versailles One of the five treaties produced at the 1919 Paris Peace Conference organized by the victors of World War I. The Treaty of Versailles imposed a harsh and punitive peace on Germany, including high reparations, restrictions on German military rearmament and activities, and the redrawing of Germany's borders, which resulted in the loss of territory.

Treblinka A labour and death camp created as part of Operation Reinhard, the German code word for the Nazi plan for murdering Jews in German-occupied Poland using poison gas. A slave labour camp (Treblinka I) was built in November 1941 near the villages of Treblinka and Małkinia Górna, about eighty kilometres northeast of Warsaw. Treblinka II, the killing centre, was constructed in a sparsely populated and heavily wooded area about 1.5 kilometres from the labour camp in 1942. From July 1942 to October 1943 more than 750,000 Jews were killed at Treblinka, making it second to Auschwitz in the numbers of Jews killed in a Nazi camp. Treblinka I and II were both liberated by the Soviet army in July 1944.

United Nations Relief and Rehabilitation Administration (UNRRA) An international relief agency created at a 44-nation conference in Washington, DC, on November 9, 1943, to provide economic assistance and basic necessities to war refugees. It was especially active in repatriating and assisting refugees in the formerly Nazi-occupied European nations immediately after World War II. *See also* International Refugee Organization.

Volksdeutsche The term used for ethnic Germans who lived outside Germany in Central and Eastern Europe; also refers to the ethnic German colonists who were resettled in Polish villages as part of far-reaching Nazi plans to Germanize Nazi-occupied territories in the East.

282 THE WEIGHT OF FREEDOM

Waldlager (German; literally, forest camp) A part of the Mühldorf camp complex in Bavaria. About 2,250 male and female prisoners were held there, living in tents or in earth huts, of which only the roofs were visible above ground. *See also* Mühldorf.

yeshiva (Hebrew) A Jewish educational institution in which religious texts such as the Torah and Talmud are studied.

Yiddish A language derived from Middle High German with elements of Hebrew, Aramaic, Romance and Slavic languages, and written in Hebrew characters. Spoken by Jews in east-central Europe for roughly a thousand years from the tenth century to the mid-twentieth century, it was still the most common language among European Jews until the outbreak of World War II. There are similarities between Yiddish and contemporary German.

Yom Kippur (Hebrew; literally, day of atonement) A solemn day of fasting and repentance that comes eight days after Rosh Hashanah, the Jewish New Year, and marks the end of the high holidays.

Zionism A movement promoted by the Viennese Jewish journalist Theodor Herzl, who argued in his 1896 book *Der Judenstaat* (The Jewish State) that the best way to resolve the problem of antisemitism and persecution of Jews in Europe was to create an independent Jewish state in the historic Jewish homeland of Biblical Israel. Zionists also promoted the revival of Hebrew as a Jewish national language.

Zionist and Jewish movements in interwar Poland Among the significant Jewish political movements that flourished in Poland before World War II were various Zionist parties – the General Zionists; the Labour Zionists (Poale Zion); the Revisionist Zionists formed under Ze'ev Jabotinsky; and the Orthodox Religious Zionists (the Mizrachi movement) – and the entirely secular and socialist Jewish Workers' Alliance, known as the Bund. Although Zionism and Bundism were both Jewish national movements and served as Jewish political parties in interwar Poland, Zionism advocated a Jewish national homeland in the Land of Israel, while Bundism advocated Jewish cultural autonomy in the Diaspora. A significant number of Polish Jews in the interwar years preferred to affiliate with the non-Zionist religious Orthodox party, Agudath Israel. *See also* Akiba, Betar, Zionism.

Photographs

1 Elka (née Hochman) Percik, Nate's maternal grandmother. Photo obtained from a gentile neighbour after the war.

2 Nate's maternal grandfather, Shimon Percik, with Nate's great-grandparents before the war. In back, Shimon; in front, Gitele and Avrum-Itzak Percik.

1 Nate's mother, Faigel Leja (Leah), 1938. Nate received this photo from his grandmother's housekeeper, Stasia, after the war.

2 Aunt Zosia (née Percik) Winiarz, 1938.

3 Aunt Rozalia (Ruzia) Percik, 1938.

4 Ruzia's husband, Antek Uziemblo, 1938.

1 & 2 Nate's paternal grandparents, Abraham Hersch and Rudel (née Biernbaum) Leipziger, circa 1930.

1

2

1 Nate's father, Jack (front, left), with his siblings Tobias (back, left), Mirla (back, right) and Leon (front, right). Chorzów, circa 1919.

2 Nate's paternal aunts and uncles. In back: Uncle Tobias (left) and Nate's father, Jack (right). In front, left to right: Aunt Mirla; Mirla's husband, Kurt Nadelberg; Aunt Dora; and Dora's husband, Samuel.

1

2

3

1 Nate's father, Jacob (Jack) Leipciger. Circa 1920s.

2 Nate's mother, Leah.

3 Engagement photo of Nate's parents, 1924.

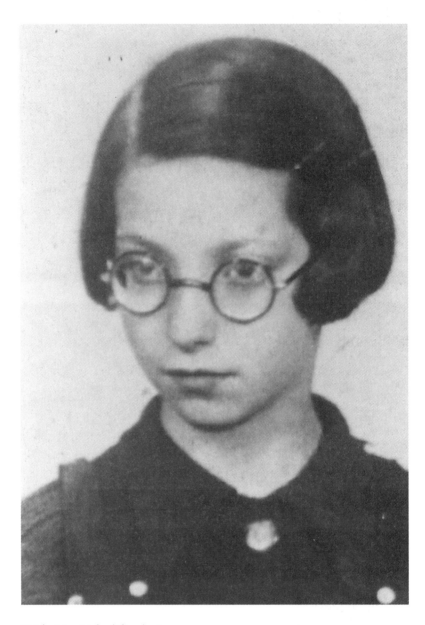

Nate's sister, Linka (Blima), circa 1933.

1

2

1 A photo of Nate's sister, Linka, that was given to him after the war by Linka's friend, Krysia. The inscription on the back of the photo reads, "To my dear Krysia, I present this photo as a souvenir of our happy time together." Sosnowiec, June 21, 1942.

2 Linka, Sosnowiec ghetto, 1942. Inscription on the back reads, "To my dear Krysia, that she may never forget me." Krysia gave this photo to Nate after the war.

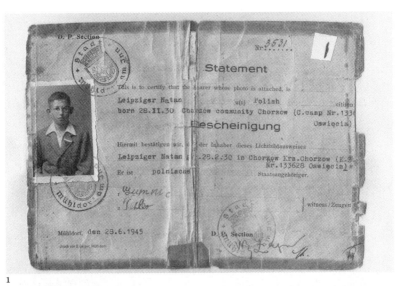

1

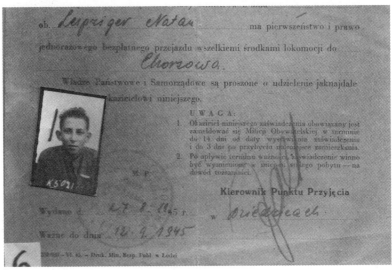

2

Nate's post-war identity documents; the earliest photos of him after liberation. 1945.

Nate, September 1945.

1 2 & 3 Nate and his father, Jack, after the war. Bamberg, 1946.

1

2

1 Jack (left), with his boss, Ed (centre), who sent Jack's letter to Uncle Dave in Canada, and the man who got Jack the job in the army (right). Bamberg, Germany, 1946.

2 Jack working for the US Army base in Bamberg, Germany, 1946.

1

2

3

4

1 Nate and his friend Ira Goetz. Bamberg, 1947.
2 Ira and Nate in Munich, 1947.
3 Nate and his friend Barbara Goldfischer. Bamberg, 1946.
4 Nate's friend Helen Ruff. Bamberg, 1946.

Nate's uncle David Leipciger (far right) who sponsored Nate and his father to come to Canada. From left to right: Nate's cousin Grace, his aunt Helen, cousin Joe and Uncle David. Toronto, 1948.

1–4 Nate in Toronto, 1948–1949.

1 & 2 Nate in Toronto, 1948–1949.
3 & 4 Nate enjoying his summer at Balfour Manor Camp in the Muskokas, 1950.

1

2

1 Nate with his stepbrother Al Waxman, who is wearing the goose sweater that
   Nate was teased about at school. Toronto, circa 1949.
2 Nate's stepbrother Benny Waxman.

The first photo Nate gave to Bernice, one year before their marriage. 1953.

1

2

3

1 Nate and Bernice on the occasion of their *aufruf*, a ritual celebration a few weeks before their wedding, 1954.

2 Nate's father, Jack, and his wife, Toby Waxman, at the *aufruf*, 1954.

3 Nate's family at the *aufruf*. From left to right: Uncle Dave, Aunt Helen, Toby and Jack. 1954.

Nate and Bernice's wedding photo. September 7, 1954.

1 Nate at Auschwitz-Birkenau, during his work on the International Council to the Museum at Auschwitz-Birkenau, circa 1990s.

2 In front of the ruins of gas chamber IV.

3 Nate and his family in the courtyard to his former residence in Sosnowiec, commemorating the fiftieth anniversary of Nate's liberation. In back, left to right: Nate, his son-in-law Zvi Litwin, and his son-in-law Steve Pinkus. In front, left to right: Bernice, and Nate and Bernice's daughters, Lisa, Ronda and Arla. Not pictured: son-in-law Cary Green. 1995.

1

2

1 Nate and Bernice's fiftieth wedding anniversary, 2004. Back row, left to right: Zvi, Arla, grandson Joshua, grandson Jason, grandson Daniel, Ronda, Cary, Lisa, Steve, and grandson Jonathan. Front row, left to right: grandson Gary, Nate, granddaughter Jennifer, grandson Adam, Nate's mother-in-law, Molly, granddaughter Jordana, Bernice, and granddaughter Mira.

2 Nate and his family on the occasion of Nate being honoured by Facing History, an educational organization Nate has been involved in since its inception in 2008. Back row, left to right: Dan Olyan, Jason Green, Cary Green, Josh Teperman, Jordana Pinkus, Jonathan Pinkus, Steve Pinkus, Joshua Litwin, and Laura Wilchesky. Middle row, left to right: Jennifer Green, Jody Nightingale, Ronda Green, Lisa Pinkus, Mira Pinkus, Lauren Greenwood, Arla Litwin, Zvi Litwin, Gary Litwin, Adam Litwin, and Samantha Landy. In front: Bernice and Nate. Toronto, 2014.

Index

The Azrieli Foundation was established in 1989 to realize and extend the philanthropic vision of David J. Azrieli, C.M., C.Q., M.Arch. The Foundation's mission is to support a wide spectrum of initiatives in education and research. The Azrieli Foundation is an active supporter of programs in the fields of Education, the education of architects, scientific and medical research, and the arts. The Azrieli Foundation's many initiatives include: the Holocaust Survivor Memoirs Program, which collects, preserves, publishes and distributes the written memoirs of survivors in Canada; the Azrieli Institute for Educational Empowerment, an innovative program successfully working to keep at-risk youth in school; the Azrieli Fellows Program, which promotes academic excellence and leadership on the graduate level at Israeli universities; the Azrieli Music Project, which celebrates and fosters the creation of high-quality new Jewish orchestral music; and the Azrieli Neurodevelopmental Research Program, which supports advanced research on neurodevelopmental disorders, particularly Fragile X and Autism Spectrum Disorders.